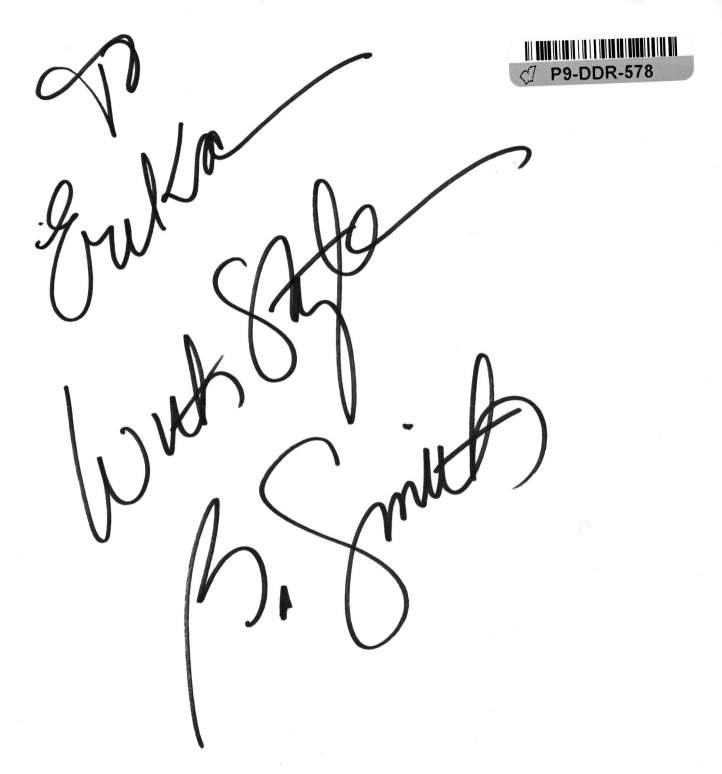

B. Smith Cooks Southern-Style

Barbara Smith

Scribner

New York   London   Toronto   Sydney

SCRIBNER
A Division of Simon & Schuster, Inc.
1230 Avenue of the Americas
New York, NY 10020

First Scribner hardcover edition November 2009

SCRIBNER and design are registered trademarks of The Gale Group, Inc.
used under license by Simon & Schuster, Inc., the publisher of this work.

For information about special discounts for bulk purchases,
please contact Simon & Schuster Special Sales at 1-866-506-1949 or business@simonandschuster.com.

The Simon & Schuster Speakers Bureau can bring authors to your live event. For more information or to book
an event contact the Simon & Schuster Speakers Bureau at 1-866-248-3049 or visit our website at www.simonspeakers.com.

DESIGNED BY ERICH HOBBING

Manufactured in the United States of America

10 9 8 7 6 5 4 3 2 1

Library of Congress Control Number: 2009021070

ISBN 978-1-4165-5354-0
ISBN 978-1-4165-9543-4 (ebook)

This book is dedicated to my father,
William H. Smith,
who loved, inspired and taught me
an appreciation for the finer things in life.

Contents

B. Smith Cooks Southern-Style

Why a Southern Cookbook Now?

"Are you from the South?" Through the years, I think I've been asked that question as much as, "How are you?"

"No, I'm not from the South but I'm from southwestern Pennsylvania," I answer, always with conviction and a smile. My family ended up in southwestern Pennsylvania by way of North Carolina and Virginia, where the first enslaved Africans arrived. Like many families, ours boasted strong Southern roots, and nowhere was it more evident than in my mother's, grandmother's, and aunts' pots and pans.

While researching this book and the heritage of Southern cooking, I discovered that there's more Southern in me than I'd realized. Eastern West Virginia borders southwestern Pennsylvania, and along with that border we also share a culture. Growing up, I never differentiated between Northern and Southern cooking; all I knew was the food we ate, and it wasn't good—it was great. My mother cooked like our neighbors cooked. I thought people all over the country ate the way we did. I didn't know the difference until I traveled north to the other side of Pittsburgh. That's where I saw for the first time cornbread inside a turkey, instead of inside my mother's iron skillet!

When I started modeling and traveling with the Ebony Fashion Fair, I was lucky to be able to explore different kinds of foods. But when I was back in New York, it had to be Southern. Trips to the Horn of Plenty, The Pink Tea Cup, Sylvia's, and Wells for its famous chicken and waffles were musts. It wasn't easy staying model thin savoring a plate of smothered chicken, but over time I learned how to enjoy the food I loved by eating in moderation. I had to choose between my taste buds and my budding career.

I've always had more than a sprinkling of Southern dishes on my restaurants' menus. At the first B. Smith's in New York, it was a tradition to have chitlins on the New Year's Eve menu. It brought back memories of my mother preparing chitlins all day to make sure they were ready and right for the New

Year. B. Smith's New York wasn't a soul food restaurant, but the funny thing about Southern food is that you put a couple of those kinds of dishes on the menu and people anoint it Southern. My goal was to always keep it eclectic. I like to think of the Southern dishes we served as inspired cooking. B. Smith's in Washington, D.C. was a different story. Since it was in the South, I had to have a great Southern chef, and I found him with the help of the famous Louisiana chef Paul Prudhomme.

Southern cuisine is bigger than crispy fried chicken and collard greens. It's a culturally rich and diverse cuisine with history in its ingredients, flavors, and textures. I like to look at it as a cultural artifact of the Old South. There's nothing like it. What other cuisine has had its journey? New settlers, enslaved Africans, enslavers, and Native Americans all had a stake in it.

In the world of food, I consider myself an explorer inside and outside the kitchen. I learn something from every bite, whether I prepared it or not. What better way to satisfy one's curiosity than with food?

I learned that the seductive flavors of Louisiana Creole cuisine have roots in France. I learned that Cajun gets its lively and spicy reputation from traditional African cooking. I respect the Upper South's penchant for pork and knowing what to do with it as much as I respect and love the Low Country's skill with seafood and various combinations.

Contrary to popular thought, enslaved Africans didn't bring their favorite foods with them. Slavery wasn't nice that way. Along with their human cargo, enslavers transported seeds to grow fruits and vegetables, like watermelon and okra. Once on land, enslaved Africans cultivated the land and planted the seeds.

And Native Americans brought a whole lot more than corn to the table. Thanks to them, early settlers' meals became more interesting and flavorful with a variety of squashes, tomatoes, and all kinds of beans, peppers, and fruits.

The big American Southern breakfast was attributed to the British fry-up, a meal heavy on pork, eggs, fried bread, and potatoes. The settlers were big hunters and didn't discriminate when it came to eating various parts of an animal, such as organ meats that included intestines, or chitterlings. Contrary to popular belief, whites, blacks, and Native Americans ate a lot of the same foods. What was different were the conditions under which they ate them. When you put all of this history together in a big pot, we call that Southern cuisine.

What I wanted to do with the recipes in this book was to bring modern eating to an old-school cuisine. Southern cooking with its rich and sometimes fat-laden qualities hasn't withstood the test of time with the health food movement. Today it's more about eating what's better for you than just what tastes good. I believe that we can have our Southern food and eat it too, with all the flavor we want and without the fat we don't need.

Let me get something straight: I like fat. It adds flavor like no other ingredient I've ever come across in all of my experience cooking. What I've done is lighten up the traditional Southern dishes we love by revisiting their original recipes, unlocking old secrets to perfect taste, and creating new ones. Talk about new ideas—anyone for Alligator Sausage Patties? We can't seem to make enough Braised Black-Eyed Peas and Greens for the restaurants; now you can make all you want in your own home. Learn my secret to how I cut down the fat when I make chitterlings; you won't be disappointed. (My husband, Dan, put a hurtin' on them.) There's a whole section on sauces and gravies, recipes so delectable it's a pity they have to go on top of something.

I love Southern food. I love the way it blankets me in comfort. I love the warm and loving memories it evokes. And there's nothing like seeing Dan and our daughter, Dana, light up when something Southern is on the table. It makes me the happiest gal from southwestern Pennsylvania.

Chapter 1

Brunch

When I moved to New York in the early 1970s, the only meal I ate before lunch was breakfast. I discovered the no-frills Pink Tea Cup when it was on Bleecker Street in the West Village. At the time it was a small storefront restaurant serving stick-to-your-ribs soul food. It was all about the food, with its down-home-style comfort. All the dancing we'd done all night long gave us huge breakfast appetites! We ordered, and our table was full of the works: eggs, sausage, bacon, ham, biscuits, and grits.

Unlike breakfast, brunch, the meal that is too late for breakfast and too early for lunch, was always served with Mimosas. By this time I had come of age, legally able to drink alcohol. I had brunch for the first time in a West Village restaurant not far from The Pink Tea Cup called Horn of Plenty. We would dress in our Sunday best and go there with friends as often as we could afford to. We would order Mimosas and take our time savoring our Southern-style brunch, abundant with waffles, chicken, sausage, eggs, bacon, ham, plenty of cornbread, and of course grits!

I love grits. What would a Southern breakfast or brunch be without grits? Thanks to Native Americans, we have them. Originally called "rockahomine" and then shortened by the colonists to "hominy," grits are the coarser part of ground cornmeal. Yellow grits include the whole kernel. We probably call them grits because of their gritty texture. The "Grits Belt" runs from Texas to North Carolina and sells three-quarters of the grits sold in the entire United States. That's a lot of grits! Grits mean so much to so many that in 2002, the state of Georgia declared grits its official food.

When we think grits, we usually think of the old-fashioned white grits. But there are stone-ground grits, yellow corn grits (also known as polenta in Italy), barley grits, and even quick grits. These are a no-no among grits purists who prefer the texture of slow-cooking grits. But I confess, I keep both in my pantry! In a fix, I've used quick grits and they're just fine. Thankfully, recipes for grits have come a long way since Native Americans served them up plain, seasoned with salt and some animal fat.

New Orleans is another brunch haunt of mine. Whenever Dan and I are in New Orleans, I make time for a good, leisurely brunch, sometimes starting with a carriage ride to the restaurant. There's something magical and romantic about a New Orleans brunch. There's nothing like grillades and grits or barbecued shrimp. Pain perdu, a.k.a. French toast, means "lost bread," which is usually leftover French bread that gets all dressed up with a custard-like coating and dusted with powdered sugar. It's simple to make, and I like it with fresh strawberries and Steen's cane syrup, the traditional syrup in New Orleans. I've included my recipe for Home-Style Cane Syrup, which is made with brown sugar, molasses, and white wine for added flavor. I watched my mother do wonders with leftovers. Back then, her French toast was made with stale Wonder Bread. She didn't believe in wasting food, and neither do I.

When we have leftover turkey, just when everyone thinks they've seen the last of it, I turn to the Turkey Hash recipe. It's hearty but not heavy, and usually there's nothing left over. You can also heat up fried fish from the night before and serve it with grits, or for a change, try the recipe for Seafood Hash. The finished dish looks much more elaborate than the actual preparation and cooking time would suggest, and it's pretty tasty any time of day.

The beauty of brunch dishes is that some of them are just right for late-night suppers. I always keep frozen biscuits in the freezer. I'll make some alligator sausage for special occasions, cook up some grits, bake the biscuits, and folks are happy. Good food knows no time of day.

Country-Style Alligator Sausage Patties and Gravy

When my husband, Dan, first ate alligator meat, he didn't ask, "What's this?" He said, "This is good." Alligator is what I call a clean, easy-cooking meat. It's low in cholesterol and fat, which makes it an excellent substitute for ground chicken, turkey, or pork. For this sausage recipe, I used ground alligator tail meat, though you can easily substitute ground chicken, turkey, or pork. What I love about making homemade sausage is that you eliminate excess fat and sodium, and can be totally creative with seasonings. Alligator meat is farm raised and can be purchased at specialty seafood and meat markets or online, including cajungrocer.com and gatorama.com.

1 pound alligator tail meat, cut into chunks (see Note)
1 tablespoon minced garlic
2 teaspoons dried thyme

2 teaspoons dried sage
1 teaspoon salt
1 teaspoon Creole seasoning
1 tablespoon vegetable oil

1. In a food processor fitted with the metal blade, place the alligator meat and grind using the pulse button, scraping down the sides as needed. Transfer the ground alligator to a large bowl and add the garlic, thyme, sage, salt, and Creole seasoning. Mix thoroughly.
2. Shape the alligator mixture into 16 small or 8 large patties, or leave in bulk to make Alligator Sausage Gravy (recipe follows). The uncooked patties can be kept in the refrigerator for up to 24 hours or frozen for up to 6 months.
3. In a large skillet, heat the vegetable oil over medium heat. Add the sausage patties (in batches if necessary) and cook for about 4 minutes on each side, until browned and cooked through. Serve immediately.

Note: Do not taste the raw alligator mixture; to taste and check the seasonings, make a small patty and cook thoroughly. Refrigerate alligator meat before and between all steps. Wash hands frequently when handling raw alligator, and wash all utensils and equipment immediately after use.

Alligator Sausage Gravy

This is a quick and easy gravy that gets loads of flavor from the seasoned cooked sausage. Use the same skillet to prepare the gravy, scraping up all the tasty, brown bits for extra flavor.

3 tablespoons vegetable oil
1 pound uncooked homemade Alligator
    Sausage (recipe above)
3 tablespoons all-purpose flour
2 cups whole milk
½ teaspoon salt

½ teaspoon freshly ground black pepper
¼ teaspoon Creole seasoning
Buttermilk Biscuits (see recipe on page
    49), optional for serving
Cooked Alligator Sausage Patties (recipe
    above), optional for serving

1. In a large nonstick or cast-iron skillet, heat the vegetable oil over medium-high heat. Crumble and add the Alligator Sausage to the skillet, cooking until completely browned and no longer pink. Using a slotted spoon, remove the Alligator Sausage to a bowl and set aside.
2. Return the skillet to medium heat and create a roux by adding the flour into the pan drippings, lightly browning while stirring constantly, until the roux begins to thicken, about 2 minutes.
3. Slowly whisk in the milk and cook, stirring constantly, until the gravy thickens. Season with the salt, pepper, and Creole seasoning. Stir in the cooked Alligator Sausage, mixing well to combine. Serve immediately, if desired over split fresh hot biscuits, with or without an Alligator Sausage Patty (recipe above).

Turkey Sausage Gravy and Biscuits

Here's another recipe for those wanting to stay on track health-wise and still enjoy their breakfast favorites. This Turkey Sausage Gravy makes a delicious low-fat and lower-calorie alternative to regular sausage gravy. Serve this up with a batch of my Buttermilk Biscuits. No time for baking from scratch? Why not serve this up with quick-and-easy Pillsbury Grands Biscuits!

1 pound ground turkey
1 tablespoon finely minced fresh sage
1 teaspoon fennel seed
½ teaspoon salt
1 teaspoon freshly ground black pepper
½ teaspoon dried thyme
½ teaspoon seasoned salt

¼ teaspoon cayenne pepper
1 tablespoon extra virgin olive oil
Buttermilk Biscuits (see recipe on page
　　49), optional for serving
Turkey Sausage Gravy (recipe follows),
　　optional for serving

1. In a large bowl, place the ground turkey, sage, fennel seed, salt, pepper, thyme, seasoned salt, and cayenne pepper. Using your hands, knead all the ingredients together.
2. Form the turkey mixture into 16 small or 8 large patties or into a log, cover tightly with plastic wrap, and refrigerate for at least 1 hour and up to 24 hours, or freeze for up to 2 months.
3. In a nonstick or cast-iron skillet over medium heat, heat the olive oil. Cook the patties in batches for about 3 to 4 minutes on each side, until browned and cooked through. Serve immediately, with split hot Buttermilk Biscuits and Turkey Sausage Gravy if desired.

Turkey Sausage Gravy

1 pound Turkey Sausage (recipe above)
3 tablespoons extra virgin olive oil
3 tablespoons all-purpose flour
1 cup chicken stock or broth
1½ cups fat-free evaporated milk

¼ cup water
Salt and freshly ground black pepper
   to taste
½ teaspoon chopped fresh sage, optional
   for garnish

1. In a large nonstick or cast-iron skillet, heat 1 tablespoon of the olive oil over medium-high heat. Crumble and add the Turkey Sausage, cooking until completely browned and no longer pink. Using a slotted spoon, remove the Turkey Sausage to a bowl and set aside.
2. Add the remaining 2 tablespoons olive oil to the skillet and place over medium heat. Add the flour and stir until lightly browned. Slowly add the chicken stock, and then the milk, stirring constantly. Add the water, 1 tablespoon at a time, if necessary to thin the gravy, smoothing any lumps with a wooden spoon. Add the cooked Turkey Sausage and mix well to combine. Season with salt and pepper, and serve immediately, garnished with chopped sage if desired.

Rich and Creamy Grits with Spicy Tomato Shrimp Gravy

YIELDS 4 SERVINGS

These rich and creamy grits are soul satisfying, and Grandma would definitely approve—but only if you use old-fashioned grits! These are great with sweet or savory dishes; make up a batch of Spicy Tomato Shrimp Gravy (recipe follows) and serve on top of the grits, or serve the grits with Buttermilk Biscuits (see recipe on page 49) right out of the oven.

2½ cups whole milk
½ cup heavy cream
4 tablespoons butter

½ teaspoon salt
1 cup old-fashioned stone-ground grits

1. In a medium saucepan over medium-high heat, bring the milk, heavy cream, butter, and salt to a simmer, stirring often to melt butter. (Do not allow mixture to boil.)
2. Slowly stir in the grits. Reduce heat to medium-low, cover, and cook, stirring occasionally, for 12 to 14 minutes or until thickened. Remove from heat and serve immediately.

Spicy Tomato Shrimp Gravy

YIELDS 4 SERVINGS

In the Low Country of South Carolina, and particularly Charleston, shrimp and grits has been considered a basic breakfast for coastal fishermen and families during the shrimp season (May through December) for decades. Simply called "breakfast shrimp," the dish consisted of a pot of grits with shrimp cooked in a little bacon grease or butter. During the past decade, this dish has been dressed up and taken out on the town to the fanciest restaurants. Not just for breakfast anymore, it is also served for brunch, lunch, and dinner.

For this recipe I use small shrimp and leave them whole, which makes for a much nicer presentation than cutting large shrimp into small pieces. I like my shrimp just cooked through. Most people like to cook it longer; you decide! If you have leftover sauce, it would add a wonderful texture and taste tucked into an omelet; in my kitchen, nothing goes to waste!

2 tablespoons butter
½ cup chopped onion
2 cloves garlic, finely chopped
¼ cup chopped celery
¼ cup chopped green bell pepper
1 cup seafood broth or stock, or bottled
    clam juice
One 28-ounce can whole peeled tomatoes,
    drained, liquid reserved, and coarsely
    chopped

1 teaspoon Old Bay Seasoning
½ teaspoon freshly ground black pepper
¼ teaspoon cayenne pepper
1 pound peeled and deveined shrimp
1 tablespoon chopped fresh basil
1 tablespoon chopped fresh parsley
Rich and Creamy Grits (recipe
    above), for serving

1. In a large saucepan, melt the butter over medium heat and sauté the onion, garlic, celery, and bell pepper until softened, about 7 minutes.
2. Add the broth, tomatoes, and reserved tomato liquid, and bring to a boil.
3. Add the Old Bay Seasoning, black pepper, and cayenne; simmer for 20 minutes. Stir in the shrimp, basil, and parsley, and simmer until the sauce is slightly thickened and the shrimp is just cooked through, about 5 to 8 minutes. Serve immediately over Rich and Creamy Grits.

Cheese Grits

This is an easy, rather rich grits recipe using old-fashioned stone-ground grits, whose texture I prefer, though you can substitute quick-cooking grits, making sure to reduce cooking time following package directions. This is the recipe I use when we have house guests; I keep printed copies on hand to pass out upon request!

3 cups chicken stock or broth, or more
    as needed
1 cup old-fashioned stone-ground grits
½ cup heavy cream

½ cup grated extra-sharp cheddar cheese
½ cup Mascarpone cheese
Salt and freshly ground white pepper
    to taste

1. In a heavy pot or saucepan, bring the chicken stock to a boil. Slowly pour in the grits, stirring constantly. Reduce heat to medium-low. Cook, stirring occasionally, for 15 to 20 minutes, until thickened.
2. Add the heavy cream and cheeses, stirring frequently, until melted and thoroughly incorporated. Season with salt and white pepper. Serve immediately or keep warm over low heat until ready to serve. Use warm chicken stock to thin the grits if necessary.

Grillades and Grits (Veal and Grits)

I read about Grillades and Grits long before I tasted them. There are many versions of this famous Louisiana dish. Many recipes call for veal, but there are also pork, beef, chicken, and even alligator versions (using tail meat thinly sliced and pounded with a meat tenderizer), as well as brown or red tomato sauce, and while the meat is almost always served with grits, there are a few who serve it with rice or mashed potatoes—you be the judge!

1½ pounds thinly sliced veal leg cutlets (sometimes labeled scaloppine)
1 cup all-purpose flour
1½ teaspoons Creole seasoning
¼ cup vegetable oil, or more as needed
1 cup chopped onion
½ cup chopped celery
½ cup chopped red bell pepper
2 large cloves garlic, finely chopped
1 bay leaf

1 teaspoon dried thyme, or 1 tablespoon fresh thyme
¼ cup white wine
2 cups beef stock or broth
Salt to taste
Creole seasoning to taste
¼ cup chopped scallion, for garnish
¼ cup chopped fresh parsley, for garnish
Rich and Creamy Grits (see recipe on page 11), for serving

1. Slice the veal into 2-inch strips.
2. In a shallow dish, mix together the flour and Creole seasoning. Dredge the veal strips in the seasoned flour. Set aside the extra flour.
3. In a large Dutch oven or stockpot, heat the vegetable oil over medium heat. Cook the veal strips in batches, browning well on both sides and adding more vegetable oil if needed. Set aside the browned veal strips.
4. Add the onion, celery, and bell pepper to the pot. Cook over medium heat, stirring frequently, for about 5 minutes, until the vegetables are softened but not browned. Stir in the garlic, bay leaf, and thyme, and let cook for 2 minutes.
5. Stir in the white wine, scraping the bottom of the pan to release the browned bits. Add 2 tablespoons of the reserved seasoned flour and stir until the flour is combined well with the vegetables.
6. Whisk in the beef stock and cook, stirring frequently, for about 10 minutes, until thickened and bubbly. Season with salt and Creole seasoning if desired.

7. Place the reserved veal slices in the sauce and simmer for about 5 minutes. Discard the bay leaf. Serve garnished with chopped scallion and parsley over freshly cooked Rich and Creamy Grits.

Lobster Grits

This recipe is so decadent and rich with the lobster and fontina cheese, it's perfect for a special brunch or served as a side dish morning, noon, or night! If you happen to be in the Low Country, or around fresh seafood, crayfish work equally well!

3½ cups seafood broth or stock, or bottled clam juice

¾ cup old-fashioned stone-ground grits

2 tablespoons butter

¼ teaspoon paprika

½ cup fontina cheese, or more to taste

1 tablespoon fresh chopped tarragon, or ½ teaspoon dried tarragon

1 cup cooked diced lobster

Salt and freshly ground white pepper to taste

Chopped scallions, for garnish

1. In a medium saucepan, bring the seafood broth to a boil and slowly stir in the grits. Reduce heat to medium-low, cover, and cook for 12 to 14 minutes or until thickened, stirring occasionally.
2. Stir in the butter, paprika, cheese, tarragon, and lobster. Continue cooking until the cheese is melted, about 2 to 3 minutes. Season with salt and pepper. Serve immediately, garnished with chopped scallions.

    Note: For thicker grits, decrease the amount of liquid; for thinner grits, increase the amount of liquid.

Jerk-Spiced Grits

For this savory side, I use quick-cooking grits. The spiced jerk seasoning is a tasty twist. Depending on the entrée the grits accompany, you can use meat, fish, or poultry stock in this recipe.

4 cups chicken or vegetable stock or broth
1½ tablespoons dried jerk seasoning,
    or more to taste
½ teaspoon salt
1 cup quick-cooking grits

2 tablespoons butter
¼ pound garlic herb cheese spread,
    such as Boursin Light
2 tablespoons chopped fresh parsley
Finely chopped scallions, for garnish

1. In a medium saucepan, bring the stock, jerk seasoning, and salt to a boil. Slowly stir in the grits. Reduce heat to medium-low, cover, and cook for 5 to 7 minutes, stirring frequently, until thickened.
2. Add the butter and cheese, stirring until melted. Add the parsley and stir to blend. Serve immediately, garnished with chopped scallions.

Pain Perdu Served with Home-Style Cane Syrup

YIELDS 6 SERVINGS

Pain perdu—elsewhere known as French toast—is a favorite in New Orleans. The name literally translates as "lost bread." In order to make use of day-old French bread that would otherwise have been wasted, chefs "rescued" the bread and made this delicious brunch menu classic. I prepare this recipe with French bread, and on special occasions when we have guests I substitute half-and-half for whole milk to create a richer version. I wouldn't think of serving this elegant dish without the cane syrup!

4 large eggs
1½ cups whole milk
1½ teaspoons vanilla
¼ cup sugar
1½ teaspoon freshly grated nutmeg
Zest of 1 lemon
One 10-ounce loaf day-old French bread
4 tablespoons melted butter

¼ cup canola oil
Fresh strawberries, cleaned and quartered,
    for garnish
Home-Style Cane Syrup (recipe follows),
    for serving
Confectioners' sugar, for garnish
Fresh mint leaves, optional for garnish

1. Preheat oven to 250°F. In a large bowl, place the eggs, milk, vanilla, sugar, nutmeg, and lemon zest. Blend the mixture together with a wire whisk until combined, and pour into a 9 x 13 x 2-inch metal or ceramic baking pan. Slice the bread on the bias into 1-inch-thick slices (you should have 12 pieces). Place the bread pieces into the egg mixture, let soak for 5 minutes, then turn the slices over and soak the flip sides for another 5 minutes. Cover with plastic wrap and refrigerate for at least 1 hour, or overnight.

2. In a small bowl, pour the melted butter and canola oil, and stir well to combine. Using a pastry brush, spread about 2 tablespoons of the butter/oil mixture on a nonstick griddle or skillet over medium-high heat. Place 4 prepared bread slices at a time on the griddle and cook for about 2 to 3 minutes per side, just until pieces are golden brown and crispy on the outside.

3. Remove the slices to a cookie sheet; place in the preheated oven to keep warm. Continue cooking the rest of the prepared bread slices in the butter/oil mixture until done.

4. To serve, place 2 slices of pain perdu on each plate and garnish with fresh strawberries. Drizzle with a generous portion of warmed cane syrup and a dusting of confectioners' sugar. Garnish each plate with fresh mint leaves, if desired.

Home-Style Cane Syrup

Traditionally, Steen's-brand syrup is served with pain perdu. It is made with pure sugarcane juice that's slow-simmered for hours in open kettles until the brown, caramel-type syrup develops with a hint of molasses flavor. This home-style sweet wine-based syrup adds that hint of Southern tradition to your breakfast or brunch.

¾ cup water, divided
½ cup dry white wine
1 cup packed dark brown sugar

1½ tablespoons cornstarch
1 teaspoon molasses

1. In a medium saucepan, pour ½ cup of the water, the white wine, and brown sugar; stir to combine. Bring the mixture to a boil over medium-high heat.
2. Meanwhile, pour the remaining ¼ cup water in a measuring cup. Add the cornstarch and molasses; stir well to combine.
3. When the brown sugar mixture boils, reduce heat to simmer and slowly add the cornstarch mixture. Stir constantly with a wire whisk until lightly thickened (if you like your syrup thicker, continue to simmer until desired thickness is achieved). Serve the syrup warm with Pain Perdu.

Note: You can make the syrup ahead and store in a tightly covered container in the refrigerator for up to 2 weeks. Before serving, gently heat the syrup in the microwave oven to warm through.

Pecan Waffles

One of my very best friends, who is originally from Louisiana, *loves* pecans. I can remember so clearly that each time she came into my restaurant in New York for brunch, she just had to have a small bowl of chopped pecans to sprinkle on her waffles. I created this recipe with her in mind, and hope you like it as much as I know she will! Serve with Home-Style Cane Syrup (see recipe on page 19) or maple syrup.

¾ cup sifted all-purpose flour
¾ cup whole-wheat flour
2 teaspoons baking powder
½ teaspoon salt
2 eggs, separated
2 tablespoons brown sugar

1¼ cups whole milk
4 tablespoons butter, melted and cooled
½ cup chopped pecans
Pecan halves, for garnish
Fresh mint leaves, optional for garnish

1. In a large bowl, sift the flour, baking powder, and salt together.
2. In a small bowl, beat the egg yolks and sugar together until thickened. Add the milk and melted butter to the egg mixture and stir well to combine. Stir the egg mixture into the dry ingredients. Add the chopped pecans and mix until blended.
3. In a large bowl, using an electric mixer, beat the egg whites until stiff, then fold gently into the batter.
4. Pour about ½ cup of the batter into a waffle iron and let cook until browned and crisp, about 4 minutes. (Cooking time and quantity of batter will vary with different waffle irons, so follow manufacturer's instructions.) Repeat for remaining waffles. Serve garnished with mint leaves, if desired.

Smothered Chicken Livers

Growing up, smothered chicken livers were always comfort food for me, and they still are today. Chicken livers are pretty rich, so I don't have them often, but when I do, I serve them over a bed of brown or white rice, mashed potatoes, or Rich and Creamy Grits.

2 cups low-sodium chicken stock or broth
½ teaspoon dried thyme
½ teaspoon dried sage
1 bay leaf
1 pound chicken livers, trimmed, cleaned, and split
½ teaspoon seasoned salt
½ teaspoon freshly ground black pepper
¼ cup all-purpose flour
2 tablespoons butter

2 tablespoons vegetable oil
1 medium onion, thinly sliced
½ cup chopped green bell pepper
Red pepper flakes to taste
Chopped scallions or minced fresh parsley, for garnish
Cooked brown or white rice, mashed potatoes, or Rich and Creamy Grits (see recipe on page 11), optional for serving

1. In a small pan, pour the chicken broth. Add the thyme, sage, and bay leaf. Bring to a boil, reduce heat, and simmer for 20 minutes.
2. Rinse the chicken livers in cool water, pat dry with paper towels, and sprinkle with the seasoned salt and pepper.
3. Lightly dredge the chicken livers in the flour, shaking off excess.
4. In a large nonstick skillet, heat the butter and vegetable oil over medium-high heat until hot. In batches, add the chicken livers and cook until lightly browned, about 3 minutes on each side. Remove the livers to a serving platter and cover to keep warm.
5. Add the onion and bell pepper to the skillet, stirring frequently, until the vegetables are just softened. Stir in the chicken broth to cover, bring to a boil, and add the chicken livers. Reduce heat, stirring often for about 3 minutes, until the livers are cooked through and the liquid has thickened to a gravy. Discard the bay leaf. Add red pepper flakes to taste, and serve immediately over cooked brown or white rice, mashed potatoes, or Rich and Creamy Grits if desired, garnished with chopped scallions or minced parsley.

Turkey Andouille Sausage and Cheese Grits Casserole

YIELDS 6 TO 8 SERVINGS

A real Southern breakfast is a decadence that we just can't indulge all of the time. For those who are very conscious about weight and health, this Turkey Andouille Sausage and Cheese Grits Casserole is a lighter version of a few of my favorites. You can't beat the flavor of fresh turkey andouille sausage. For this recipe, it should be removed from the casing, crumbled, and cooked before being added to the grits.

3 cups low-sodium chicken stock or broth
½ teaspoon salt
1 cup uncooked quick grits
1½ cups shredded sharp cheddar cheese
2 tablespoons butter, plus more for
 greasing pan

2 eggs, beaten
½ pound cooked crumbled turkey andouille
 sausage
1 tablespoon chopped fresh parsley
Hot pepper sauce to taste, optional

1. Preheat oven to 350°F. Butter the inside of a 2-quart casserole or 8-inch square baking dish, or coat with nonstick cooking spray.
2. In a large saucepan, heat the chicken broth and salt to boiling over high heat. Slowly stir in the grits and reduce heat to low. Cover and simmer, stirring occasionally, until thickened, 5 to 7 minutes.
3. Remove pan from heat; stir in 1 cup of the cheese and the butter, stirring until melted. Set aside to cool slightly, about 5 minutes.
4. Stir in the eggs, sausage, parsley, and hot sauce, if using. Pour the grits mixture into the prepared casserole and spread evenly.
5. Bake uncovered for 30 minutes. Sprinkle the top evenly with the remaining ½ cup of cheese. Continue baking until the center is slightly puffed and set (when a knife comes out clean or it springs back when lightly pressed) and the top is golden brown, about 20 minutes.

Turkey Hash

This is a good dish to make with leftover turkey and fresh mushrooms. Hash is a Southern breakfast staple. Fresh Lacy-Edged Batty Cakes (see recipe on page 24) or Buttermilk Biscuits (see recipe on page 49) are a must to accompany this savory, healthy hash!

4 tablespoons butter
2 tablespoons vegetable oil
1 cup finely diced onion
½ cup diced celery
¼ cup finely diced green bell pepper
½ pound fresh mushrooms, sliced
¼ cup all-purpose flour
2 cups turkey or chicken stock or broth

4 cups finely diced or shredded roasted turkey
¼ cup finely chopped fresh parsley
1 tablespoon Worcestershire sauce
1 teaspoon salt
½ teaspoon freshly ground black pepper
½ cup heavy cream, as needed

1. In a large skillet, melt the butter and oil over medium heat. Add the onion, celery, and bell pepper, and stir for 5 minutes, until vegetables are soft. Add the mushrooms and continue cooking, stirring occasionally, for 8 to 10 minutes, until the mushrooms are cooked and the liquid has evaporated.
2. Stir in the flour, incorporating well, then add the stock or broth to the pan. Stir with a whisk until the sauce comes to a boil, thickens slightly, and is smooth. Reduce the heat to low.
3. Add the turkey, parsley, Worcestershire, salt, and pepper. Simmer, stirring frequently, for 3 to 4 minutes, until the hash is heated through. If it looks a little dry, add heavy cream by the tablespoonful until the hash reaches the desired consistency. Serve immediately.

Lacy-Edged Batty Cakes

In an online edition of John Thorne's book *Simple Recipes,* he gives instructions to make Southern Lacy-Edge Corn Cakes, and the headnote reads, "There are various recipes for this corn cake, made famous by the once-annual 'Batty Cake Brekfus' on the morning of the Kentucky Derby, where they were served along with 'sawsidges, 'lasses, sputterin' coffee and fried apples.'"

¾ cup white cornmeal
½ teaspoon baking powder
½ teaspoon baking soda
½ teaspoon salt
1 cup buttermilk

1 egg, slightly beaten
4 tablespoons butter, melted and cooled slightly
Vegetable oil, for cooking as needed

1. In a medium bowl, combine the cornmeal, baking powder, baking soda, and salt.
2. In a separate bowl, combine the buttermilk and egg. Stir in the cornmeal mixture until the cornmeal absorbs the liquid. Gently fold in the melted butter.
3. Preheat a griddle or cast-iron skillet over medium-high heat, and lightly oil the surface. Using 1 tablespoon of batter for each cake, fry 4 at a time for 2 to 3 minutes, until cakes begin to bubble and bottoms are golden. Flip the cakes with a spatula and cook for 2 to 3 minutes longer, until golden. Serve immediately.

Seafood Hash

I am a bit spoiled: I like to prepare this dish in the summertime when we're in Sag Harbor, because after all, it is a historical fishing village. For this recipe, use cooked, skinned, and boned fresh or left-over fish of your choice—just about any combination works. Years ago, I would have flavored this hash with salt pork or bacon. Now, to keep the sodium and fat content low, I use Old Bay Seasoning and salt-free fish seasonings that can be found in the seasoning section of your grocery store. Even without the added pork, this hash really adds a new twist on a classic brunch staple.

2 tablespoons butter
2 tablespoons vegetable oil
1 medium sweet yellow onion, diced
½ cup diced green bell pepper
1¾ cups diced boiled potatoes
¼ teaspoon Old Bay Seasoning
½ teaspoon salt-free fish seasoning,
    or to taste
¼ teaspoon white pepper

½ cup diced cooked scallops
½ cup cooked fish, skinned, boned,
    and flaked
¾ cup diced cooked shrimp
Pinch of cayenne pepper
Salt and freshly ground black pepper
    to taste
Chopped scallions and fresh minced
    parsley, for garnish

1. In a large skillet or Dutch oven, heat the butter and oil over medium heat. Add the onion, bell pepper, potatoes, Old Bay Seasoning, fish seasoning, and white pepper. Cook, stirring occasionally, about 5 minutes, until vegetables are cooked and lightly browned.
2. Stir in the scallops, fish, and shrimp, and cook until the fish is heated through. Add the cayenne pepper, salt, and black pepper. Taste and adjust seasonings. Place on a warm platter and serve immediately, garnished with scallions and parsley.

Chapter 2

Appetizers

At some point shortly after I was accepted to become a model at the Wilhelmina Modeling Agency in New York City, invitations to private parties and club events started arriving on a regular basis. Though not quite prepared socially for the New York party scene, I adapted rather quickly. And who wouldn't? Back in the early seventies, there were numerous sophisticated receptions and cocktail parties for business and pleasure, and they all seemed to serve champagne, cocktails, and hors d'oeuvres.

Thinking back to home in western Pennsylvania, I guess the mixed nuts and/or relish tray with olives and carrots and celery that my mother put out before dinner were appetizers. My culinary travels have taken me a long way from western Pennsylvania! All those parties and venturing into the restaurant business made me a firm believer in waking up the taste buds before dinner with appetizers. They give your guests an inkling of things to come. Even when I lived in a tiny apartment, I'd always serve a couple of appetizers with drinks before dinner. "You should always have nibbles for people when they're having cocktails," my mom would say. On a trip I took to Charleston, South Carolina, a few years ago, I still remember the taste of some savory little benne wafers my friend Rhetta Mendolson served with an adult-style iced tea on her porch. They were the perfect bite before dinner.

Appetizers are incredibly versatile. If you're serving them before dinner, the serving size should be smaller. They should also pair well with the meal. I don't like crowding one's taste buds before dinner, or for that matter, even during a meal. For parties, variety is the key. I'll put several appetizers on a table or make up a few to pass around on trays. Of course, I'm partial to my recipes. Even if I'm having a party catered, I'll provide the caterer my recipes. This way there are no surprises for my guests or me.

Many Southern foods are natural-born appetizers. You can never go wrong with chicken. Sugarcane-Skewered Chicken can be grilled, baked, or fried. I've included my special recipe for Sweet and Spicy Ginger Pineapple Dipping Sauce; it adds a sweet yet tangy touch. Arranged on a platter, they look as festive as they are simple and elegant. The Sweet Chili Spiced Chicken Wings are always a big hit and are also easy to prepare and eat, so make plenty. To avoid cutting up the wings, you can buy just drumettes.

I always try to serve hors d'oeuvres that I think my guests don't have the time to make or have never had. Vegetables are appetizers' best friends, and they can be transformed into some of the most interesting bites. Spicy Baby Okra and Olives are much more interesting than a plain bowl of olives and can also be used as a relish with a meal or as a tasty garnish in a martini or Bloody Mary. Fried Green Tomatoes are really big sellers in our restaurants; now they can be made at home. Eggplant Fries are also unusual, not to mention full of texture and flavor, especially dipped in my Tomato Truffle Ketchup!

Appetizers are a great way to experiment with recipes or ingredients. Everything about Alligator-Stuffed Eggplant is new and different. Try a new group of sliders, using recipes for Codfish Cakes, Bourbon Brown Sugar–Brushed Ham Loaf, Alligator Sausage Patties, and Root Beer Barbecued Pulled Pork for a change of pace. Calamari may not be the most Southern of appetizers, but with the recipe for Seasoned Fried Calamari with Spicy Creole Dip you can give them a Cajun or Creole twist. Crispy Catfish Fingers with Guinness Tartar Sauce gives guests a choice of two different kinds of seafood.

You'll know when you've found your favorite appetizer recipes; they're the ones you make again and again because everyone wants more, more, more!

Alligator-Stuffed Eggplant

Eggplant grows extremely well in my garden. It's known as the "garden egg" in Africa, but I thought I'd give it a Southern twist, stuffing it with seasoned ground alligator meat. Served as an hors d'oeuvre or appetizer, this starter makes a great-tasting conversation piece!

1 medium or 2 small whole eggplants
2 tablespoons extra virgin olive oil
½ cup diced onions
2 teaspoons chopped garlic
2 cups ground cooked alligator tail meat
   (see Note)
5 canned plum tomatoes, diced, liquid
   reserved

¾ teaspoon salt
1 teaspoon freshly ground black pepper
1 teaspoon cayenne pepper, or to taste
¾ cup breadcrumbs
¾ cup cheddar cheese
¼ cup chopped fresh parsley

1. Preheat oven to 350°F. In a large pot, cover the eggplants with water and boil until slightly tender.
2. Cut each eggplant in half lengthwise. Using a paring knife, cut a border so that ¼ inch of flesh and skin remain around the edge. Slice the flesh within the border lengthwise and crosswise, then scoop out and cube the eggplant pulp (you should have 1 to 2 cups eggplant cubes). Reserve the eggplant cubes and the hollowed-out eggplant halves.
3. In a large skillet, heat the olive oil over medium heat, and sauté the onions and garlic until transparent, about 4 to 5 minutes. Stir in the cooked alligator meat, eggplant cubes, diced tomatoes, and reserved tomato liquid. Add the salt, pepper, and cayenne. Cook over medium heat for 15 to 20 minutes, until eggplant is cooked.
4. Add the breadcrumbs to the meat mixture and toss to coat. Place equal amounts of the meat mixture into each reserved eggplant half. Sprinkle each eggplant half with cheddar cheese.
5. Bake for about 20 minutes, until lightly browned. Sprinkle with parsley and serve immediately.

> Note: Place alligator meat in a food processor fitted with the metal blade. Grind using the pulse button, scraping down the sides as needed. Heat vegetable oil over medium-high heat in a large nonstick or cast-iron skillet. Crumble the sausage meat into the skillet, cooking until completely browned and no longer pink.

Catfish Fingers with Guinness Tartar Sauce

YIELDS 4 TO 6 SERVINGS

Catfish fingers are popular at our restaurants, which is no surprise since Americans consume 120 million pounds of this Southern favorite a year! Here I'm serving it with a light Guinness Tartar Sauce. Any firm white fish, such as grouper or tilapia, can be substituted for the catfish, but not at my house or restaurants!

1½ pounds catfish fillets, cut into
    1½- to 2-inch strips
1 cup all-purpose flour
1 teaspoon salt
1 teaspoon freshly ground black pepper
2 large eggs
2 tablespoons water

1½ cups yellow cornmeal
1 teaspoon garlic powder
1 teaspoon Creole seasoning
¼ teaspoon cayenne pepper
Vegetable oil for frying
Guinness Tartar Sauce (recipe follows),
    for serving

1. Have ready 3 shallow dishes or bowls. In one bowl, combine the flour, salt, and pepper.
2. In another bowl, lightly beat together the eggs and water.
3. In the last bowl, stir together the cornmeal, garlic powder, Creole seasoning, and cayenne pepper.
4. In a deep skillet or electric fryer, pour the vegetable oil to a depth of 2 inches. Heat the oil to about 375°F.
5. Dredge the fish strips in the flour mixture. Dip them in the egg and then roll in the cornmeal mixture, shaking off the excess.
6. Without overcrowding the pan, place the fish strips in the hot oil. Fry for about 2 minutes, then turn over and cook for another 2 minutes, until golden brown.
7. Drain the fish on paper towels. Serve immediately, or keep warm in a 200°F oven until serving. Serve with Guinness Tartar Sauce.

Guinness Tartar Sauce

½ cup mayonnaise
½ cup sour cream
3 tablespoons Guinness Stout
2 tablespoons chopped dill pickles
   or dill pickle relish
2 tablespoons capers, drained

2 tablespoons minced scallion, white
   and green parts
1 tablespoon minced fresh tarragon,
   or 1 teaspoon dried
2 dashes hot pepper sauce

In a small bowl, mix together the mayonnaise, sour cream, Guinness Stout, pickles, capers, scallion, tarragon, and hot pepper sauce, and stir until well blended. Cover and store in the refrigerator until serving. To thin the sauce, stir in additional Guinness Stout to desired consistency.

Eggplant Fries with Tomato Truffle Ketchup

Eggplant Fries are very versatile. Pass them around as hors d'oeuvres, or serve them as a side with sandwiches or entrées. Don't forget the Tomato Truffle Ketchup, served warm or at room temperature.

1 medium eggplant (about 1½ pounds)
2½ teaspoons kosher or fine sea salt
¼ teaspoon cayenne pepper
¾ cup flour
3 large eggs, beaten
¾ cup yellow cornmeal

¾ cup finely grated Parmigiano-Reggiano
   cheese
Vegetable oil, for frying
Lemon wedges, for garnish
Tomato Truffle Ketchup (recipe follows),
   for serving

1. Peel the eggplant, cut into ½-inch rounds, then slice the rounds into ½-inch slices so they look like fries. In a colander, toss the eggplant with ½ teaspoon of the salt and allow to sit for about 15 minutes to extract water. Blot the eggplant with a paper towel to dry before frying.
2. On a small plate, combine the cayenne and remaining 2 teaspoons salt and set aside.
3. Set up 3 plates, one with the flour, one with the egg, and the third with the cornmeal and Parmigiano-Reggiano cheese combined. Coat the eggplant with flour, then egg, then the cornmeal mixture.
4. Heat a skillet with ½ inch of oil on medium-high heat. Fry the eggplant in batches, not crowding the pan, for about 3 to 4 minutes, until golden. Drain on paper towels, then while hot, sprinkle with the cayenne-salt mixture and place on a serving platter. Garnish the platter with lemon wedges, and serve with Tomato Truffle Ketchup.

Tomato Truffle Ketchup

Tomatoes grow in abundance in my garden. They bring out the country girl in me. I kick off my shoes and enjoy the warm summer soil while eating them fresh, right in the garden. Other times I stew them and use them in various recipes. You can add garlic and herbs, depending on your favorite flavors. Here I'm using canned plum tomatoes, which are available year round, and they taste great in this Truffle Tomato Ketchup.

1 to 2 tablespoons extra virgin olive oil
1 teaspoon minced garlic
¼ cup diced onions
¼ cup diced red bell pepper
One 14.5-ounce can diced Muir Glen
    tomatoes, crushed with juices,
    or stewed fresh tomatoes

1 teaspoon brown sugar
¼ teaspoon salt
¼ teaspoon paprika
¼ teaspoon cayenne pepper
1 tablespoon truffle oil, or more to taste

1. In a small saucepan, heat the olive oil over medium heat. Add the garlic, onion, and bell pepper, and cook, stirring frequently, until the vegetables are soft but not brown, about 4 minutes. Add the tomatoes and their juices to the pan. Stir in the brown sugar, salt, paprika, and cayenne, and simmer for about 4 to 5 minutes, until the sauce has thickened.
2. In the bowl of a mini food processor or blender, place the vegetables and pulse until smooth. Add the truffle oil and blend until combined.
3. Serve immediately with Eggplant Fries, or place in a resealable container and refrigerate until using. Serve at room temperature.

Fried Green Tomatoes with Roasted Red Pepper Aioli

YIELDS 4 SERVINGS

Fried Green Tomatoes are one of the most popular side dishes in our restaurants. It's a traditional Southern dish made from unripe green tomatoes dipped in buttermilk, flour, egg, and breadcrumbs. It's delicious garnished with ricotta salata cheese and Roasted Red Pepper Aioli.

4 medium, firm green tomatoes
Salt
Freshly ground black pepper
½ cup buttermilk
⅔ cup all-purpose flour
2 eggs, beaten

¾ cup fine dry breadcrumbs or cornmeal
½ cup olive oil
Grated ricotta salata cheese, for garnish
Roasted Red Pepper Aioli (see recipe on page 239), for garnish
Chopped scallion, for garnish

1. Preheat oven to 200°F.
2. Cut the unpeeled tomatoes into ½-inch slices. Sprinkle the slices with salt and pepper to taste. Let the tomato slices stand for 15 minutes.
3. Meanwhile, have 4 shallow dishes or bowls ready. Place the buttermilk in the first dish, flour in the second dish, and eggs in the third dish. Place the breadcrumbs in the last dish, and season with salt and pepper.
4. Heat 3 tablespoons of the olive oil in a nonstick skillet on medium heat. Dip the tomato slices in the milk, then flour, then eggs, then breadcrumbs.
5. Fry the tomatoes in batches (do not crowd the pan) on each side for 3 to 4 minutes, or until brown. Place in the heated oven as you cook the remaining tomatoes. Add more olive oil to the skillet as needed.
6. Serve immediately, garnished with grated ricotta salata cheese, a drizzle of Roasted Red Pepper Aioli, and chopped scallion.

Seasoned Fried Calamari with Spicy Creole Dip

Calamari, also known as squid, is another popular appetizer at the restaurants, and is easy to prepare. I've given this version a Southern twist with spicy Cajun or Creole seasoning and buttermilk. Once you serve this at home, friends and family will put in a request for more, and frequently!

¾ pound fresh calamari
¼ cup buttermilk, or more as needed
1 cup all-purpose flour, or more as needed
2 teaspoons Cajun or Creole seasoning
½ teaspoon seasoned salt, or to taste

¼ teaspoon freshly ground black pepper,
   or to taste
Vegetable oil, for frying
Spicy Creole Dip (recipe follows),
   for serving

1. Cut the calamari body into rings approximately ¼ inch thick. Rinse the rings and tentacles well in cold water, then blot dry on paper towels.
2. In a shallow bowl, pour the buttermilk. Add a teaspoon or more of water to thin the buttermilk if needed.
3. In a large plate or pan, combine the flour, Cajun or Creole seasoning, seasoned salt, and pepper.
4. Add ¼ inch of oil to a skillet, and heat over medium-high heat.
5. Dip the calamari rings and tentacles first into the buttermilk and then into the seasoned flour, turning to coat evenly. Using a slotted spoon, immediately lower the rings into the hot oil. Cook, turning occasionally, until the calamari is golden brown on all sides, 2 to 3 minutes. Remove the calamari from the oil and drain on paper towels. Serve immediately with Spicy Creole Dip.

Spicy Creole Dip

3 ripe plum or Roma tomatoes, halved,
    seeded, and chopped
1 small clove garlic, minced
2 tablespoons freshly squeezed lemon juice
2 tablespoons mayonnaise or light canola
    mayonnaise

2 tablespoons extra virgin olive oil
½ teaspoon Creole seasoning
½ teaspoon salt
½ teaspoon freshly ground black pepper
⅛ teaspoon cayenne pepper

1. In a blender, combine all the ingredients and process on high speed until smooth. Scrape down the sides and blend again. Taste to adjust seasonings.
2. Remove to a bowl or resealable container. Serve immediately with Seasoned Fried Calamari, or cover and refrigerate until ready to use.

Sweet Chili Spiced Chicken Wings

YIELDS 8 SERVINGS

We serve these wings in all of our restaurants, and folks cannot get enough. Use whole wings cut at the joint to make three pieces, or purchase drumettes. The marinade infuses layers of flavor, and the chili sauce adds just the right amount of sweetness and spice. Be careful, you may need to double the recipe, because these wings are truly addictive!

¼ cup reduced-sodium soy sauce
1½ to 2 tablespoons sesame or vegetable oil
½ teaspoon onion powder
½ teaspoon garlic powder
2 teaspoons five-spice powder
½ teaspoon freshly ground black pepper

24 chicken wing pieces or drumettes
    (2½ to 3 pounds)
¾ cup all-purpose flour, more if needed
Canola oil, for frying
1 bottle store-bought sweet chili sauce
2 tablespoons toasted white sesame seeds,
    optional for garnish

1. To make the marinade, in a small bowl, combine the soy sauce, sesame oil, onion powder, garlic powder, five-spice powder, and black pepper.
2. If using whole wings, cut the chicken at the joints to make 3 pieces. Discard the tips. In a resealable gallon-size plastic food storage bag, place the chicken wing pieces or drumettes.
3. Add the marinade to the plastic bag. Seal the bag and turn to coat the chicken wings. Refrigerate for at least 1 hour and up to 12 hours, turning the bag occasionally.
4. Remove the wings from the marinade. In a clean resealable plastic food storage bag, pour the flour. Add the wings a few pieces at a time, shake to coat, then shake off excess flour.
5. In a deep skillet, pour canola oil and heat to 350°F. Fry the wings in batches until crisp and the juices run clear when pierced near the bone with a sharp knife. Drain on paper towels.
6. In a large bowl, pour the chili sauce. While warm, add the chicken wings to the bowl and toss them to coat with the chili sauce. Serve warm or at room temperature, garnished with toasted sesame seeds if desired.

Spicy Baby Okra and Olives

Serve these as a relish with the meal, or offer as cocktail nibbles. They can be prepared in advance of serving, and also can be jarred for a great little hostess gift!

6 ounces fresh baby okra or small okra

2 tablespoons halved, pitted Kalamata olives

2 tablespoons halved, pitted cracked green olives

2 tablespoons pimiento-stuffed green olives

¼ cup freshly squeezed lemon juice

¼ cup extra virgin olive oil

1½ tablespoons fresh thyme leaves

1 garlic clove, thinly sliced

¼ teaspoon coarse kosher salt

¼ teaspoon red pepper flakes

1. In a 1-quart resealable plastic bag, combine the okra and olives.
2. In a medium bowl, whisk the lemon juice, olive oil, thyme, garlic, salt, and red pepper flakes to blend. Pour the marinade over the okra and olives. Tightly seal the bag, and turn it to distribute the marinade evenly.
3. Refrigerate for at least 1 day and up to 2 weeks, turning occasionally. Serve cold or at room temperature.

Sugarcane-Skewered Chicken with Sweet and Spicy Ginger Pineapple Dipping Sauce

YIELDS 6 TO 8 APPETIZER SERVINGS OR 4 TO 6 ENTRÉES

This is one of my favorite appetizers, which also can be served as an entrée. Sugarcane skewers (see Box), hot sauce, and Old Bay Seasoning add Southern flair to this chicken dish. If you cannot find sugarcane, use 6-inch metal skewers or bamboo skewers that have been presoaked in water. All of the above work fine, as this dish is really about the flavorful marinade and the Sweet and Spicy Ginger Pineapple Dipping Sauce.

2 tablespoons peanut oil

2 tablespoons pineapple juice

2 tablespoons oyster sauce

¼ teaspoon hot sauce

1 tablespoon light brown sugar

1 teaspoon Old Bay Seasoning

1 teaspoon salt

½ teaspoon freshly ground black pepper

One 2-inch piece fresh ginger, peeled and grated

1 clove garlic, minced

2 pounds boneless, skinless chicken tenderloins (tendons removed), or chicken breasts cut into ½-inch-wide strips

Sweet and Spicy Ginger Pineapple Dipping Sauce (recipe follows), for serving

1. In a medium bowl, combine the peanut oil, pineapple juice, oyster sauce, hot sauce, brown sugar, Old Bay Seasoning, salt, pepper, ginger, and garlic, and stir to combine. Add the chicken and toss to coat.
2. Thread the chicken onto skewers, then place in an 8 x 12-inch rectangular pan or on a cookie sheet. Pour any remaining juices onto the chicken skewers. Cover with plastic wrap and marinate in the refrigerator for at least 2 hours, but no longer than 6 hours, before cooking.
3. Grill the skewers for 3 to 5 minutes per side on an outdoor gas or charcoal grill, or an indoor grill pan on medium-high heat, until cooked through and lightly browned. Or, to bake the skewers, preheat oven to 350°F. Place the skewers on a lightly oiled baking sheet and bake for 6 to 7 minutes. Turn the skewers with tongs and cook for 6 to 7 minutes more, until chicken is cooked through.
4. Serve immediately with Sweet and Spicy Ginger Pineapple Dipping Sauce.

Sweet and Spicy Ginger Pineapple Dipping Sauce

1 cup freshly grated pineapple, or one
    8-ounce can crushed pineapple
½ cup pineapple preserves
1 tablespoon light brown sugar

One 1-inch piece of fresh ginger, peeled
    and grated
¼ teaspoon red pepper flakes
¼ teaspoon salt

1. In a medium saucepan, place all the ingredients and stir to combine. Bring the mixture to a boil on medium-high heat; cook, stirring constantly, for 2 minutes.
2. Remove from heat, cool to room temperature, and place in a bowl or resealable container. Cover and refrigerate until serving.

How to Make Sugarcane Skewers

Check out the produce section at Whole Foods or specialty food stores for fresh sugarcane; it makes a wonderful sweet organic skewer. Simply peel a 6-inch length of sugarcane and cut it into thin skewers. Be sure to cut a pointed V-shape at the tip of each skewer for easy assembly when spearing with chicken or other foods.

Southern Slider Sandwiches

I had my first sliders at the Ritz-Carlton on Central Park South in New York City, not far from our apartment. My husband raved about them, saying they were a perfect accompaniment to cocktails, and so much better than bar snacks! They are usually served as a trio of mini burger–sized sandwiches. What a creative, elegant way to serve a burger with style and the right amount of satisfaction! There are so many recipes in this book that would make exciting sliders, especially served as passed hors d'oeuvres at a cocktail party or a make-it-yourself mini buffet. Use the recipes for the Whole-Wheat Potato Rolls or the Yeast Rolls—just to name a couple of ideas. And for the filling, try Bourbon Brown Sugar–Brushed Ham Loaf, Root Beer Barbecued Pulled Pork, Codfish Cakes, or Alligator Burgers (as shown below) or turkey burgers, seafood, or Seafood Hash (see recipe on page 25) with any number of tasty sauces and edible garnishes. I think sliders are here to stay! I even have dessert sliders in this book—B. aims to please!

Alligator Sliders

20 Alligator Sausage Patties (see recipe on page 7)

Twenty 3-inch Yeast Rolls (see recipe on page 61) or Whole-Wheat Potato Rolls (see recipe on page 59), or store-bought buns
Your favorite barbecue sauce

1. Cook Alligator Sausage Patties according to directions, using 1½ tablespoons of meat per patty.
2. Slice the buns and place 1 patty and a dollop of barbecue sauce on each. Serve immediately.

Ham Sliders

Twenty 2-inch rounds Bourbon Brown
  Sugar–Brushed Ham Loaf (see recipe
  on page 127)

Twenty 3-inch Yeast Rolls (see recipe
  on page 61) or Whole-Wheat Potato
  Rolls (see recipe on page 59)
Your favorite barbecue sauce

1. Preheat oven to 200°F. Prepare Bourbon Brown Sugar–Brushed Ham Loaf according to directions. Cut the loaf into ½-inch slices, then create 20 rounds using a 2-inch biscuit cutter. Place the rounds on a nonstick or lightly sprayed baking sheet and bake until warmed through.
2. Slice the rolls and place 1 Ham Loaf round and a dollop of barbecue sauce on each. Serve immediately.

Pulled Pork Sliders

Root Beer Barbecued Pulled Pork (see
  recipe on page 147)

Twenty 3-inch Yeast Rolls (see recipe
  on page 61) or Whole-Wheat Potato
  Rolls (see recipe on page 59),
  or store-bought buns
Cole slaw, optional

1. Prepare Root Beer Barbecued Pulled Pork according to directions.
2. Slice the rolls and place 1½ tablespoons pulled pork and a dollop of cole slaw, if desired, on each. Serve immediately.

Codfish Sliders

20 mini Codfish Cakes (see recipe on page
  44)

Twenty 3-inch Yeast Rolls (see recipe
  on page 61) or Whole-Wheat Potato
  Rolls (see recipe on page 59),
  or store-bought buns
Your favorite sauce

1. Prepare Codfish Cakes according to directions, using 1½ tablespoons of fish per cake.
2. Slice the rolls and place 1 Codfish Cake and a dollop of sauce on each. Serve immediately.

Codfish Cakes

When I was growing up, my mother never made codfish cakes. After I tasted them at a friend's home, I decided to create my own recipe adding a spicy dash of Creole or Old Bay Seasoning and cayenne pepper for a Southern take. These versatile, tasty cakes are perfect served small as an appetizer on salad greens, or large on a sandwich or as an entrée. Try serving them with a fruit sauce or salsa.

1 pound cod fillets, steamed and flaked
1 tablespoon freshly squeezed lemon juice
2 tablespoons butter
½ cup finely chopped onion
¼ cup finely chopped celery
¼ cup finely chopped red bell pepper
½ teaspoon chopped garlic
¾ cup breadcrumbs, or more as needed

¼ cup chopped fresh parsley
1 teaspoon Creole or Old Bay Seasoning
½ teaspoon dry mustard
½ teaspoon salt
½ teaspoon freshly ground black pepper
Cayenne pepper to taste
1 egg, lightly beaten
2 tablespoons canola oil, for frying

1. In a large bowl, place the cooked flaked cod. Be sure to remove any stray bones. Toss with the lemon juice.
2. In a small pan, melt the butter over medium heat. Sauté the onion, celery, red pepper, and garlic until softened, about 5 minutes; cool slightly.
3. Add the breadcrumbs, parsley, Creole or Old Bay Seasoning, mustard, salt, pepper, cayenne, egg, and cooled onion mixture to the steamed fish. Mix gently until combined, making sure not to pack the mixture together too much. (If mixture is too sticky, add more breadcrumbs as needed.) Gently form the mixture into 8 small or 4 large cakes.
4. In a large skillet, heat the oil over medium heat. Add the codfish cakes and cook in batches if necessary, for 4 to 5 minutes on each side, until the cakes are a light golden brown. Serve immediately.

Pork Tenderloin Brochettes with Warm Mincemeat Sauce

YIELDS 8 APPETIZER SERVINGS OR 4 ENTRÉES

When I was a child, my favorite cookies were my dad's homemade mincemeat cookies. Mincemeat historically was developed as a way to preserve meats in a mixture of fruits and spices cooked with brandy, rum, or whiskey. English settlers introduced this traditional preparation to the South when settling in the colonies. You can purchase mincemeat dried, but I prefer the jarred liquid version, which makes a terrific warm sauce for the savory Pork Tenderloin Brochettes.

1½ pounds pork tenderloin
2 tablespoons extra virgin olive oil
2 tablespoons Worcestershire sauce
2 tablespoons grated fresh ginger
1 teaspoon minced garlic
¼ teaspoon hot sauce
Vegetable oil, for wiping pan

1 small orange bell pepper, seeded
*   and cubed*
1 small yellow bell pepper, seeded
*   and cubed*
Warm Mincemeat Sauce (recipe follows),
*   for serving*

1. Have ready four 12-inch metal skewers, or eight 6-inch bamboo skewers that have been presoaked in water for 15 minutes (see box).
2. Trim the fat and silver skin from the pork. Cut the pork into twenty-four 2½-inch x ½-inch-thick cubes.
3. To make the marinade, in a small bowl, combine the olive oil, Worcestershire sauce, ginger, garlic, and hot sauce. Place the pork in a large resealable plastic bag. Pour the marinade over the pork and seal the bag. Shake the bag a few times to be sure all pork is coated with the marinade. Refrigerate for at least 3 hours and up to 24 hours.
4. Preheat oven to 350°F. Coat or spray a large baking sheet with oil. Thread the pork onto the skewers (use 3 pieces per skewer for an appetizer, or 6 pieces per skewer for an entrée), alternating each cube of pork with a piece of bell pepper.
5. Lay the skewers on the prepared baking sheet, leaving space between the skewers. Bake for 8 minutes. Turn with a pair of tongs and continue to bake until cooked through, about 8 more minutes. Serve immediately with Warm Mincemeat Sauce.

Warm Mincemeat Sauce

YIELDS 2 TO 2½ CUPS

½ cup chicken stock or broth
1 teaspoon minced fresh ginger
½ cup apple juice or white wine
1 to 1½ cups jarred mincemeat

1 tablespoon cornstarch
1 tablespoon cold water
1 tablespoon orange zest

1. In a small saucepan, heat the chicken stock over medium heat. Stir in the ginger, bring to a simmer, and cook until ginger is tender, about 5 minutes.
2. Strain out the ginger and place the strained stock back in the saucepan. Add the apple juice or white wine and the mincemeat to the pan. Bring to a boil, then reduce to a simmer and cook for 5 minutes.
3. In a small cup, mix together the cornstarch and cold water until dissolved. Stir the cornstarch mixture into the sauce and cook until slightly thickened, about 3 to 4 minutes. Add the orange zest, mix, and serve warm with Pork Tenderloin Brochettes.

Using Bamboo Skewers

Bamboo skewers are readily available in supermarkets and can typically be found in 6-inch, 8-inch, 10-inch, and 12-inch lengths. They are easy to use for all sorts of brochettes; however, to avoid burning during cooking, bamboo skewers must first be hydrated. Simply place the skewers in a baking pan or other shallow dish in which they can lie flat, cover with water, and let soak for at least 15 minutes before threading with foods and grilling or baking.

Chapter 3

Breads and Dressings

One of my favorite family kitchen memories will always be of the women preparing and baking bread. It was in my mom's mother's home; back then it wasn't uncommon to have married adult family members live under one roof. And since Grandma had a big house, Mom's sister Hattie and her husband Clint as well as her brother Jessie and his wife Mable all lived there. Neither couple had kids, so my brothers and I really were treated royally! All the women baked delicious breads, biscuits, and desserts, and I don't recall ever seeing a recipe. I was too young to help out much but I certainly was a good taster, especially when it came to the sweet, rich cinnamon sticky buns.

My mom was a great cook, but unlike my aunts she had four kids to feed. The 1950s were a time of convenience foods. She made cornbread from scratch in her iron skillet and most of the time she made muffins from scratch, but she also purchased muffin mix and showed us kids how to prepare the packaged goods. Many a morning my brothers and I would share the breakfast muffin–making duties. One of us would mix up a batch of muffins and put them in the oven while the others prepared lunch or dressed for school. Betty Crocker was definitely one of our best friends when it came to making pancakes, waffles, and biscuits!

Being involved in our restaurants and many other businesses, unless it's a vacation or a dedicated baking day, yeast breads and homemade biscuits just aren't my thing! But I do like to make quick-and-easy sweet breads and give them as gifts. The Tomato Drop Biscuits are an exception and say it all for me: they taste of savory spices, and I can use a scoop or just drop them on a cookie sheet and they're out of the oven in 10 to 12 minutes!

Just like there's room for dessert after a good, old-fashioned Southern meal, there's always room for bread during the meal. Even at the end of the meal, bread has its place—how else can you sop up the gravy? Baking your own bread or rolls has always been commonplace in the South. My Grandmother Hart made yeast rolls like people make toast (see her recipe on page 61). She made them frequently and effortlessly. And that's how we ate them!

Give me a piece of piping-hot cornbread smothered with butter any day. While Native Americans were first to use maize, the early settlers made a cornbread out of it. In the North, we tend to like our cornbread made with yellow cornmeal and on the sweet side; in the South, cornbread is more commonly made with white cornmeal and it's more on the savory side. The Southern Cornbread recipe I've included in this chapter calls for white cornmeal. A piece of cornbread gives a nice boost to a salad or soup. Speaking of salads, give your next one a Southern twang with Cornbread Croutons. If you don't have time to make them from scratch, let Betty Crocker cornbread and muffin mix help you.

I also love biscuits, and not all biscuits are created beige. Add a splash of color to a meal with Pumpkin Biscuits or Tomato Drop Biscuits. You'll find both recipes easy, and you can have them piping hot on your table in no time.

Spoon bread is so moist, it's close to a pudding and can be eaten with a spoon or a fork. The classic Southern spoon bread is made with cornmeal, which is what I use in my Sweet Potato Spoon Bread. It makes a great side dish along with meat and a vegetable. On the sweeter side, you'll find the Fig and Pistachio Tea Bread just plain scrumptious. There's nothing light and fluffy about it, but it has great depth of flavor.

Like many people today, I don't eat as much bread as I used to. And when I do, it can't be any old piece of bread. But when I see good homemade rolls, biscuits, or breads on the table, I have but one thing to say: "Pass the bread, please."

Buttermilk Biscuits

Originally, buttermilk was the liquid left over from churning butter from cream. It's slightly tart and thicker than plain milk, with a flavor similar to that of yogurt.

2 cups all-purpose flour
2 teaspoons baking powder
¼ teaspoon baking soda
1 teaspoon salt

4 tablespoons chilled butter or shortening,
cut into pieces
¾ cup buttermilk

1. Preheat oven to 450°F.
2. In a food processor fitted with the metal blade, sift together the flour, baking powder, baking soda, and salt until well combined. Add the butter or shortening and pulse until it is the texture of coarse meal. Add the buttermilk to the flour mixture. Pulse briefly, only until the dough is soft and easy to handle (do not overprocess, or biscuits will be tough).
3. Turn the dough onto a lightly floured work surface. Knead the dough gently until smooth. Roll it out to ½-inch thickness, sprinkling more flour on the work surface as necessary to prevent sticking, and cut the dough into rounds with a 2-inch biscuit cutter or the top of a 2-inch glass. (Scraps can be rerolled and cut into more rounds.)
4. Place the biscuits on a lightly greased baking sheet. Bake for 10 to 12 minutes, or until lightly browned. Serve warm or at room temperature.

How to Make a Buttermilk Substitute

Buttermilk substitute can be made by adding 1 tablespoon of lemon juice or vinegar or 1¾ teaspoons cream of tartar to each cup of whole milk. The soured milk should be allowed to sit for 10 minutes before being used.

Pumpkin Biscuits

These pumpkin biscuits bake up quickly and beautifully. They're a nice addition to soups, salads, and suppers. The key to great biscuit-making is to use chilled butter or shortening. Be careful not to over-mix or pulse the dough—just combine the ingredients together enough to make a coarse textured mixture—so biscuits are light and flaky.

2 cups all-purpose flour
2 teaspoons baking powder
½ teaspoon baking soda
1 teaspoon salt

4 tablespoons chilled butter or shortening,
    cut into pieces
½ cup canned pumpkin purée
½ cup buttermilk

1. Preheat oven to 450°F.
2. In a food processor fitted with the metal blade, sift together the flour, baking powder, baking soda, and salt. Add the butter or shortening and pulse briefly, just until it is the texture of coarse meal. Add the pumpkin and buttermilk to the flour mixture. Pulse just until the dough is soft and easy to handle (do not overprocess, or biscuits will be tough).
3. Turn the dough onto a lightly floured work surface. Knead the dough gently until smooth. Roll it out to ½-inch thickness, sprinkling more flour on the work surface as necessary to prevent sticking, and cut the dough into rounds with a 2-inch biscuit cutter or the top of a 2-inch glass. (Scraps can be rerolled and cut into more rounds.)
4. Place the biscuits on a lightly greased baking sheet. Bake for 10 to 12 minutes, or until lightly browned. Serve warm or at room temperature.

Tomato Drop Biscuits

Biscuits are a Southern staple for almost every meal. "Drop" biscuits get their name because you literally drop the dough onto a baking sheet by the spoonful, rather than rolling out and cutting it. This recipe is a snap to make, and the combination of tomato paste and tomato juice adds a really nice flavor to these savory bites.

Nonstick baking spray or parchment paper
2 cups all-purpose flour
2½ teaspoons baking powder
1 teaspoon salt
1 teaspoon onion powder
1 tablespoon sweet paprika
¼ teaspoon cayenne pepper, or more to taste
5 tablespoons cold unsalted butter, cut into small pieces
1 tablespoon tomato paste
¾ cup whole milk
½ cup tomato juice

1. Preheat oven to 400°F. Prepare a large baking sheet by spraying with nonstick spray, or by lining with parchment paper.
2. In a large bowl, sift the flour, baking powder, salt, onion powder, paprika, and cayenne pepper.
3. Add the butter to the flour mixture and blend in with a fork, pastry blender, or your fingers until the texture resembles coarse breadcrumbs.
4. In a separate bowl, whisk together the tomato paste, milk, and tomato juice. Add the tomato-milk mixture gradually into the flour mixture, stirring with a wooden spoon just until the dough forms, about 30 seconds (do not overmix, or biscuits will be tough).
5. Drop about 2 tablespoons of biscuit dough 1 inch apart on the baking sheet (you could also use a ¼-cup measuring cup or an ice-cream scoop sprayed with nonstick baking spray to drop biscuits). Bake for 15 to 18 minutes, until lightly golden. The biscuits are best served hot.

Down-Home Cornbread

Cornbread was first discovered by Europeans during their exploration of North America. European settlers, who had to use the local resources for food, fashioned cornmeal into cornbread. It was also popular during the Civil War, because it was very cheap and could be made in many different forms. Southerners traditionally prefer to use white cornmeal in their cornbread recipes, which is lighter than the yellow cornmeal we Northerners are used to. White cornmeal is readily available in the grocery store. If you prefer a sweeter cornbread, add some more sugar to the batter.

1 cup all-purpose flour
1 cup white or yellow cornmeal
¼ cup sugar
1 tablespoon baking powder
½ teaspoon salt

3 large eggs
1 cup milk
½ cup canola oil
Nonstick baking spray

1. Preheat oven to 400°F. Prepare a heavy 8-inch ovenproof skillet (such as a cast-iron skillet, an enamel-coated skillet such as those made by Le Creuset, a heavy-bottomed ovenproof nonstick skillet, or an 8-inch square baking pan) with nonstick spray.
2. In a large bowl, stir together the flour, cornmeal, sugar, baking powder, and salt to combine.
3. In a medium bowl, whisk together the eggs, milk, and canola oil to combine. Add the egg mixture to the flour mixture; stir to combine just until the lumps disappear.
4. Pour the batter into the prepared skillet or baking pan and bake for 25 to 30 minutes, until golden brown and a toothpick inserted in the center comes out clean. Serve warm from the skillet. (If you wish to remove the cornbread from the pan for serving, cool 5 minutes, then turn out to a serving dish.)

Cornbread Croutons

YIELDS 8 CUPS

These croutons are easy to make and liven up everyday soups and salads. They can be stored in an airtight container until ready to use, and will keep for up to 2 weeks.

1. Bake Cornbread as directed above. Cool to room temperature. Preheat oven to 325°F.
2. Cut cornbread into 1-inch cubes. Space evenly in a single layer on a large baking sheet. Bake for 35 to 40 minutes, until crisp and lightly browned. Allow to cool completely before storing in an airtight container.

Cornbread Muffins

To make standard-size Cornbread Muffins, prepare a 12-cup muffin pan with nonstick baking spray and divide the batter equally into each cup. Bake at 400°F for 15 to 20 minutes, or until golden brown and a toothpick inserted in the center comes out clean. For Mini Cornbread Muffins, prepare a 24-cup mini-muffin pan with nonstick baking spray and divide the batter equally into each cup. Bake for 10 to 12 minutes, or until golden brown and a toothpick comes out clean. Serve warm.

Cornbread Oyster Dressing

I didn't grow up on oysters, but once I discovered them, there was no turning back. The oysters take this cornbread dressing to new heights. The recipe makes enough stuffing for one 12½-pound turkey, with a small amount left over. If the stuffing is going inside the bird, it is best to barely moisten it, since it will get plenty of juices during the roasting. If your family and friends are stuffing fans, then the recipe should be doubled and the leftover dressing baked in a casserole. One tip: this dressing prefers not to be overmixed!

4 tablespoons butter
1 cup chopped onion
½ cup chopped celery
½ cup chopped red bell pepper
½ cup chopped green bell pepper
6 to 8 cups 1-inch-cubed cornbread
   (day-old is best)
1 teaspoon low-salt seafood seasoning

½ teaspoon salt
½ teaspoon freshly ground pepper
¼ to ½ teaspoon cayenne pepper, or more
   to taste
1 tablespoon finely chopped fresh parsley
2 eggs, beaten
3 dozen oysters, drained, liquid reserved,
   and chopped

1. In a heavy skillet, melt the butter over medium heat and add the onion, celery, and peppers. Sauté until the vegetables are tender, about 5 minutes.
2. In a large bowl, toss the cornbread cubes with the vegetables and seasonings. Gently stir in the eggs, chopped oysters, and only enough reserved liquid to slightly moisten and barely bind the ingredients.
3. Use the dressing to stuff Roast Turkey (see recipe on page 168), or place in a buttered casserole dish, cover, and bake in a preheated 350°F oven for 30 to 40 minutes.

Corn Fritters

Whether I'm at my home in Sag Harbor or at my apartment in New York City, I always have a pantry of staples on hand, just in case guests drop by at the last minute. These corn fritters are great dressed up with crème fraîche and caviar to serve as an hors d'oeuvre. Golden brown on the outside with a soft savory center, they're addictive!

Canola oil, for frying
3 cups (19.5 ounces) store-bought
    cornbread and muffin mix
1 egg, beaten
⅓ cup whole milk

1 tablespoon butter, melted
½ cup canned or frozen corn kernels
2 tablespoons finely diced red bell pepper
½ teaspoon seasoned salt with black
    pepper

1. In a deep saucepan or stockpot, heat 3 to 4 inches of oil to 365°F.
2. In a large bowl, place the cornbread mix.
3. In a medium bowl, combine the egg, milk, and melted butter, and whisk it into the cornbread mix. Then stir in the corn, red bell pepper, and seasoned salt. Allow the batter to rest for 10 minutes before frying.
4. Using 2 spoons (to protect hands), drop tablespoons of batter into the hot oil. Fry for 3 to 4 minutes, until the fritters puff and are browned on all sides.
5. Remove the fritters from the oil with a slotted spoon or tongs, and drain on paper towels (see Note). Serve hot.

Note: When I'm frying the fritters, I keep a muffin tin with paper muffin cups nearby; they absorb some of the oil and make a nice presentation.

Fig and Pistachio Tea Bread with Zesty Orange Glaze

Tea breads are sweet quick breads (breads made without yeast), but don't let the word "bread" fool you—they are actually cakes traditionally served with afternoon tea. Similar to pound cakes but moister, richer, and fuller, they come in a variety of delicious flavors. In this recipe, the combination of Mission figs and pistachio gets an extra boost of sweet flavor with the zesty orange glaze.

Nonstick cooking spray
1 packed cup roughly chopped dried
    Mission figs, stems removed
1½ cups orange juice
1½ teaspoons baking soda
1½ cups sugar
3 tablespoons unsalted butter, softened
2 large eggs
2½ cups all-purpose flour

½ teaspoon salt (omit if using salted
    pistachios)
1 cup unsalted shelled pistachios,
    plus more chopped pistachios for
    garnish
1 cup confectioners' sugar, sifted
Zest of 1 orange
1 tablespoon plain yogurt, or 1 to 2
    tablespoons milk

1. Preheat oven to 350°F.
2. Spray two 8 x 3 x 2-inch metal or disposable aluminum baking pans with nonstick baking spray.
3. Place the chopped figs in the bowl of a large food processor (or if you don't have a processor, in a medium bowl).
4. In a microwave oven or a small saucepan, heat the orange juice for 1 minute, or just until hot. Pour the warm juice over the figs. Add the baking soda, cover with the processor lid (or plastic wrap if using bowl), and let sit for 30 minutes to soften the figs. After 30 minutes, pulse the figs 8 to 10 times, just until they are finely chopped with bits remaining but not completely puréed. (Or, drain the juice off the chopped figs and reserve. Finely chop the figs by hand, and add the figs back into the reserved juice.) Set aside.
5. In a large bowl, combine the sugar, butter, and eggs. Beat with an electric mixer on medium speed for about 5 minutes, or by hand until the mixture is light and fluffy.
6. Sift together the flour and salt. Add the flour and fig mixture alternately to the sugar mixture, ending with the flour. Fold in the cup of pistachios until just combined.
7. Pour the batter equally into the 2 prepared baking pans.

8. Bake the bread on the middle rack of the oven. Check the bread at 45 minutes, and to prevent overbrowning, if necessary loosely tent it with aluminum foil. Continue baking for an additional 10 to 15 minutes, or until a toothpick comes out clean and the surface is golden brown and slightly cracked. Remove from oven, and allow bread to cool for 15 minutes in the pan. Turn the bread out of the pan and allow to cool completely before glazing.
9. In a small bowl, place the confectioners' sugar, orange zest, and yogurt or milk and stir well to combine; if the glaze is too thick to pour, thin it by stirring in a little more milk. Pour the glaze over the cooled breads. Garnish with the remaining orange zest and chopped pistachios.

Sweet Potato Spoon Bread

YIELDS 8 SERVINGS

Spoon bread, also known as "batter bread," is a sweet, moist cornmeal-based dish closer in consistency and taste to pudding than bread. I like to serve this sweet potato–flavored version as a side dish with meat and poultry.

Nonstick cooking spray
3 cups whole milk
1 cup yellow or white cornmeal
4 tablespoons butter, cut into pieces

2 cups mashed sweet potatoes
1 tablespoon baking powder
3 large eggs, beaten

1. Preheat oven to 350°F. Spray a round 2-quart baking dish with nonstick cooking spray.
2. In a large saucepan, pour the milk and cook over medium heat. Slowly whisk in the cornmeal to avoid any lumps. Continue whisking; as the milk heats to steaming, the mixture will thicken, about 3 to 4 minutes. Allow to come to a gentle boil and cook for about 1 minute. Turn off the heat and add the butter, whisking until it melts.
3. In a large bowl, stir together the mashed sweet potatoes and baking powder. Stir in the warm milk mixture and mix until smooth. Beat in the eggs a little at a time, blending well after each addition.
4. Pour the batter into the prepared baking dish. Bake for about 45 to 50 minutes, until the edges are golden brown and a toothpick inserted in the center comes out clean. Serve immediately.

Whole-Wheat Potato Rolls

YIELDS TWENTY 3-INCH ROLLS

These rolls contain mashed potatoes and come from an old recipe that stands the test of time. The mini size makes them perfect as dinner rolls, or for serving Southern Slider Sandwiches (see recipe on page 41).

1 large potato, peeled and cubed
2 packages (4 teaspoons) active dry yeast
1 tablespoon sugar
2¾ cups all-purpose flour
2¼ cups whole-wheat flour
1½ teaspoons salt

⅔ cup whole milk, warmed to 105°F
2 large eggs, lightly beaten
2 tablespoons unsalted butter, melted
    and cooled
Vegetable oil, for greasing pans

1. In a small saucepan, cook the potato in boiling salted water until tender. Drain, reserving ¼ cup of the cooking liquid, and mash the potato until very smooth. Set aside.
2. Cool the reserved potato cooking liquid to between 105° and 115°F, so it is very warm to the touch, then stir the yeast and sugar into the liquid and allow the mixture to stand until frothy, about 10 minutes.
3. Meanwhile, in a large bowl, mix the flours and salt together. In another large bowl or the bowl of a stand mixer, mix the yeast mixture, warm milk, eggs, melted butter, and mashed potato until well blended.
4. Add 3 cups of the flour mixture and beat for 5 minutes, until very smooth. Gradually add the remaining flour mixture to form a dough.
5. Turn the dough out onto a floured surface, and gradually knead the dough until it is smooth. It should be soft but not sticky; if necessary, add more flour, 1 tablespoon at a time, until dough is no longer sticky.
6. Grease a large bowl with vegetable oil, place the dough in the bowl, and turn it over once to coat all sides lightly with oil. Cover the bowl loosely with oiled plastic wrap and allow dough to rise in a warm place for 1 hour, or until doubled in size.
7. Generously oil a large baking sheet. Divide the dough into 20 pieces. Roll each piece of dough into a ball and tuck the edges under to create a smooth, flat top to the roll. Arrange the dough balls on the baking sheet with the edges of the dough touching.

8. Cover loosely with oiled plastic wrap and allow dough to rise in a warm place for 45 minutes, or until doubled in size.

9. When the dough has nearly risen, preheat oven to 400°F. Bake the rolls for 20 minutes, until they are golden on top and sound hollow when tapped on the bottom. Serve warm, or transfer the rolls to a wire rack to cool completely before serving.

Yeast Rolls

My Grandmother Hart made these rolls all the time. She would knead a big batch of dough, then put it on a heating grate, which was common in western Pennsylvania. These grates were in every room and helped to heat the house. She would cover the dough with a kitchen towel and let it rise. I'd watch the dough rise and see her punch it down, over and over—a process that resulted in these tasty, fragrant rolls. This recipe is well suited for a dinner roll, or as a bun for Southern Slider Sandwiches (see recipe on page 41). The recipe can easily be doubled (see Note).

1 package quick-rise active dry yeast
½ teaspoon sugar
1½ cups warm water (105°F to 115°F)
1 teaspoon salt
2 cups all-purpose flour, plus more for counter

1 teaspoon canola oil
White or yellow cornmeal, for sprinkling pan
Nonstick baking spray
1 large egg, beaten with 1 teaspoon water

1. In a large bowl of a stand mixer, stir the yeast and sugar into the warm water until dissolved. Allow to sit for 15 minutes, when the mixture should bubble up, which tells you the yeast is activated.
2. With the mixer on low speed fitted with a dough hook, add the salt, then gradually add the flour and mix until the dough comes together, about 1 minute. Increase the speed to medium and knead until the dough is smooth and elastic, about 5 minutes. (If doing this step without a stand mixer, follow steps 1 and 2 and stir with a wooden spoon until the dough comes together.)
3. Turn the dough out onto a clean counter that has been dusted with extra flour and knead by hand to form a smooth, round ball. The dough should be soft but not sticky.
4. In a large, deep bowl, pour the canola oil. Using a paper towel, spread the oil to the bottom and sides of the bowl. Add the dough; turn it once or twice in the bowl so the dough is lightly covered with the oil. Cover the bowl tightly with plastic wrap. Allow the dough to rise in a warm place for at least 1 hour, or until doubled in size. (If your kitchen is cool, fill a large pot half full with water and bring to a boil. Turn heat off. Invert the lid and place it on top of the pot. The surface of the lid should be flat and stable so that you can place the bowl with the dough on top of it. The bowl will stay warmer with this method and help the dough rise.)
5. Meanwhile, prepare a 9 x 13-inch baking sheet by spraying with nonstick baking spray, and sprin-

kle it lightly with cornmeal. Gently punch the raised dough down. Remove the dough to a lightly floured countertop and cut into 12 equal pieces. Roll each piece of dough into a ball and tuck the edges under to create a smooth, flat top to the roll.

6. Place the dough balls on the prepared baking sheet, making sure to space them equally. Spray a sheet of plastic wrap cut larger than the baking sheet with nonstick baking spray, and place it loosely on top of the dough balls. Let the dough rise in a warm place for 30 minutes, or until doubled in size.

7. When the dough has risen, preheat the oven to 375°F. Beat the egg and water until combined. Using a pastry brush, gently brush the tops of the rolls with the egg wash. Bake for 30 to 35 minutes, or until the rolls are crusty, golden on top, and the bottoms sound hollow when tapped. Serve warm, or transfer the rolls to a wire rack to cool completely before serving.

> *Note:* This recipe can be easily doubled to make 24 rolls. Use a full sheet pan (12 x 18 inches) for baking. If you make a double batch, you also have the option to freeze half of the dough by placing it in a sealed plastic bag and storing in the freezer. When you want to bake additional rolls, defrost the dough in the bag overnight in the refrigerator, and follow the recipe at step 5 to continue the baking process.

Chapter 4

Soups and Stews

No matter where you go in the South, you can always find a sturdy soup or stew simmering with the flavors of that region. Many were born out of necessity—you made do with what you had in the larder. The results were always democratic. Every ladle was chockful of meats and vegetables.

In the South, stews were and still are served at big events such as rallies, family reunions, and church gatherings. When an event calls for a large quantity of stew, there are actually stew masters who preside over huge pots. Southerners take their stews seriously; there've even been stew wars over who made a particular stew first.

No one seems to know where the "burgoo" came from in Kentucky Burgoo, but it's a must-have at Kentucky Derby parties and barbecues. It can also warm up a cold winter's day. Recipes vary, some calling for mutton, wild game, and in pioneer times, squirrel, possum, or raccoon. I've always made burgoo with beef, lamb, and chicken and mixed vegetables. I like that it's ready to serve in less than two hours.

Frogmore Stew isn't made with frogs and it's really not a stew in the traditional sense, it's more of a Low Country boil. Frogmore was the name of a town near St. Helena, an island near Beaufort, South Carolina. The stew is made with plenty of shrimp, fresh corn, and smoked sausage. This recipe is more stew than boil.

When I first had jambalaya in New Orleans, I didn't know that there were two types; all I knew was that every jambalaya I ate was delicious. I learned that Creole jambalaya has tomatoes and Cajun doesn't. The Duck Jambalaya recipe I've created is Creole. It's a favorite in my family. You don't have to buy a whole duck; just buy duck legs and split them in two. Jambalaya could be intimidating for someone who's never made one, but it's really a simple dish to prepare and to serve—at a sit-down dinner or a party.

An étouffée can take a little more time and involve more steps—and every step is worth it. A strictly undisputed Cajun dish, étouffée comes from the French word *étouffer*, which means "to smother." Since I love seafood, my favorite étouffée is made with crab and shrimp. I've included that recipe and also one for Vegetarian Étouffée. Why should we seafood lovers have all the fun?

I'm an all-year-round soup lover, maybe because of the fond memories I have of soup when I was growing up. My mother used to make a big pot with vegetables from our garden and sometimes leftover meat from dinner the night before. I loved the way her soup made the house smell. We'd come home from school and have a bowl, and then she'd send us off to do our homework. After a bowl of her soup, we didn't mind. Homework seemed easier.

Chestnut Soup also conjures up fond memories. The aroma of chestnuts always reminds me of my first fall in New York City. I bought a small bag from a street vendor and loved them at first bite. As soon as I get the first whiff of chestnuts roasting on street carts, I know it's chestnut soup season. The first time I made the soup for Dan, he loved it. I can't remember a Christmas dinner in our home without it.

At all of our restaurants, Braise of Black-Eyed Peas and Greens is the soup star. It's slow cooked, so the peas and greens are tender but not overcooked until they become mushy. It's as healthy as it is tasty. I've seen customers order it twice! She Crab Soup is another favorite because of its creaminess.

If you like the texture of lobster and frog legs, then you'll like Turtle Soup. It's a popular delicacy of Louisiana. This rich, heavy soup can be a meal in itself. The recipe calls for snapping turtle. The meat is easy to find and order online.

To me, soups and stews do more than just bring all kinds of good foods and seasonings together in one pot. A good soup or stew is a gift that keeps giving to family and friends.

Andouille-Spiced White Bean Soup

Chilly days are a perfect excuse to make this rich, hearty soup. Paired with a loaf of French bread and a salad, this recipe satisfies 6 to 8 hungry appetites. It's a great do-ahead dish. After cooking, simply cool, cover, and refrigerate the soup for up to 2 days or freeze for up to 1 month. Reheat over low heat, adding more broth to adjust the consistency.

3 cups uncooked Great Northern white beans

2 tablespoons extra virgin olive oil

¾ pound andouille sausage or andouille spiced smoked sausage, cut into ½-inch cubes

3 small zucchini, cut into ¾-inch cubes

½ cup finely chopped onion

½ cup finely chopped carrot

½ cup finely chopped celery

2 cloves garlic, finely chopped

6 cups chicken stock or broth

1 bay leaf

2 teaspoons ground cumin

1 teaspoon salt

½ teaspoon freshly ground black pepper

½ cup packed fresh parsley leaves, chopped

¼ cup dry sherry

1 tablespoon freshly squeezed lemon juice

½ teaspoon hot sauce, or to taste

Lemon zest, minced parsley, and sour cream, for garnish

1. The day before cooking the soup, in a large bowl, place the beans and cover with cold water. Set aside to soak overnight.
2. The day of cooking, rinse and drain the presoaked beans.
3. In a large Dutch oven or heavy stockpot, heat the olive oil over medium-high heat. Add the andouille sausage to the pot and sauté until lightly browned, about 4 minutes. Remove the sausage with a slotted spoon and drain on paper towels, leaving the olive oil and rendered fat in the pot.
4. Add the zucchini to the pot and sauté for about 3 to 5 minutes, until lightly browned; remove and set aside. Add the onion, carrot, celery, and garlic and sauté for about 5 minutes, until soft. Add the presoaked beans, chicken stock, bay leaf, ground cumin, salt, and pepper; stir to combine. Bring the soup to a boil, cover, and simmer for 45 minutes, or until the beans are tender. Remove and discard the bay leaf.
5. Remove 2 cups of beans from the pot with a slotted spoon and set aside. Using a potato masher, mash the remaining beans in the pot until smooth and creamy.

6. Add the reserved beans, andouille sausage, zucchini, parsley, sherry, lemon juice, and hot sauce to the pot; stir to combine. Cook, uncovered, over medium heat for 30 minutes, or until the mixture is slightly thickened. Serve immediately, cool and store in a tightly covered container in the refrigerator for up to 2 days, or freeze for up to 1 month.

Braise of Black-Eyed Peas and Greens Soup

YIELDS 6 SERVINGS

Braising is a method of cooking that involves first browning an ingredient such as meat or vegetables, then finishing cooking in a liquid over low heat. This slow style of cooking allows you to create dishes with incredible flavor and tenderness. While this dish isn't a traditional braise, I use the term because there's a whole lot of slow cookin' goin' on in this soup of vegetables, black-eyed peas, meat, and greens. I like to use kale or collard greens in the recipe because they hold up well to this type of slow cooking. Serve this hearty soup with a loaf of crusty bread for dipping!

1¼ cups (about 10 ounces) dried black-eyed peas, or two 15-ounce cans cooked black-eyed peas, drained and rinsed

2 tablespoons olive oil

1 cup diced sweet onion, such as Vidalia

2 cloves garlic, minced

1 cup diced celery

½ cup diced carrots

2 bay leaves

1½ cups chopped kale or collard greens, stems discarded

1 cup diced pork, ham, or smoked turkey breast

6 cups low-sodium chicken stock or broth

2 teaspoons Creole seasoning

½ teaspoon dried oregano

Sea salt and freshly ground black pepper to taste

1 cup cooked barbecued rib meat, shaved off the bone and chopped, optional for garnish

1. The day before serving, in a large bowl, place the dried black-eyed peas. Cover with water and let soak overnight. Drain and rinse thoroughly. Or, to quick-soak the peas, place them in a large pot or Dutch oven, cover with water, and bring to a boil over high heat. Remove from the heat, cover tightly, and let stand for 1 hour, then drain and rinse thoroughly.

2. In a large Dutch oven or saucepan, heat the olive oil over medium heat. Add the onion, garlic, celery, and carrots, and sauté for about 5 minutes, until tender. Add the bay leaves, kale or collard greens, and meat to the pot, and sauté, stirring frequently, for 2 to 3 minutes.

3. Add the chicken stock, soaked dried black-eyed peas or drained and rinsed canned black-eyed peas, Creole seasoning, and oregano to the pot. Bring the mixture to a boil, reduce heat to low, and simmer, partially covered, for 45 minutes to 1 hour, or until the peas are tender.

4. Remove the bay leaves, and season with salt and pepper. Ladle the soup into bowls and serve immediately, garnished with chopped rib meat if desired.

Cajun Veal Stew

YIELDS 6 TO 8 SERVINGS

This simple one-pot stew is enhanced with the flavors of a brown roux that creates rich, delicious gravy. You will think you are eating your grandmother's stew! By slow-cooking the seasoned veal with leeks, turnips, and red bell pepper, this recipe creates a succulent and tender stew. Serve it with cooked rice, grits, or Down-Home Cornbread (see recipe on page 52).

2 pounds veal stew meat, cut into 2-inch
    pieces
2 tablespoons Cajun seasoning
1 teaspoon kosher salt
½ teaspoon freshly ground black pepper
⅓ cup plus 2 tablespoons extra virgin olive
    oil, divided
1 cup chopped leeks
1 cup chopped celery
1 cup chopped carrots

1 cup chopped turnips
1 cup chopped red bell pepper
2 cloves garlic, finely chopped
⅓ cup all-purpose flour
2 cups chicken stock or broth
1½ cups water
1 teaspoon tomato paste
½ tablespoon Worcestershire sauce
⅛ teaspoon hot sauce, optional
Freshly chopped celery leaves, for garnish

1. Place the veal on a large sheet of parchment or wax paper. Dry the veal by pressing gently with paper towels, then sprinkle with the Cajun seasoning, salt, and pepper. Toss the veal pieces with your hands to distribute seasonings.
2. In a large Dutch oven or heavy stockpot, heat 2 tablespoons of the olive oil over medium-high heat. Add the veal and sauté for about 5 to 8 minutes, until browned on all sides. Using a slotted spoon, remove the veal and place in a large bowl; set aside. Leave remaining oil in the pot.
3. Add the leeks, celery, carrots, turnips, red pepper, and garlic to the pot and sauté for about 3 to 4 minutes, until the leeks and celery are translucent. Remove the vegetables with the slotted spoon and add to the bowl with the veal; set aside.
4. To make the roux, add the remaining ⅓ cup olive oil and the flour to the pot; stir together with a wire whisk to combine. Place heat on medium and cook, stirring constantly with the whisk, for 12 minutes, or until the mixture is dark brown and has a strong, nutty flavor. The roux will be very thick.
5. Whisk the chicken stock, water, tomato paste, Worcestershire sauce, and hot sauce into the roux;

whisk well to combine until the mixture is smooth, without any lumps. Turn the heat up to medium-high and continue to whisk until bubbles form at the edges of the pot. Carefully add the reserved veal and vegetables back into the pot; stir to combine. Bring the mixture to a boil and cover the pot. Reduce heat to low and simmer for 1½ to 2 hours, or until the veal is tender and the sauce is thickened. Serve immediately, garnished with freshly chopped celery leaves.

Cioppino

When you think of Southern cooking, Italian dishes don't usually come to mind. However, during the peak immigration years, the American South attracted its share of Italian immigrants who were all looking to follow the American Dream. They brought their culinary skills with them, and Italian influence can be seen in the pasta, eggplant, and artichoke dishes that are so popular in south Louisiana and across the rest of the South. Cioppino is a seafood stew, and is traditionally made from the catch of the day, usually crab, clams, shrimp, scallops, mussels, and fresh fish. What better place to get a fresh catch than the Low Country?

⅓ cup olive oil

1 large yellow onion, diced

4 cloves garlic, minced

One 2-ounce can anchovy fillets, diced, or to taste

2 bay leaves

1 teaspoon red pepper flakes, or to taste

2 cups dry white wine

2 cups fish stock or broth, or bottled clam juice

One 15-ounce can tomato sauce

One 28-ounce can crushed tomatoes

1 teaspoon dried basil

1 teaspoon dried oregano

2 small cooked lobsters, claws and tails separated

2 cooked king crab legs, cut into pieces

10 ounces firm white fish such as catfish, halibut, or red snapper, cut into 1½-inch chunks

16 mussels, scrubbed and debearded

16 clams, scrubbed

16 raw shrimp, peeled and deveined

Salt and freshly ground pepper to taste

Chopped fresh parsley, for garnish

1. In a large pot, heat the olive oil over medium-high heat. Add the onion and cook, stirring frequently until soft, about 3 minutes. Stir in the garlic and cook for 2 to 3 minutes. Add the anchovies, bay leaves, red pepper flakes, and wine to the pot, reduce the heat, and simmer for 5 minutes. Add the fish stock, tomato sauce, crushed tomatoes, basil, and oregano, stirring well to combine.

2. Cover the pot and simmer for about 20 minutes, until slightly thickened. (At this point, the soup can be cooled to room temperature, covered, and refrigerated or frozen until ready to use. Reheat the soup before proceeding.)

3. Add the lobster and crab legs to the soup and heat through, about 5 minutes. Remove the lobster and crab to a large warm bowl.

4. Return the soup to a boil and add the fish, mussels, clams, and shrimp. Reduce heat, cover, and simmer gently until the mussels and clams open and the shrimp turn pink. Discard any unopened mussels and clams and the bay leaves. Season with salt and pepper. Divide the reserved lobster and crab legs into individual serving bowls, pour the remaining shellfish and the soup over the lobster and crab, and serve immediately, garnished with parsley.

Chestnut Soup

The first roasted chestnuts I tasted were from a street vendor in New York City. The earthy aroma is definitely synonymous with fall holiday recipes. Fresh chestnuts work particularly well for this recipe, but since they are available only seasonally from October through December, canned or vacuum-packed chestnuts are an acceptable substitute.

1½ pounds fresh chestnuts, or 14 ounces
   vacuum-packed peeled chestnuts
2 tablespoons olive oil
½ cup diced onion
¼ cup diced celery
1 leek, white and light green stem only,
   rinsed well and chopped
2 cloves garlic, finely diced
5 cups chicken stock or broth

1 bay leaf
1 teaspoon dried thyme
2 tablespoons brandy
¾ cup half-and-half
½ teaspoon salt, or to taste
¼ teaspoon freshly ground black pepper,
   or to taste
Ground nutmeg to taste

1. If using fresh chestnuts, preheat the oven to 400°F, or bring a large pot of water to a boil. Using the tip of a sharp knife, slice an X on the flat side of each chestnut. Place the chestnuts on a baking sheet to roast them in the oven, or boil them for 10 to 12 minutes, until the outer skin begins to curl. Remove the chestnuts from oven or drain them, and allow to cool enough to handle. Remove the outer and inner layers of skin from the chestnuts and set aside.

2. In a large saucepan, heat the olive oil over medium heat. Add the onion, celery, leek, and garlic, and cook, stirring frequently, for about 5 minutes, until soft. Stir in the chicken stock, bay leaf, thyme, and peeled chestnuts. Bring to a boil, reduce heat, and simmer, partially covered, for 30 minutes, or until chestnuts are tender. Discard the bay leaf.

3. In a blender, carefully purée the soup in batches, and add the purée back to the saucepan. Stir in the brandy, half-and-half, salt, pepper, and nutmeg. Place over medium heat until just heated through, and serve immediately.

Crab and Shrimp Étouffée

YIELDS 6 TO 8 SERVINGS

Étouffée comes from the French word meaning "to smother or braise." It is traditionally prepared with seafood but can be done with a variety of meats, poultry, and game. Always begin with a roux, and include the holy trinity: onions, peppers, and celery.

¼ cup butter

2 tablespoons olive oil

⅓ cup all-purpose flour

1 cup chopped onion

¼ cup chopped green bell pepper

¼ cup chopped poblano chile pepper

½ cup chopped celery

2 tablespoons minced garlic

1 cup chopped scallion, divided

2 cups chicken or shrimp stock or broth, warmed

⅓ cup dry white wine

1 tablespoon low-salt Creole seasoning

1 tablespoon tomato paste

5 tablespoons chopped fresh curly parsley, divided

2 teaspoons Worcestershire sauce

½ teaspoon hot sauce

2 pounds unpeeled medium-size raw shrimp, or two 16-ounce packages frozen unpeeled raw shrimp, thawed according to package directions

1 pound fresh lump or claw crabmeat, drained and flaked

5 cups hot cooked long-grain rice, for serving

1. To make the roux, in a wide, heavy Dutch oven or pot, melt the butter and olive oil over medium-high heat. Stir in the flour and cook, stirring constantly, for 5 minutes, or until the roux is caramel colored.
2. Add the chopped onion, bell pepper, poblano pepper, and celery to the pot and cook, stirring constantly, for 4 minutes, or until the vegetables are tender. Add the garlic and ¼ cup of the scallion, and sauté for 1 to 2 minutes.
3. Slowly stir the warm broth and white wine into the pot. Add the Creole seasoning, tomato paste, 2 tablespoons of the parsley, the Worcestershire sauce, and hot sauce. Bring to a boil, reduce heat to medium-low, and simmer, stirring occasionally, for 30 minutes.
4. Add the shrimp, 2 tablespoons of the parsley, and ¼ cup scallion to the pot. Cover and simmer, stirring occasionally, for 5 minutes, until the shrimp turn pink and are just cooked.

5. Stir the crabmeat into the pot and continue to cook, stirring often, until heated through, about 5 minutes. Divide the hot cooked rice into individual serving bowls. Spoon the Crab and Shrimp Étouffée on top of the rice. Garnish with the remaining 2 tablespoons parsley and serve immediately with the remaining ½ cup of the scallion.

B. Smith Cooks Southern-Style

Vegetarian Étouffée

I think it's important to include vegetarian recipes that entire families will enjoy. This étouffée could turn the staunchest naysayer into a convert! The recipe calls for sunchokes, also known as Jerusalem artichokes, a root vegetable that grows as small underground tubers that resemble gingerroot. Sunchokes are actually a type of sunflower and have been cultivated in the United States for centuries, originally by the Native Americans. They have a distinctive sweet, almost nutty taste and crisp texture. Sunchokes may be difficult to find, so mushrooms may be substituted; the dish becomes quite different, but equally satisfying!

2 teaspoons canola oil
2½ cups diced okra
2 cups diced eggplant
3 tablespoons butter or canola oil
3 tablespoons all-purpose flour
1 cup chopped onion
1 cup chopped celery
¼ cup chopped red bell pepper
¼ cup chopped yellow bell pepper
¼ cup chopped green bell pepper
¼ cup chopped seeded poblano chile pepper
1 tablespoon chopped garlic
1 tablespoon Creole seasoning
¼ teaspoon cayenne pepper
½ cup low-sodium chicken broth

⅓ cup white wine
One-half 14-ounce can diced tomatoes
*   with Italian seasoning*
½ cup diced carrots
1 cup peeled, diced sunchokes (Jerusalem
*   artichokes)*
1½ teaspoons dried thyme leaves or
*   1½ tablespoons chopped fresh thyme*
4 scallions, chopped and divided
3 tablespoons chopped fresh parsley, divided
Salt and freshly ground black pepper to taste
2 teaspoons Worcestershire sauce, or
*   golden sherry to taste*
Cooked long-grain white rice or sautéed
*   firm tofu, optional for serving*

1. In 2 medium saucepans, add 1 teaspoon of the canola oil to each and heat over medium-high heat. When the oil is hot, add the okra to one pan and the eggplant to the other. Sauté the vegetables for about 10 minutes each, or until they start to brown. Set aside.
2. To make a roux, in a large heavy Dutch oven or stockpot, melt 3 tablespoons butter or canola oil over medium heat, stir in the flour, and cook, stirring constantly, for 5 to 10 minutes, or until the

roux is a rich medium brown with a nutty aroma. During this time, watch carefully and regulate the heat to achieve a nice brown color without burning.

3. To stop the roux from cooking, immediately add the onion, celery, peppers, garlic, Creole seasoning, and cayenne. Stir to combine and cook over medium heat, stirring frequently, for 10 to 15 minutes, or until vegetables are soft.

4. Add the broth, wine, tomatoes, carrots, sunchokes, thyme, half the scallions, 2 tablespoons of the parsley, and the reserved okra and eggplant to the pot. Season with salt and pepper. Bring the mixture to a boil, then lower heat to a simmer, cover, and cook, stirring frequently, for 30 to 45 minutes.

5. Stir in the Worcestershire sauce or the golden sherry and serve the Vegetarian Étouffée immediately, over a bed of cooked rice or sautéed firm tofu if desired. Garnish with the remaining 1 tablespoon parsley and the remaining scallions. (The Vegetarian Étouffée can be made a day ahead; store tightly covered in the refrigerator and reheat to a simmer before serving.)

Duck Jambalaya

Jambalaya is a Louisiana Creole dish of Spanish and French heritage. It is traditionally made in one pot with meats and vegetables, and is completed by adding stock and rice. This is different from a gumbo or étouffée because the rice is added uncooked during cooking, and the flavor of the jambalaya is absorbed into the cooking rice.

5 duck legs	1 tablespoon minced garlic
1 teaspoon salt, plus more for seasoning duck	½ teaspoon dried thyme
¼ teaspoon freshly ground black pepper, plus more for seasoning duck	2 cups uncooked long-grain white rice
	Two 14½-ounce cans diced tomatoes
	Chicken or duck stock or broth, as needed
12 ounces andouille sausage, cut into ½-inch dice	2 small bay leaves
¾ cup chopped onion	¼ teaspoon cayenne pepper, optional
¾ cup chopped green bell pepper	½ cup thinly sliced scallions
½ cup chopped celery, with a few leaves	1 tablespoon chopped fresh parsley, for garnish

1. Cut each duck leg into 2 pieces (drumstick and thigh). Trim excess skin and fat from the duck; season well with salt and freshly ground pepper.
2. In a large Dutch oven or stockpot, brown the duck pieces over medium-high heat, turning them to brown evenly, about 5 minutes on each side. Remove the duck from the pan and set aside. Remove all but 2 tablespoons of drippings from the pot.
3. Add the sausage to the pot and cook over medium-high heat, stirring frequently, for about 4 to 5 minutes, until browned. Remove the sausage from the pot and set aside. Reduce heat to medium and add the onion, bell pepper, celery, garlic, and thyme to the pot. Cook, stirring frequently, for about 5 minutes, until softened. Stir in the rice and cook, stirring frequently to coat rice, for 1 to 2 minutes.
4. Drain the tomatoes and reserve the liquid. Pour the tomato liquid into a large measuring cup, add enough chicken or duck stock to make 3½ cups, and pour into the pot. Add the tomatoes, bay leaves, salt, ¼ teaspoon black pepper, and cayenne pepper and bring to a boil.

5. Return the duck pieces and sausage to the pot. Reduce heat to low and simmer, covered, for about 25 minutes, until the duck is cooked through and the rice has absorbed most of the liquid. Remove the bay leaves. Stir in the scallions and serve immediately, garnished with chopped parsley.

B. Smith Cooks Southern-Style

Fricassee of Pork

It's time to revive a memory of special Sunday lunches from years past with this old-fashioned dish called fricassee. This recipe stars pieces of tender pork tenderloin, shallots, parsnips, and green peas. It cooks to perfection in a sophisticated wine and cream sauce in only 30 minutes! Want a quick, special dish for those you care about? This foolproof recipe is the one for you! It's delicious served with boiled new potatoes.

¼ cup all-purpose flour

1 teaspoon paprika

1 teaspoon kosher salt

½ teaspoon freshly ground black pepper

2 pounds pork tenderloin, trimmed
    of sinew and fat and cut into 2-inch
    cubes

4 tablespoons unsalted butter

½ cup finely chopped shallot

1 cup chicken stock or broth

½ cup dry white wine

½ pound (about 3 large) parsnips,
    cut into julienne strips

½ cup heavy cream

½ cup fresh or frozen green peas

Finely chopped chives, for garnish

1. In a gallon-size resealable plastic bag, combine the flour, paprika, salt, and pepper. Add the pork pieces, seal the bag, and toss well to coat each piece of meat with the flour mixture.

2. In a large nonstick sauté pan, melt the butter over medium heat. Add the shallots and cook until translucent, about 2 to 3 minutes. Add the pork pieces and sauté for 5 minutes, or just until the pork is pale golden in color. Remove the pork to a plate; set aside.

3. Add the chicken broth and white wine to the pan, stirring constantly with a wire whisk for 2 to 3 minutes over medium-high heat, until the mixture slightly thickens and turns into a sauce. Add the pork and parsnips to the pan, gently stirring to combine. Lower heat to a simmer, cover the pan, and simmer for 30 minutes, or until the meat is cooked. Gently stir in the cream and continue to simmer, uncovered, for 5 more minutes (if you like a thicker sauce, simmer an additional 5 minutes).

4. Just before serving, add the green peas to the pan and simmer 1 to 2 minutes, or until peas are cooked. Serve immediately, garnished with chives. (Reheat leftovers with ½ cup of hot chicken stock to maintain the original sauce consistency.)

Frogmore Stew

YIELDS 6 TO 8 SERVINGS

There are no frogs in Frogmore Stew, and there's no shortage of flavor! This Low Country South Carolina recipe gets its name from a small coastal town. The name of the town has since been changed, but the ingredients of shrimp, corn, and whatever else you have on hand have remained the same in this traditional seafood boil. This one-pot meal is perfect for sharing with family and friends.

2 teaspoons vegetable oil
1½ pounds spicy smoked sausage, cut into
*   ½-inch dice*
2 medium green bell peppers, cut into
*   ½-inch chunks, optional*
8 cups chicken stock or broth
Salt and freshly ground black pepper to taste
3 bay leaves
2 teaspoons Old Bay Seasoning
1 teaspoon dried thyme

18 small new potatoes, halved
2 medium onions, sliced lengthwise into
*   ⅓-inch wedges*
3 ears corn, shucked and silks removed,
*   each cut into 4 pieces*
One 15-ounce can diced tomatoes,
*   drained*
36 large raw shrimp, heads on if available
1 tablespoon chopped fresh parsley,
*   for garnish*

1. In a large Dutch oven or heavy pot, heat the vegetable oil over medium-high heat. Add the sausage and bell peppers, stirring to coat with the oil. Cook, stirring occasionally, for about 8 to 10 minutes, until the peppers have softened and the sausage is lightly browned. Remove the sausage and peppers from the pot and set aside.
2. Pour the chicken stock into the Dutch oven, scraping up any browned bits stuck to the bottom of the pot. Bring to a boil, reduce heat to medium-low, and season with salt and pepper. Add the bay leaves, Old Bay Seasoning, thyme, potatoes, and onions and cook, partially covered, for 10 minutes. Add the cooked sausage and peppers, the corn, and tomatoes to the pot and simmer, uncovered, for about 10 minutes, until the potatoes and corn are tender.
3. Adjust the seasonings—the stew should be highly flavored. Add the shrimp and cook for 3 to 5 minutes, just until they are cooked through. Remove the bay leaves.
4. Serve the Frogmore Stew immediately in heated soup plates, equally dividing the shrimp, sausage, and vegetables with some of the broth ladled over, garnished with parsley.

Kentucky Burgoo

YIELDS 10 TO 12 SERVINGS

This dish is particularly popular for large Southern gatherings. People bring one or two ingredients and add them to one big community pot. Depending on the time of year, fresh, frozen, or canned vegetables can be used in this recipe. I like to serve mine with Down-Home Cornbread (see recipe on page 52).

One 3- to 3½-pound whole chicken, split
1 pound beef shank, trimmed of excess fat
1 pound lean boneless lamb, trimmed
    of excess fat
Generous pinch of red pepper flakes
1 tablespoon plus 1 teaspoon salt, divided
3 quarts water, plus more as needed
2 cups finely chopped onion
4 cloves garlic, chopped

3 cups your favorite frozen mixed
    vegetables or two 15-ounce cans
    mixed vegetables, drained
One 15-ounce can butter beans, drained
8 ounces frozen sliced okra
2 tablespoons Worcestershire sauce
½ teaspoon freshly ground black pepper
1 cup chopped fresh parsley

1. In a heavy 6- to 8-quart Dutch oven, combine the chicken, beef shank, lamb, red pepper flakes, 1 tablespoon salt, and the water. Bring to a boil over high heat, skimming off the foam as it rises to the surface.
2. Reduce the heat to low and simmer, partially covered, for 45 minutes, or until the chicken is tender. Remove the chicken with tongs or a slotted spoon to a plate and let cool to room temperature. Refrigerate until ready to use.
3. Partially cover the Dutch oven and continue to simmer for about 1½ hours, until the beef and lamb are tender. With a slotted spoon, remove the beef and lamb from the Dutch oven.
4. Remove any beef shank bones and discard them. Strain the broth into a large measuring cup, and add some water to the broth if necessary to measure 6 cups. Pour the 6 cups of broth back into the Dutch oven.
5. Stir the onion, garlic, mixed vegetables, butter beans, okra, Worcestershire sauce, 1 teaspoon salt, and pepper into the broth. Bring to a boil, reduce the heat to low, and simmer, uncovered, stirring occasionally, for 1½ hours.

6. Meanwhile, remove the chicken meat from the bones, and cut the beef and lamb into 1-inch pieces. Cover and refrigerate the meat until the vegetables have cooked.
7. Once the vegetables have cooked for 1½ hours, stir the chicken and meat into the pot. Simmer over low heat until heated through. Stir in the parsley, and season with salt and pepper. Serve immediately.

Red Bean Soup

Red beans are a popular member of the kidney bean family, with the same rich red color, but are smaller and more rounded. Over the years, kidney beans have become the popular bean for this dish, but the Cajuns originally used small red beans, which can still be found canned or dried.

3½ quarts water, plus more as needed
1 pound dried small red beans or red
    kidney beans
1½ pounds smoked ham hocks
2 medium onions, coarsely chopped
1 cup coarsely chopped celery, including
    some leaves

1½ teaspoons dried thyme or
    1½ tablespoons chopped fresh thyme
1 large bay leaf
2 teaspoons Creole seasoning
Salt and freshly ground black pepper to taste
¼ cup dry red wine
2 scallions, including the green tops,
    trimmed and sliced, for garnish

1. In a heavy 8- to 10-quart Dutch oven or soup pot, bring 3½ quarts of water to a boil over high heat. Add the beans and boil them for 2 minutes, then turn off the heat and let the beans soak for 1 hour.
2. Drain off the liquid from the beans into a large measuring cup, adding enough fresh water to measure 3½ quarts. Return the liquid and the beans to the pot, add the ham hocks, onion, celery, thyme, and bay leaf, and bring to a boil over high heat.
3. Reduce the heat to low and simmer, partially covered, for 3 hours, or until the ham is tender and shows no resistance when pierced deeply with the point of a sharp knife.
4. Transfer the ham hocks to a plate, cut off the meat, and discard the skin and bones. Cut the meat into ¼-inch pieces.
5. Discard the bay leaf. Purée the beans and vegetables and their cooking liquid through the medium blade of a food mill, or use a potato masher, and return them to the pot.
6. Add the ham and Creole seasoning to the pot and stir to combine. Taste the soup, and season with salt and pepper.
7. Bring the soup to a boil over high heat. Remove the pot from the heat, stir in the wine, and pour the soup into a heated tureen or in individual soup plates. Serve immediately, garnished with sliced scallion.

Seafood Gumbo

In my opinion, gumbo is one of the greatest contributions of Louisiana kitchens to Southern cuisine. Gumbo originated in New Orleans, and is a result of the melding of many cultures in Louisianan history. The dish is based on the French soup bouillabaisse, but the use of okra is West African in origin, and many recipes call for filé powder (ground sassafras leaves), which is of Native American origin. According to some sources, the word *gumbo* comes from the Bantu (Angolan) word *gombo*, meaning "okra," while other sources claim it comes from the Choctaw word *kombo*, meaning "sassafras." Any way you say it, you can't talk about Southern soups and stews without mentioning gumbo! When serving gumbo, pass around Creole seasoning, filé powder, and hot sauce. Some like it hot!

½ cup bacon fat or canola oil
½ cup all-purpose flour
1½ cups diced onion
1 cup diced celery
1 large poblano chile pepper, stemmed, seeded, and diced
1 red jalapeño pepper, stemmed, seeded, and finely diced
1 cup canned fire-roasted diced tomatoes with green chiles
1 tablespoon tomato paste
½ cup chopped fresh parsley, divided, plus more for garnish
½ cup chopped scallion, divided
2 bay leaves
2 tablespoons chopped fresh thyme
2 tablespoons chopped fresh sage
¼ teaspoon red pepper flakes
1 tablespoon minced garlic

¼ teaspoon cayenne pepper (omit if using andouille sausage)
4 cups simmering Gumbo Stock (recipe follows)
Salt and freshly ground black pepper to taste
Meat from one 3-pound cooked chicken, reserved from making stock
1 pound medium whole shrimp or crawfish, peeled and deveined (reserve heads, shells, and tails for Gumbo Stock)
1 pound crabmeat, picked over
1 pound andouille or turkey sausage, cooked and diced
8 cups hot cooked long-grain white rice, for serving
Creole seasoning, filé powder, and hot sauce, for serving

1. To make a roux, in a medium Dutch oven or heavy stockpot, melt the bacon fat or canola oil over medium-high heat. Stir in the flour. Cook, stirring continuously, for about 15 to 20 minutes, until the roux is deep brown in color. Watch the mixture closely and adjust the heat to keep the roux from burning.
2. When the roux is done, immediately stir in the onion, celery, poblano and jalapeño peppers, and cook over medium heat, stirring frequently, for about 8 minutes.
3. Stir the diced tomatoes, tomato paste, ¼ cup of the parsley, ¼ cup of the scallions, the bay leaves, thyme, sage, red pepper flakes, garlic, and cayenne into the pot. Add the 4 cups of simmering Gumbo Stock to the pot. Stir well and season with salt and pepper. Cover and simmer over medium-low heat, stirring occasionally, for 40 minutes or longer.
4. While the gumbo is simmering, remove the skin and bones from the cooled chicken reserved from making the Gumbo Stock. Tear the chicken into bite-size pieces.
5. Add the chicken, shrimp or crawfish, crabmeat, sausage, and remaining scallions and parsley to the pot. Add more Gumbo Stock if needed, and cook over medium-high heat for 5 minutes, until the shrimp or crawfish are cooked through. Remove and discard the bay leaves.
6. In large soup bowls, ladle the gumbo over scoops of hot rice. Sprinkle each serving with chopped parsley, and serve immediately with hot sauce on the side.

Gumbo Stock

YIELDS ABOUT 9 TO 10 CUPS

One 3-pound chicken, whole or cut up
1 onion, roughly chopped with skin
1 rib celery, roughly chopped
1 bay leaf
2 sprigs fresh parsley
1 large clove garlic, smashed
2 sprigs fresh thyme

¼ teaspoon salt
¼ teaspoon red pepper flakes
Water, to cover chicken
4 to 6 small whole live blue crabs
Heads, shells, and tails from 1 pound
    medium shrimp or crawfish (reserved
    from Seafood Gumbo ingredients)

1. In a large stockpot, place the chicken. Add the onion, celery, bay leaf, parsley, garlic, thyme, salt, and red pepper flakes. Fill the pot with enough water to fully cover the chicken. Bring to a boil,

reduce heat to medium-low, and simmer for 30 to 45 minutes, until the chicken is cooked through. Using tongs or a slotted spoon, remove the chicken from the pot, set aside to cool, and reserve for making Seafood Gumbo.

2. Add the live crabs to the simmering stock and cook for a few minutes, until just cooked. Then remove. Add the shrimp or crawfish shells, heads, and tails to the stock and keep simmering over low heat until ready to use. Strain the stock before using.

3. Any stock remaining after making gumbo can be strained, cooled, and stored in a tightly sealed container in the freezer for 3 months.

She-Crab Soup

I first tasted she-crab soup with blue crabmeat in Charleston, South Carolina. We sampled different versions in quite a few restaurants in that charming city. While some Southerners have been known to garnish it with chopped egg yolks, I prefer to wait to prepare this soup until I find live blue crabs, and add color and flavor with a sprinkle of the rich red roe.

4 tablespoons unsalted butter
1 cup finely chopped onion
½ cup finely chopped celery
3 tablespoons all-purpose flour
½ cup dry sherry
1 cup bottled clam juice, or 1 cup fish
    stock or broth
2 cups heavy cream

2 cups milk
¼ teaspoon ground mace or nutmeg
1½ teaspoons Worcestershire sauce
1 cup lump crabmeat, from fresh blue
    crabs if possible
¼ cup crumbled crab roe, plus more
    for garnish, or 2 hard-boiled eggs
Salt and freshly ground black pepper to taste

1. In a large stockpot, melt the butter over medium-high heat. Add the onion and celery and sauté for about 3 minutes, until soft and golden. Add the flour, stirring constantly, for about 2 to 3 minutes, until golden.
2. Stir the sherry into the pot and cook for about 1 minute, allowing it to reduce a little. Stir in the clam juice, heavy cream, and milk. Simmer over medium or medium-low heat for 20 minutes, stirring occasionally.
3. Add the mace, Worcestershire sauce, crabmeat, and ¼ cup roe to the pot and stir to combine. Allow to heat through for about 5 minutes. Season with salt and pepper. Serve immediately, garnished with additional crab roe. If crab roe is unavailable, finely chop 2 hard-boiled eggs and distribute evenly among individual soups bowls before ladling in the soup.

Southern Peanut Soup

George Washington Carver was known as "the peanut wizard," in part because he developed more than three hundred peanut-based products while working at the Tuskegee Institute in Alabama. He also saved many Southern farmers from losing their land by convincing them to grow peanuts when their cotton crops were destroyed. This peanut soup is creamy and delicious, with loads of spices. If you want to add a bit more heat, increase the amount of white pepper. I think Mr. Carver would approve!

2 teaspoons peanut oil
2 tablespoons butter
2 celery stalks, chopped with some leaves
1 large onion, chopped
2 medium cloves garlic, crushed
3½ cups chicken stock or broth
1 tablespoon brown sugar
1½ teaspoons ground cumin
½ teaspoon ground coriander
½ teaspoon ground ginger

⅛ teaspoon ground white pepper, or more
   to taste
⅛ teaspoon ground nutmeg
1 cup unsalted smooth peanut butter
½ cup fat-free half-and-half
1 teaspoon salt, or more to taste
1 cup chopped peeled and seeded tomatoes,
   optional for garnish
2 tablespoons chopped fresh cilantro,
   optional for garnish

1. In a medium saucepan, heat the peanut oil and butter over medium heat. Add the celery, onion, and garlic, and cook, stirring frequently, for about 5 minutes, until the vegetables are tender. Stir in the chicken broth, brown sugar, cumin, coriander, ginger, white pepper, and nutmeg. Whisk in the peanut butter. Bring to a boil, then reduce heat and simmer, covered, for 20 minutes.

2. Remove the saucepan from the heat. Pour the soup through a strainer placed over a large bowl. Return the cooking liquid to the saucepan. In a blender or food processor fitted with a metal blade, purée the solids, adding some cooking liquid if necessary. Stir the vegetable purée back into the cooking liquid, and stir in the half-and-half and salt. Heat over low heat until just heated through. (Do not allow to boil, or soup will curdle.) Pour the soup into a warmed tureen or into 6 individual soup bowls. Serve immediately, garnished with chopped tomato and cilantro if desired.

Sweet Parsnip Soup

Parsnips are root vegetables that resemble ivory-colored carrots, brought to America by the Europeans in the 1600s. Parsnips are complex, combining sweetness with earthy herbal notes. Look for small to medium, well-shaped roots free of pitting. The nutmeg in this recipe really brings out the sweetness of the parsnips and makes for a delicious soup. Fresh snipped chives are a pretty, flavorful garnish.

2 tablespoons butter

2 large leeks, white parts only, sliced and
    cleaned well

1 clove garlic, finely chopped

1 pound parsnips, peeled and cubed

2 small (about 1 pound) sweet potatoes,
    peeled and cubed

4 cups low-sodium chicken broth

1 cup fat-free half-and-half

Pinch of nutmeg

Salt and freshly ground black pepper
    to taste

Snipped fresh chives, for garnish

1. In a large stockpot or Dutch oven, melt the butter over medium heat. Add the leeks and garlic to the pot and sauté for about 5 minutes, until soft.
2. Add the parsnips, sweet potatoes, and chicken broth to the pot. Bring to a boil, reduce heat, and simmer until the vegetables are soft, about 20 minutes.
3. Remove pot from heat. In a blender, carefully purée the soup in batches, or use an immersion blender. Stir in the half-and-half and nutmeg, and season with salt and pepper to taste. Heat over low heat until just heated through. (Do not allow to boil, or soup will curdle.)
4. Pour the soup into a warmed tureen or into individual soup bowls and serve immediately, garnished with chives.

Turtle Soup

Turtle Soup with a sherry splash! This Southern favorite is historically a nod to the hunter. Snapping turtles (*Chelydra serpentina*) are the type of turtle used for this recipe. Farm-raised turtle meat can be ordered from multiple online sources. The turtle has the texture of frog legs or lobster, and is truly delicious.

2 pounds fresh, frozen, or canned turtle
    meat, thawed if frozen
8 cups water
1 small onion, peeled and quartered,
    plus 1½ cups finely chopped onion
1 bay leaf
½ teaspoon cayenne pepper
2 teaspoons salt
Chicken stock or broth, as needed
8 tablespoons (1 stick) butter

½ cup all-purpose flour
¼ cup canned tomato purée
¼ cup Worcestershire sauce
2 hard-boiled eggs, finely chopped
2 tablespoons finely chopped fresh parsley,
    preferably flat-leaf Italian variety
¼ cup dry sherry, for garnish
1 lemon, sliced crosswise into ¼-inch-thick
    rounds

1. In a large Dutch oven or heavy stockpot, combine the turtle meat and the water and bring to a boil over high heat, skimming off the foam and scum from the surface. Add the quartered onion, bay leaf, cayenne pepper, and salt, and reduce the heat to low. Simmer, partially covered, for about 2 hours, or until the turtle meat is tender and shows no resistance when pierced with the point of a sharp knife.

2. Using a slotted spoon, transfer the meat to a plate, and when cool enough to handle cut the meat into ½-inch cubes. Strain the contents of the Dutch oven through a fine sieve set over a large bowl and reserve 4 cups of the cooking stock. (If there is less than 4 cups, pour the cooking stock into a large measuring cup and add enough chicken stock to measure 4 cups.)

3. Rinse the Dutch oven, add the butter, and melt over low heat. When the foam subsides, turn up the heat to medium-low, add the 1½ cups chopped onion, and cook, stirring frequently, for about 20 minutes, or until the onion is soft and golden. Watch carefully and regulate the heat so that the onion colors without burning.

4. Mix the flour into the pot and cook, stirring occasionally, over low heat to medium-low for about

30 minutes, until the flour-and-butter mixture turns deep brown. During this time, watch carefully and regulate the heat to achieve a nice brown color without burning.

5. Stirring constantly with a wire whisk, pour the reserved 4 cups of stock into the pot and cook over high heat for about 10 minutes, until the mixture comes to a boil, thickens slightly, and is smooth.

6. Reduce the heat to low, stir in the tomato purée and Worcestershire sauce, and simmer uncovered for 10 minutes. Add the cubed turtle meat and the chopped hard-boiled eggs and, stirring gently, simmer the soup for 2 or 3 minutes longer to heat the meat through. Add the parsley and taste for seasoning. Ladle the soup into a heated tureen or individual soup plates. Stir in 1 to 2 teaspoons of sherry per serving, garnish with the lemon slices, and serve immediately.

Watercress Soup with Roasted Red Pepper Aioli

YIELDS 6 SERVINGS

Watercress has been eaten since ancient times but has been cultivated only since the nineteenth century. Its Latin name, *Nasturtium*, comes from *nasum tortus*, meaning "twisted nose," because of its sharp, peppery kick. This succulent plant grows wild alongside slow-running waterways in Britain, Europe, Asia, and America, and is grown for both its delicious gold-to-scarlet blossoms and its lily pad–shaped leaves. To give this soup an additional layer of flavor, try garnishing it with some chopped roasted red pepper and/or a drizzle of Roasted Red Pepper Aioli.

4 tablespoons butter
1 cup diced onion
1 cup chopped celery, with some leaves
3 cups low-sodium chicken stock or broth, or more as needed
1 large potato (about 12 ounces), peeled and diced
4 bunches watercress
1 cup fat-free half-and-half

Salt and freshly ground black pepper to taste
½ cup chopped roasted red pepper, optional for garnish
Roasted Red Pepper Aioli (see recipe on page 239), optional for garnish
Edible (pesticide-free) nasturtium flowers, optional for garnish

1. In a large pot, melt the butter over medium heat. Add the onion and celery, and sauté for about 5 minutes, until tender. Add the chicken stock and the potato, bring to a boil, then reduce the heat and simmer for about 15 minutes, partially covered, until the potatoes are tender.

2. Rinse the watercress well and trim away the heavy stems. Stir the watercress into the pot. Cover and simmer for 5 minutes. Remove the pot from the heat. In a blender or a food processor fitted with the metal blade, carefully purée the soup until smooth, adding more chicken stock as necessary to achieve desired consistency. Return the purée to the pot, stir in the half-and-half, and add salt and pepper to taste. Heat the soup over medium-low heat until just heated through. (Do not allow soup to boil, or it will curdle.)

3. Serve soup immediately, if desired garnishing each bowl with 1 tablespoon chopped roasted red pepper, a drizzle of Roasted Red Pepper Aioli, or a few edible nasturtium flowers.

Homemade Stocks

The restaurant business has taught me so much. It's all about flavors, and that's where I really learned about stocks and broths. I love seeing those huge restaurant pots simmering very slowly. Whether it's meat, poultry, fish, or vegetable stocks and broths, they all add flavor to dishes as well as have nutritional value. Browning the ingredients in fat or roasting them in the oven or under the broiler before adding to the stock adds a rich color and loads of flavor.

Shrimp Stock

YIELDS ABOUT 5½ CUPS

Anytime I purchase shrimp for various recipes, I peel the shrimp to use right away and refrigerate or freeze the shells, heads, and tails in a heavy resealable bag until I'm ready to use them to make Shrimp Stock. They infuse a rich shrimp flavor, especially with the addition of all the seasonings in this recipe.

6 cups water
Shells from 2 pounds of shrimp
½ onion, roughly chopped with skin
1 clove garlic, smashed with skin
½ rib celery, roughly chopped

1 sprig fresh thyme, or 1 teaspoon dried
  thyme
1 sprig fresh parsley or 1 teaspoon dried
  parsley
1 fresh bay leaf or 2 dried bay leaves
1 teaspoon red pepper flakes

1. In a large stockpot with 6 cups of water, place the shrimp shells, onion, garlic, celery, thyme, bay leaf, parsley, and red pepper flakes. Bring the pot to a boil, then lower heat and simmer for 30 minutes or longer.
2. Strain the stock to use in recipes or allow strained stock to cool, store in a tightly sealed container, and refrigerate for up to 1 week or freeze for up to 3 months.

Duck Stock

YIELDS ABOUT 5½ CUPS

2 pounds duck wings, neck, and bones
1 onion, quartered
2 stalks celery with leaves, chopped
2 bay leaves

6 peppercorns, crushed
1 teaspoon dried thyme
6 cups Poultry Stock (recipe follows),
    or more as needed

1. In a large stockpot, place the duck bones, onion, celery, bay leaves, peppercorns, and thyme. Add the Poultry Stock. Bring the stock to a boil, reduce heat to medium-low, and simmer uncovered for 4 hours.
2. Skim any foam from the surface as it develops. Add more Poultry Stock as needed if the liquid evaporates.
3. Strain the stock through a mesh sieve and allow to cool. Use immediately, or place in a tightly covered container and refrigerate for up to 1 week or freeze for up to 3 months.

Poultry Stock

YIELDS ABOUT 5½ CUPS

2 tablespoons olive oil
Turkey, duck, and chicken bones, necks,
    and wingtips
1 onion, chopped, with skin

Chopped carrots
Chopped celery
2 quarts chicken stock or water, or more
    to cover

1. In a large roasting pan, heat the oil and add the reserved bones of the turkey, duck, and chicken. Brown the bones slightly. Add the onion, carrots, and celery, stirring frequently until the vegetables are softened.
2. In a large stockpot, place the bones and vegetables. Add the chicken stock or water to cover. Sim-

mer the stock for at least 1½ to 2 hours, or until reduced by half. Skim the surface occasionally with a large spoon or ladle to remove any foam.

3. Strain the stock and cool to room temperature. Cover and refrigerate until ready to use. The Poultry Stock will keep refrigerated for up to 5 days or frozen for up to 2 months.

Chapter 5

Salads

The Southern salad that usually comes to mind first is potato salad. But the list of Southern-style salads is actually long and varied. That's probably due to the Southern garden. It's the best place for all the right fixings for a great salad. Thomas Jefferson had a wonderful one he referred to as his "kitchen garden." It covered the length of three football fields—ample space to experiment with growing more than three hundred varieties of vegetables and herbs!

Southern gardens today still burst with the best greens grown to man—collards and cabbage. They're also rich in root vegetables, like beets and sweet potatoes, as well as fresh, juicy tomatoes and plump strawberries.

Salads are wonderfully flexible. They can begin a meal or end a meal. You can have one for brunch, lunch, or dinner, or for a late-night repast. A salad can even be a breakfast, like my recipe for Frisée Salad with Smoked Bacon, Mushrooms, and Quail Eggs. Like any other course, they should be planned with the right mix of ingredients. And I do like a new take on old favorites.

We've all had potato salad, and everyone has a favorite version or at least knows where to find it. But if you're ready for a change, I think you'll appreciate the recipe for Sweet Potato Salad with Orange-Maple Dressing. When we think collards, we don't think of a salad. But Collard Greens Slaw is delicious, and it's a great way to get the nutritional value of collards into your diet. Warm Cabbage Cashew Apple Slaw takes the place of cole slaw when temperatures begin to drop.

I'll take okra any day, any way. If I'm already grilling, I'll put on some okra and make Grilled Okra and Tomato Salad. This recipe includes a dressing that can go Creole or Cajun. Slow-Roasted Beets and Arugula Salad with Sunflower Vinaigrette aren't your mother's beets, which usually came out of a jar or can. You'll need fresh beets for this recipe. It's a healthy, flavorful salad, and the sunflower seeds give it a nice crunch.

On special occasions, my mother always made a gelatin mold. We ate it as a side, as we would a salad. The Nutty Fruit Gelatin Salad adds a light, sweet touch to a meal with its combinations of different fruit-flavored gelatins and canned fruits. I wanted to do something different with watermelon, my favorite fruit. I originally created my Watermelon Mint Salad to pair with grilled lamb chops. I just love the warmth of the chops and coolness of the salad.

I also like dishes that successfully marry the sweet with the savory, as in the Grilled Chicken and Strawberry Salad with Toasted Sugared Pecans and Strawberry Vinaigrette. Make sure you use the juiciest strawberries you can find.

You may wonder why there's a lobster salad in this book—it doesn't seem very Southern. I've noticed something about my Southern friends when they entertain: they don't always serve the expected down-home Southern meal. I find that they up the ante with more expensive meats and fish. So I thought I'd do the same and included Fifties-Style Lobster Salad. At our Sag Harbor restaurant we serve it in a half lobster shell on a bed of summer greens. Fried Calamari has always been a popular appetizer at our restaurants, so why not create a calamari salad for my family and friends? Add cornbread or crusty French bread and it makes a nice, well-rounded entrée, served with a spicy tomato dressing. Salad days are here to stay. Start tossing!

Collard Greens Slaw

YIELDS 6 SERVINGS

I wanted to do something different with collard greens, a Southern staple for well over a century, so I created this recipe as an accompaniment for my Seafood Salad (see recipe on page 114). It's easy to prepare and makes a great side salad for any meal. This salad is best prepared ahead and refrigerated until the greens are softened and wilted. Serve slightly chilled or at room temperature, or quickly sauté it for an extra flavorful, warm side dish.

¼ cup white wine vinegar
¼ cup extra virgin olive oil
1 tablespoon sugar
1½ teaspoons dry mustard
1½ teaspoons celery seed
1 teaspoon sweet Hungarian paprika
Salt and freshly ground black pepper
   to taste

1 large bunch (about 1 pound) collard
   greens, thick stems trimmed and
   leaves halved lengthwise, then thinly
   sliced crosswise (about 8 cups)
4 cups (about ½ medium head) thinly
   sliced Napa cabbage
1 cup (about 2 large) coarsely grated
   peeled carrots

1. To make the dressing, in small bowl, whisk the vinegar, olive oil, sugar, mustard, celery seed, and paprika to blend. Season with salt and pepper. (Dressing can be made 1 day ahead; place in a sealed container and refrigerate until ready to use.)
2. In a large bowl, combine the collard greens, cabbage, and carrots. Pour the dressing over the vegetables; season generously with salt and pepper, and toss well to coat. Cover and refrigerate until the collard greens soften and wilt slightly, tossing occasionally, at least 1 hour and up to 3 hours. Serve chilled or at room temperature.

Fried Calamari Salad with Spicy Tomato Dressing

Fried calamari, also known as squid, is such a popular appetizer in all of our restaurants that I decided to create a salad that showcases a seasoned version of it with a Cajun or Creole twist. The peppery taste of the arugula and the tender, mild flavor of the baby spinach is a delicious combination with the fried calamari. Drizzle the spicy dressing slowly . . . a little goes a long way!

1 pound fresh calamari	Bottled clam juice or water, as needed
2 cups all-purpose flour, or more as needed	Vegetable oil, for frying
1 tablespoon salt-free Cajun or Creole seasoning blend	2 cups arugula
	2 cups baby spinach
1 teaspoon seasoned salt, or to taste	6 cherry tomatoes, halved
1 teaspoon freshly ground black pepper, or to taste	6 pear tomatoes, halved
½ cup buttermilk	Spicy Tomato Dressing (recipe follows), for serving

1. Cut the calamari body into rings approximately ¼ inch thick, reserving the tentacles. Rinse the rings and tentacles well in cold water, then blot dry on paper towels.
2. In a large shallow plate or pan, combine the flour, Cajun or Creole seasoning, seasoned salt, and pepper. Pour the buttermilk into a shallow bowl; if needed, add a small amount of clam juice or water to thin the milk.
3. In a large skillet, pour ¼ inch of oil and heat over medium-high heat. Dip the calamari rings and tentacles first into the buttermilk and then into the seasoned flour, turning to coat evenly.
4. Using a slotted spoon, immediately lower the rings into the hot oil. Cook, turning occasionally, for 2 to 3 minutes, until golden brown on all sides. Remove the calamari from the oil and drain on paper towels. Keep warm until ready to serve.
5. Divide the arugula and spinach evenly onto large salad plates or shallow bowls, using ½ cup of each for each salad. Arrange the tomatoes on the salad, and evenly top with fried calamari. Drizzle with Spicy Tomato Dressing and serve immediately.

Spicy Tomato Dressing

3 plum or Roma tomatoes, halved, seeded, and chopped

1 teaspoon minced garlic

2 teaspoons fresh lemon juice

2 tablespoons mayonnaise

2 tablespoons extra virgin olive oil

½ teaspoon salt-free Creole or Cajun seasoning

½ teaspoon salt

¼ teaspoon freshly ground black pepper

⅛ teaspoon cayenne pepper, or to taste

1. In a blender or mini food processor, combine all the ingredients and process on high speed until smooth. Scrape down the sides and blend again.
2. Serve immediately over Fried Calamari Salad, or place in a sealed container and refrigerate until needed. Dressing will keep in the refrigerator for up to 3 days.

Frisée Salad with Smoked Bacon, Mushrooms, and Quail Eggs with Spicy Dijon Vinaigrette

YIELDS 4 SERVINGS

One great thing about this salad is its versatility: it would be perfect for a breakfast buffet, as a small appetizer, or even as an entrée salad for lunch. The shiitake mushrooms, with their distinctive smoky aroma, enhance the flavors of the bacon, and the dressing adds just the right amount of kick to this salad. Quail eggs are available at most specialty stores. While the eggs are small in size—4 quail eggs equal 1 chicken egg—they have a big yolk that yields lots of flavor.

16 large shiitake mushrooms, or fresh
    mushrooms of your choice, stems
    removed
3 tablespoons plus 1 teaspoon extra virgin
    olive oil
Salt and freshly ground black pepper
    to taste

6 ounces smoked slab bacon, or 10 slices
    smoked bacon, cut into 1/4-inch pieces
3 cups frisée lettuce, torn into pieces
2 cups arugula, torn into pieces
2 cups baby spinach
Spicy Dijon Vinaigrette (recipe follows)
16 Poached Quail Eggs (recipe follows)

1. Preheat oven to 425°F. Arrange the mushrooms on a roasting pan, drizzle with 3 tablespoons olive oil, and season with salt and pepper to taste.
2. Roast the mushrooms for 8 to 10 minutes, until they are soft, fragrant, and slightly browned. Remove from oven, and when they are cool enough to handle, slice into pieces. Transfer the mushrooms to a bowl and set aside.
3. In a sauté pan, warm the remaining teaspoon of olive oil over medium heat. Add the bacon and cook, stirring often, for about 6 to 8 minutes, until crisp. Remove the bacon with a slotted spoon and allow to drain on paper towels.
4. In a salad bowl, combine the frisée, arugula, and spinach, dress with Spicy Dijon Vinaigrette, season to taste with salt and pepper, and toss lightly to coat. Divide the salad greens among 4 plates.
5. Arrange the mushrooms and carefully place 4 quail eggs on each salad. Garnish each salad with crumbled bacon, and serve immediately.

Poached Quail Eggs

1 teaspoon white vinegar
⅛ teaspoon salt

16 quail eggs

1. Fill a small nonstick skillet halfway with water. Bring the water to a slow simmer over medium heat. Add the vinegar and salt.
2. One at a time, gently break 4 of the quail eggs into a small saucer or ramekin. Slide the eggs into the water. Continue with the remaining eggs, 4 at a time, adding each ramekin of eggs to a different spot in the skillet, creating 4 groups of eggs.
3. Gently spoon the simmering water over the eggs. Place the lid on the skillet to gently poach the eggs for about 1½ to 2 minutes. Carefully remove each group of eggs with a slotted spoon, and serve over Frisée Salad.

Spicy Dijon Vinaigrette

2 tablespoons fresh lemon juice
1 tablespoon balsamic vinegar
1½ teaspoons Dijon mustard
1 clove garlic
1 teaspoon Worcestershire sauce

¼ to ½ teaspoon hot pepper sauce,
   or to taste
Salt and freshly ground black pepper
   to taste
⅓ cup extra virgin olive oil

1. In a blender, purée the lemon juice, vinegar, mustard, garlic, Worcestershire sauce, hot pepper sauce, salt, and pepper. Slowly add the olive oil in a thin stream, while blending.
2. Serve immediately over Frisée Salad, or place in a sealed container and refrigerate until needed. Dressing will keep in the refrigerator for up to 3 days.

Grilled Chicken and Strawberry Salad
with Toasted Sugared Pecans and Strawberry Vinaigrette

YIELDS 4 SERVINGS

This recipe was a big hit at my D.C. restaurant, and is one of my favorite dishes. When the chef took it off the menu, as chefs often do to rotate items, I knew I was going to put it in one of my cookbooks. Since fresh strawberries are readily available year round, and grilled chicken is so quick to prepare, this is one of those recipes that's easy to put together. I have included Strawberry Vinaigrette to go with it; however, there are quite a few great store-bought options if you prefer not to make your own. The homemade Strawberry Vinegar in this recipe is really delicious, but if you are pressed for time, feel free to substitute store-bought raspberry vinegar or red wine vinegar.

4 skinless, boneless chicken breast halves
    (about 1½ pounds)
¼ cup extra virgin olive oil
2 tablespoons Strawberry Vinegar (recipe
    follows) or red wine vinegar
1 teaspoon fresh thyme leaves,
    or ½ teaspoon dried thyme
2 cloves garlic, minced

1 teaspoon salt
½ teaspoon freshly ground black pepper
4 cups mixed salad greens (about 3 ounces)
1½ cups sliced fresh strawberries
Strawberry Vinaigrette (recipe follows),
    or store-bought salad dressing
½ cup toasted sugared pecans halves,
    chopped

1. Place the chicken in a 1-gallon-size plastic resealable bag. In a small bowl, whisk together the olive oil, Strawberry Vinegar, thyme, garlic, salt, and pepper. Pour the marinade over the chicken breasts. Seal the bag and refrigerate for up to 1 hour.

2. Prepare a charcoal or gas grill to high heat. Grill the chicken breasts for 4 to 5 minutes on each side, until cooked through. Remove from grill to a clean platter, cover with foil, and allow to stand for 5 minutes before serving, to retain juices.

3. Divide the salad greens on 4 salad plates. Slice the chicken breasts thinly on the diagonal and arrange one chicken breast half on each plate. Evenly distribute the strawberries on each of the salad plates.

4. Drizzle each salad with 2 tablespoons of Strawberry Vinaigrette and sprinkle with 2 tablespoons chopped toasted sugared pecans. Serve immediately.

Strawberry Vinaigrette

YIELDS 1 CUP

This is one of those recipes I like to prepare at my home in Sag Harbor when I have the time. It brings back memories of being in my mother's kitchen when she and Dad used to can up as much of the produce from our garden as possible. You can purchase strawberry vinegar, but if you have fresh strawberries and thyme on hand, it is well worth the time and energy to make it yourself—plus it makes for a personal host or hostess gift when presented in a pretty bottle!

½ cup extra virgin olive oil
¼ cup seedless strawberry jam or
*   sweetened puréed fresh strawberries*

¼ cup Strawberry Vinegar (recipe follows)
*   or red wine vinegar*

In a small bowl, whisk all the ingredients together. Place in a sealed container and refrigerate until needed. Dressing will keep stored in the refrigerator for up to 3 days.

Strawberry Vinegar

YIELDS 2 CUPS

½ cup sliced strawberries, stems removed
6 to 8 sprigs fresh thyme

2 cups red wine vinegar

1. In a sterilized glass jar, combine the strawberries and thyme.
2. In a small nonreactive saucepan, heat the vinegar just until warm. Pour the warm vinegar over the strawberries and thyme. Allow to cool to room temperature, and seal jar with a lid. Refrigerate for at least 6 days. Strain before using. Vinegar will keep stored in the refrigerator for up to 2 weeks.

Toasted Sugared Pecans

YIELDS ½ CUP

½ cup pecan halves

1 tablespoon butter

2 teaspoons sugar

½ teaspoon salt

In a small skillet, toast the pecans over medium heat, stirring until browned and fragrant, about 5 minutes. Pour the pecans into a small dish or bowl. Toss the hot pecans with the butter, sugar, and salt. Spread on a plate to cool.

Grilled Okra and Tomato Salad

YIELDS 4 SERVINGS

This recipe was developed for an outdoor charcoal or gas grill to give it a smoky flavor; a wire grill basket with small openings will help to ensure the okra doesn't fall during cooking. Because the okra gives off a lot of liquid, it is precooked to crisp-tender, then lightly charred so it does not overcook. For indoor cooking you can use a grill pan; while it doesn't offer quite the same flavor, it works equally well. Make sure to toss the okra and tomatoes with the vinaigrette just before serving to keep the color bright green.

¼ cup plus 2 tablespoons extra virgin olive oil

2 tablespoons red wine vinegar

1 teaspoon brown sugar

½ teaspoon dry mustard

½ teaspoon Cajun or Creole seasoning

½ teaspoon salt

½ teaspoon freshly ground black pepper

1 pound fresh okra

4 medium plum tomatoes, quartered

4 cups mixed salad greens

¼ cup chopped fresh basil

½ cup sliced scallions, white and green parts

6 strips bacon, cooked crisp and crumbled

1. Heat a charcoal or gas grill or stovetop grill pan to medium-high heat.
2. Meanwhile, to make the salad dressing, in a small bowl, whisk together ¼ cup olive oil with the vinegar, brown sugar, mustard, Cajun or Creole seasoning, salt, and pepper. Set aside.
3. Rinse the okra and trim the stems without cutting the pods. Bring a small pot of salted water to a boil over high heat. Add the okra and boil for about 3 minutes, until crisp-tender. Drain and rinse with cold water to retain the bright green color.
4. Toss the okra and tomatoes with the remaining 2 tablespoons olive oil and place in a grill basket. Grill the vegetables until lightly charred, turning occasionally, about 3 to 4 minutes. Remove the vegetables from grill and cool slightly.
5. Divide the salad greens among 4 plates. Toss the grilled okra and tomatoes with the dressing and divide among the salad plates. Sprinkle with the fresh basil, sliced scallions, and crumbled bacon and serve immediately.

Fifties-Style Lobster Salad

Lobster is one of the most popular items on the menu at my Sag Harbor restaurant, and the Fifties-Style Lobster Salad served in a lobster shell is definitely our most popular and impressive presentation. To make this salad at home, look for lobsters that are active and lively. If live lobsters are not available, use whole frozen lobsters, thaw, and cook according to package directions. For an alternative presentation, the lobster salad can be served on a bed of salad greens garnished with red and yellow cherry tomatoes.

Two 1½- to 2½-pound fresh live lobsters
    (2 cups finely chopped cooked lobster)
½ cup finely chopped celery
2 scallions, finely sliced, white and green
    parts
½ to ¾ cup mayonnaise

½ teaspoon dry mustard
2 tablespoons freshly squeezed lemon juice
½ teaspoon sea salt
Freshly ground black pepper to taste
Old Bay Seasoning to taste
Chopped fresh parsley, for garnish

1. To cook the lobsters, in a large pot, bring 6 quarts of salted water to a boil over high heat. Add the live lobsters, head first, one at a time, careful to grasp just behind the claw. Return water to a boil and cook for 12 to 14 minutes, or until lobsters are bright red. Using tongs, remove the lobsters from the pot, and allow to drain until cool enough to handle.
2. Turn a lobster on its back, make a deep cut through the length of the body with a heavy sharp knife, and spread the halves apart. Scoop out and set aside the green liver—also known as tomalley—and the coral roe, found in the female lobster. Discard the lungs and stomach. Carefully remove the lobster meat from the body halves and set aside. Repeat with the remaining lobster.
3. To prepare the lobster salad, finely chop the lobster meat and place in a large bowl. Add the celery, scallions, mayonnaise, mustard, lemon juice, sea salt, pepper, and Old Bay Seasoning, and toss until well combined. Taste to adjust seasonings.
4. Divide the lobster salad among the four lobster body halves, garnish with chopped fresh parsley, and serve immediately.

Nutty Fruit Gelatin Salad

YIELDS 6 TO 8 SERVINGS

Gelatin salads were popular when I was growing up, and always looked beautiful when placed on our buffet table. Back in the day, my mother and aunts used fruit cocktail and nuts in their gelatin salads. There was always that moment of anticipation before the salads came out of the molds as we waited to see if they would make it out in one piece—and they usually did. My mom would give the bottom of the mold a quick dip in some warm water and run a knife around the edge to break the seal, though I find a warm towel placed over the mold works well, too. In my Nutty Fruit Gelatin Salad, the colors of the gelatin studded with apricots, peaches, and pecans create a tasty texture and elegant addition to any table!

1 package apricot-flavored gelatin
1 package mango-flavored gelatin
2 cups water
2 cups cold ginger ale

6 canned apricot halves, drained
12 canned peach slices, drained
½ cup chopped pecans or walnuts

1. In a medium mixing bowl, place the apricot and mango gelatin. Bring 2 cups of water to a boil. Pour over the gelatin and stir to dissolve for at least 2 minutes. Gradually stir in the ginger ale until thoroughly incorporated. Cover the bowl and refrigerate for about 2 hours, until the mixture starts to gel.
2. In the bottom of a ring mold, decoratively place half the apricots and peaches. Dice the remaining fruit, then stir the diced fruit and the nuts into the gelatin. Pour the mixture slowly into the ring mold, cover, and refrigerate for at least 4 hours, until firm.
3. Unmold by inverting the mold over a serving plate or cake stand. Place a warm wet dish towel over the mold until it loosens, then gently pull off the mold. Serve immediately.

Seafood Cobb Salad with Basil-Dill Vinaigrette

YIELDS 4 TO 6 SERVINGS

Cobb salads have become popular again, which is no surprise since they are so delicious. This salad is practically a meal in itself, with its variety of ingredients. I have made a few slight changes to the traditional recipe, substituting fresh seafood for the meat, and created a Basil-Dill Vinaigrette that complements the seafood perfectly. If you love fresh seafood, this recipe is a must!

1 head bibb lettuce	1 ripe avocado, peeled and diced
6 cups mixed salad greens	1 medium red onion, minced
1 head endive, sliced	4 boiled eggs, diced
Basil-Dill Vinaigrette (recipe follows)	2 medium red tomatoes, diced
2 cups flaked cooked salmon	2 medium yellow tomatoes, diced
2 cups diced cooked shrimp	½ cup Roquefort (or other blue) cheese
2 cups flaked cooked crabmeat	¼ cup chopped fresh chives

1. Separate the leaves of the bibb lettuce, wash, and dry them on paper towels. Arrange the leaves on a serving platter.
2. In a large bowl, toss the mixed greens and endive with ½ cup of the Basil-Dill Vinaigrette. Evenly place the mixed greens over the bibb lettuce.
3. Lay a row each of salmon, shrimp, and crabmeat across the top of the greens. Arrange rows of avocado, onion, boiled eggs, and tomato on all sides of the seafood. Sprinkle the blue cheese and chives on top of the salad and drizzle with the remaining Basil-Dill Vinaigrette.

Basil-Dill Vinaigrette

½ cup extra virgin olive oil
¼ cup white wine vinegar or freshly
    squeezed lemon juice
2 teaspoons anchovy paste

2 teaspoons minced garlic
2 teaspoons chopped fresh basil leaves
2 teaspoons chopped fresh dill

In a small bowl, place all the ingredients and whisk until well blended. Use immediately to dress Seafood Cobb Salad.

Seafood Salad with Collard Greens Slaw

YIELDS 6 SERVINGS

Southerners love their seafood—but no matter where you live, this salad is sure to please your palate. Its beauty is in the combination of the clams and mussels in their shells along with the sea scallops and shrimp. This dish would look beautiful on a buffet, or as part of a large spread. The seafood tossed with herbs and spices is the perfect combination of flavors, and when served over the Collard Greens Slaw makes for a gorgeous dish, flavorful and elegant!

1 pound small littleneck clams or Manila
clams, scrubbed
1 pound mussels, scrubbed and debearded
1 cup dry white wine
1 pound sea scallops, connective side tissue
trimmed
¾ pound uncooked large shrimp, peeled
and deveined
¼ cup extra virgin olive oil
2 tablespoons white wine vinegar

2 tablespoons packed chopped fresh basil
1½ tablespoons chopped fresh parsley
1½ tablespoons drained capers
1½ large cloves garlic, minced
1½ teaspoons Dijon mustard
¼ teaspoon dried crushed red pepper
Salt and freshly ground black pepper
to taste
Collard Greens Slaw (see recipe on
page 101), for serving

1. In large wide pot, combine the clams, mussels, and wine. Cover lid tightly, and cook over high heat for about 4 to 5 minutes, until the clams and mussels open. Discard any clams and mussels that do not open. Using a slotted spoon, transfer the clams and mussels to a very large bowl. Strain the cooking liquid into a medium bowl and set aside.

2. In a large saucepan of boiling salted water, cook the scallops until just opaque in the center, about 3 minutes. Using a slotted spoon, remove the scallops from the saucepan and add to the clams and mussels.

3. Return the water in the saucepan to a boil. Add the shrimp and cook just until opaque in the center, about 3 minutes. Drain the shrimp and transfer to the bowl with the shellfish. (Seafood can be prepared 4 hours ahead and refrigerated until serving.)

4. In a small bowl, whisk together the olive oil, vinegar, basil, parsley, capers, garlic, mustard, and crushed red pepper. Season with salt and pepper. Whisk ⅓ cup of the reserved cooking liquid into

the dressing (reserve remaining cooking liquid for another use). Dressing can be made up to 4 hours ahead; cover tightly, refrigerate, and bring to room temperature before using.

5. Pour the dressing over the shellfish and toss to combine. Serve over Collard Greens Slaw.

Slow-Roasted Beets and Arugula Salad with Sunflower Vinaigrette

YIELDS 4 SERVINGS

Beets are very sweet—they have the highest sugar content of any vegetable—but are very low in calories. Common beets are dark red, and the betacyanin dye turns hands a brilliant magenta when handling, so use latex or rubber gloves and a plastic cutting board when preparing them. This recipe is all about presentation and the layers of flavor and texture from the sweet beets, the crunch of the walnuts, and the peppery spice of the arugula. The Sunflower Vinaigrette and Balsamic Reduction are a must.

4 medium beets

3 tablespoons extra virgin olive oil

1 tablespoon plus 1 teaspoon red wine vinegar

2 tablespoons unsalted, toasted sunflower seeds

½ teaspoon salt

Pinch of freshly ground black pepper

6 cups arugula, stems removed

½ cup walnut halves

½ cup crumbled goat cheese

Salt and freshly ground black pepper to taste

Sunflower Vinaigrette (recipe follows)

Balsamic Reduction (recipe follows)

1. Preheat oven to 350°F. Wash the beets well and trim the roots and stems without piercing the skin. Place the beets on a sheet of aluminum foil, fold into an airtight packet, and place on a cookie sheet. Bake for 45 to 60 minutes, until beets are tender.
2. Cool the beets, remove the skin, and cut into small cubes (you should have about 2 cups of diced beets). Cover the beets and chill until ready to prepare salad.
3. In a small bowl, whisk together the olive oil, red wine vinegar, sunflower seeds, salt, and pepper.
4. In a large bowl, toss the arugula with the Sunflower Vinaigrette and distribute among four salad plates. Distribute the beets, walnuts, and crumbled goat cheese evenly over the top of each salad. Drizzle the rim of each plate with Balsamic Reduction. Serve immediately.

Sunflower Vinaigrette

YIELDS ABOUT ¼ CUP

Sunflower seeds are rich in calcium and minerals. For this vinaigrette, use whole unsalted toasted sunflower seeds.

3 tablespoons extra virgin olive oil
1 tablespoon plus 1 teaspoon red wine
  vinegar

2 tablespoons unsalted, toasted sunflower
  seeds
½ teaspoon salt
Pinch of freshly ground black pepper

In a mixing bowl, whisk together all the ingredients. Serve immediately with Slow-Roasted Beets and Arugula Salad, or store in a sealed container and refrigerate for up to 3 days.

Balsamic Reduction

YIELDS ½ CUP

1½ cups balsamic vinegar

In a small stainless steel saucepan, bring the vinegar to a boil. Lower heat to medium and allow the vinegar to reduce down to ½ cup, about 20 minutes. Allow the Balsamic Reduction to cool completely and serve with Slow-Roasted Beets and Arugula Salad, or store in a sealed container and refrigerate for up to 2 weeks.

Sweet Potato Salad with Orange-Maple Dressing

Sweet potatoes are high in vitamins A and C. These edible roots come in many varieties, and interestingly enough are *not* related to yams as widely thought. I enjoy cooking them many different ways, and I think they make a surprisingly tasty, colorful salad with my Orange-Maple Dressing.

3 pounds red-skinned sweet potatoes, peeled and cut into ¾-inch cubes	¼ teaspoon salt
½ cup extra virgin olive oil	½ cup chopped green onion
2 tablespoons pure maple syrup	½ cup chopped fresh parsley
¼ cup orange juice	¼ cup coarsely chopped toasted pecans
2 tablespoons balsamic vinegar	¼ cup golden raisins
2 tablespoons minced peeled fresh ginger	¼ cup brown raisins
¼ teaspoon ground nutmeg	Salt and freshly ground black pepper to taste

1. In a large pot, steam the sweet potatoes in batches until just tender, about 15 minutes per batch. Transfer them to a large bowl and let cool to room temperature.
2. Meanwhile, in a small bowl, make the Orange-Maple Dressing by whisking together the olive oil, maple syrup, orange juice, vinegar, ginger, nutmeg, and salt.
3. Add the green onion, parsley, pecans, and raisins to the cooled sweet potatoes. Pour the Orange-Maple Dressing over the potato mixture, and toss gently to combine. Season to taste with salt and pepper. This salad can be made several hours ahead of time; cover and refrigerate until serving.

Warm Cabbage Cashew Apple Slaw

I originally developed this recipe as a side for pork chops, but it stands well on its own and can be served warm or at room temperature. The tartness of the apples and texture of the cabbage and the chopped cashews give the slaw the perfect crunch.

2 tablespoons butter
1 tablespoon extra virgin olive oil
1 small head (about 2 pounds) green
    cabbage, finely shredded
2 Granny Smith apples, cored and
    shredded

½ cup apple cider
¼ cup freshly squeezed lemon juice
½ teaspoon sugar
Salt and freshly ground black pepper
    to taste
1 cup chopped roasted unsalted cashews

1. In a large skillet, melt the butter and olive oil over medium-high heat. Add the shredded cabbage and apples, tossing to coat well.
2. Add the apple cider, lemon juice, and sugar to the cabbage mixture. Continue cooking, tossing, for about 5 minutes, until crisp-tender. Season with salt and pepper, and mix in the cashews. Serve warm or at room temperature.

Watermelon Mint Salad

I love watermelon, and this simple salad is great for cooling off on a hot day. With lots of flavor and just the right amount of spice, it packs a punch and looks beautiful. Red diced watermelon combined with lime juice and the fresh green colors of scallions, jalapeño peppers, and fresh julienned mint leaves, this salad has a great balance of coolness, warmth, sweetness, and citrus tang.

4 cups (about 1 pound, 3 ounces)
1-inch-diced watermelon

2 teaspoons freshly squeezed lime juice

2 teaspoons finely chopped seeded jalapeño
pepper

1½ teaspoons finely chopped scallions,
white and green parts

6 large fresh mint leaves, finely
julienned

In a large bowl, gently toss the watermelon with the lime juice, jalapeño, scallions, and mint leaves. Cover and refrigerate until ready to serve.

Chapter 6

Meat

In our small town in western Pennsylvania, there was just one small store and it sold everything. The owner's name was John, and he usually could be found working behind the meat counter. Everyone referred to him as John the Butcher. My father didn't hunt, so if John the Butcher didn't have it, we didn't eat it. I didn't eat venison until I was a grown woman. Our family had an account at John's and when my mother had to work late, on my way home after school I would buy the meat for dinner. Often, I bought liver, because I loved liver smothered with onions and I knew how to make it. I'd make plenty of rice, too. I ate so much rice, my mother used to call me "Geechee" after the Gullah of Low Country South Carolina. The Gullah are ancestors of enslaved Africans who came from rice-growing regions in West Africa. Their rice-growing skills created a successful rice business in the South.

When I first went on the road with the Ebony Fashion Fair, I discovered soul-satisfying dishes like chicken fried steak. As much as I loved chicken fried steak and its comforting powers, I had to learn moderation quickly.

The Southern love affair with meat began with the early settlers. They had to hunt for their dinner and there was plenty to hunt. White-tailed deer, rabbits, squirrels, cattle, and the almighty hog were in abundance. No part of the animal was off-limits. No popular Southern dish demonstrates this more than chitterlings. I've included two recipes; one is basic and was how my mom prepared them, with plenty of vinegar, while the other brings a taste of sophistication to this down-home favorite using shallots and white wine.

The Baby Back Ribs with Southern Dry Rub are simple and come out tasting just as good baked in your oven or over charcoal. I'm careful about the cuts of pork I eat. Pork chops are fine because they don't have to be fatty. They're an easy meat to cook with and absorb seasonings well. The recipe for Pork Chops with Glazed Sweet Potatoes is comforting, with a wonderful savory/sweet flavor. The Cajun Fried Pork Chops have a tasty kick. Ham Steak with Red Eye Gravy needs no occasion, nor does Bourbon Brown Sugar–Brushed Ham Loaf.

I don't remember having lamb until I lived in New York. Some of my favorite recipes, Pecan Roasted Rack of Lamb and Madeira-Braised Leg of Spring Lamb, are both rich in aroma and flavor. When I first came to New York, it didn't take me long to get used to eating lamb whenever I wanted; no special occasion was necessary. A friend of mine used to call me Lamb Chop.

Jerk seasoning has gone mainstream and beyond chicken. Jerk-Spiced Beef Tenderloin is easy to make because jerk spices are now accessible. When I went to Jamaica to shoot my show with Mama Marley Booker (she taught me how to make a vegetable dish called "rundown"), I visited Walkerswood Caribbean Foods in St. Ann. Their Traditional Jerk Seasoning is outstanding, as are their other spices, and they're easy to find.

The variety of meats available to us on a daily basis has come a long way since I shopped at John the Butcher. If you don't find them at the butcher, you can go online and what you want is a click away. And anyway, who has time to hunt for dinner?

Baby Back Ribs with Southern Dry Rub

I love baby back ribs prepared with a spiced dry rub. These ribs are first rubbed with a flavorful mix of spices and sugar, and are cooked dry with no basting sauces or mops during cooking; they are grilled over hickory chips for added flavor. If you have the time, coat the meat with the dry rub the night before.

1 tablespoon smoked paprika	1 tablespoon garlic powder
1/3 cup sweet paprika	1 tablespoon onion powder
2 tablespoons kosher salt	1/2 teaspoon cayenne pepper
2 tablespoons brown sugar	Hickory wood chips or chunks, for grilling
2 tablespoons freshly ground black pepper	3 slabs pork back ribs, about 1 1/2 pounds
1 tablespoon chili powder	each

1. To make the dry rub, in a small bowl, mix together the paprikas, salt, brown sugar, pepper, chili powder, garlic powder, onion powder, and cayenne. Set aside. (See Note.)
2. Soak hickory wood chips or chunks in a large pan of water. Prepare a 200°F to 250°F indirect charcoal fire on an outdoor charcoal grill. Place a large handful of the soaked wood chips on the charcoal, or if using a gas grill, fill a smoker box with wood chips.
3. Using a small paring knife, remove the membrane from the underside of the ribs. In a small bowl, place 1 cup of the dry rub, and set aside the remainder for another use (see Note). Use caution not to contaminate the unused dry rub with raw meat juices. Liberally coat both sides of the ribs with rub. Stack the ribs on a large baking sheet and let sit for about 30 minutes at room temperature.
4. Place the ribs on the grill rib-side-down and allow to cook over indirect low heat for about 4 to 5 hours, until the meat is tender and pulls easily from the bone. Turn the ribs about every 45 minutes during the cooking time. During this time the heat will need to be replenished with hot coals and soaked hard wood. Serve the ribs hot from the grill.

   Note: Make a double batch of dry rub; it can be stored in a sealed container in the pantry for up to 3 months. I like to use it for meat, poultry, and fish.

Beer-Braised Rabbit

Rabbit has become quite popular again. The meat is fine grained and mild flavored, and can be prepared in recipes much like young poultry. Here I've brined the meat and then added lots of vegetables and spices; the beer takes it over the top—not only does it tenderize the meat, it gives great flavor, too!

2 cups hot water	1 tablespoon brown sugar
1/2 cup kosher salt	1/2 teaspoon dry mustard
1/4 cup granulated sugar	1 cup dark beer
2 cups cold water	1 tablespoon Worcestershire sauce
One 3- to 3 1/2-pound rabbit, rinsed and cut into 8 pieces	2 sprigs fresh thyme
	16 peeled pearl or cipollini onions
4 slices bacon	16 peeled baby carrots
1/2 cup all-purpose flour	1 cup button mushrooms, stems trimmed
2 tablespoons butter or olive oil	Salt and freshly ground black pepper to taste
1/2 cup finely chopped onion	
1/4 cup finely chopped green bell pepper	1 tablespoon finely chopped fresh parsley, preferably Italian flat-leaf variety
1 tablespoon finely chopped garlic	

1. To make the brine, in a large bowl, dissolve the kosher salt and granulated sugar in the hot water; add the cold water, and allow the mixture to cool to room temperature. Place the rabbit pieces in a 1-gallon resealable plastic bag resting in a bowl; add the brine to the bag, seal the bag tightly, and refrigerate for 3 to 4 hours.
2. In a large heavy skillet, fry the bacon over medium heat, turning the slices frequently with tongs until they are crisp and brown and have rendered all of their fat. Transfer the bacon to paper towels to drain, then crumble it into small bits and set aside. Reserve the skillet with bacon fat.
3. Remove the rabbit pieces from the brine, rinse, and pat dry with paper towels. In a shallow dish, place the flour and dredge one piece of rabbit at a time to coat lightly, then shake off the excess flour.
4. Place the reserved skillet with bacon fat over medium-high heat. Brown the rabbit skin-side-down

in the fat in the skillet, turning frequently, about 5 minutes on each side. Transfer the cooked rabbit to a plate.

5. Add the butter or olive oil to the remaining bacon fat in the skillet and heat over medium heat. Add the chopped onion, green pepper, and garlic to the skillet; stirring frequently, cook until the vegetables are soft but not brown. Stir the brown sugar and mustard into the pan. Add the beer, Worcestershire sauce, thyme, pearl onions, and carrots; bring to a boil over high heat, scraping up the browned bits on the bottom and sides of the skillet.

6. Return the rabbit and the accumulated juices from the plate to the skillet. Reduce the heat to low and simmer, covered, for 45 minutes. Add the mushrooms to the pan. Continue simmering, covered, for about 15 more minutes, or until the rabbit is tender and shows no resistance when pierced deeply with the point of a small sharp knife. Taste and season with salt and pepper.

7. To serve, arrange the rabbit in a large heated bowl or platter; ladle the sauce and vegetables over it. Garnish the top with the reserved bacon bits and chopped parsley, and serve immediately.

Bourbon Brown Sugar–Brushed Ham Loaf

YIELDS 6 SERVINGS

Authentic aged Virginia ham has a rich mahogany color and firm texture, and is highly flavorful. Smithfield, Virginia's ham capital, was named after Arthur Smith, who owned the land the town was founded on in 1752. The soil was too poor for tobacco-growing but was perfect for growing peanuts, which the hogs loved to eat. For this ham loaf, I use two types of ham. Virginia ham is drier, more like country ham, and smoked ham is more moist, sometimes injected with water or natural juices. If only Virginia ham is available, it is fine to substitute for the smoked ham.

Vegetable oil or nonstick cooking spray, for
    greasing pans
1 pound cooked Virginia ham
½ pound cooked smoked ham
1 cup cooked mashed potatoes
2 eggs, well beaten
1 medium onion, chopped
¾ cup plain breadcrumbs

2 tablespoons milk
½ cup Bourbon Brown Sugar Barbecue
    Sauce (see recipe on page 232),
    divided
¼ teaspoon salt
½ teaspoon freshly ground black pepper
Whole cloves, if desired

1. Preheat oven to 350°F. Grease an 8½ x 4½ x 2 ½-inch loaf pan or 6 individual 4½ x 2½ x 1½-inch loaf pans with vegetable oil or nonstick cooking spray.
2. In a food processor or blender, grind both hams to desired consistency.
3. In a large bowl, mix the Virginia ham and smoked ham together. Add the mashed potatoes and mix well to combine. Stir in the eggs, onion, breadcrumbs, milk, 2 tablespoons of the Bourbon Brown Sugar Barbecue Sauce, the salt, and pepper. Turn the ham mixture into the prepared pan or pans and press down to remove air pockets. Insert whole cloves across the surface, if desired. Spread the remaining barbecue sauce over the top.
4. Bake the large loaf at 350°F for 50 to 60 minutes, or the smaller loaves for 40 to 45 minutes, until brown around the edges. Serve immediately or at room temperature.

Cajun Fried Pork Chops

Choose thick, bone-in pork chops, which are very flavorful and retain moisture during cooking. Spice them up with a generous sprinkling of Cajun or Creole seasoning. Serve with Warm Cabbage Cashew Apple Slaw (see recipe on page 119) or your favorite side dishes.

Four 1-inch-thick bone-in pork chops
Salt and freshly ground black pepper
to taste

4 teaspoons Cajun or Creole seasoning,
or to taste
2 tablespoons olive oil

1. Sprinkle both sides of the pork chops with salt and pepper. Using 1 teaspoon per chop, coat both sides of each chop with the Cajun or Creole seasoning.
2. In a large skillet, heat the olive oil over medium heat. Add the pork chops and cook for 5 to 6 minutes per side, or until cooked through. Remove the chops to a warm platter and serve immediately.

Chicken Fried Steak

Chicken Fried Steak is also known as Country Fried Steak. Thin-cut, bottom round steak is pounded with a meat mallet, dredged in seasoned flour, and pan-fried like chicken, more often than not served with a cream gravy, vegetables, biscuits, and mashed potatoes.

1¼ cups all-purpose flour, divided
1 teaspoon salt
½ teaspoon garlic powder
1 teaspoon cayenne pepper
3 eggs, lightly beaten
1¼ pounds bottom round steak,
  ¼ to ½ inch thick

½ cup vegetable oil, for frying
2½ cups whole milk
1 tablespoon chili powder
¾ teaspoon celery salt
1 cube beef bouillon, crumbled

1. In a shallow bowl, combine 1 cup of the flour with the salt, garlic powder, and cayenne pepper; set aside. In a small bowl, beat together the eggs and remaining ¼ cup flour.
2. Cut the steak into 4 pieces and pound each with a meat mallet until about ¼ inch thick. Dredge the steaks first in the flour mixture, then in the egg mixture, then back in the flour mixture. Place the coated steaks on a wax paper–lined baking sheet and refrigerate for 20 minutes to allow coating to set. Reserve 2 tablespoons of the leftover flour mixture.
3. Heat the oil in a large skillet over medium-high heat. Working in batches, fry the coated steaks until golden brown, about 3 minutes on each side. Remove the steaks from the skillet, transfer to a platter, and keep warm while making the gravy.
4. Pour off all but 2 tablespoons of the oil from the skillet, and whisk in 2 tablespoons of the leftover flour mixture. Cook over medium heat, stirring constantly, until the flour is browned. Remove the pan from the heat and stir in the milk, chili powder, celery salt, and crumbled bouillon cube. Return pan to the heat and bring to a simmer, stirring constantly, until gravy thickens. Serve immediately over Chicken Fried Steak.

Make It Light

For a lighter version of Chicken Fried Steak, use egg substitute or egg whites instead of eggs for the coating. Substitute fat-free evaporated milk for the regular milk in the gravy. To reduce the salt content, replace the celery salt with ½ teaspoon celery seed, and use low-sodium beef bouillon.

Chitterlings

When I was growing up, "chitlins" (pigs' intestines) were always on the table New Year's Day, Thanksgiving, Christmas, and any other time my parents had a taste and the time to prepare them. Cleaning the chitterlings is always time-consuming, especially for large crowds. These days they can be purchased cleaned and precooked, but I prefer to clean and cook them myself. Thaw the chitterlings, then remove as much of the fat as possible when cleaning them to prepare this recipe.

10 pounds frozen or fresh chitterlings
1 cup cider vinegar, divided
1 tablespoon salt
1½ cups cubed potato
1 cup coarsely chopped onion
3 cloves garlic, minced
4 bay leaves

1 teaspoon chopped fresh thyme leaves,
    or ½ teaspoon dried thyme
1 teaspoon crushed red pepper flakes
Salt and freshly ground black pepper
    to taste
Hot sauce, to taste

1. Thaw then clean the chitterlings in slightly warm water. Remove the fat and any residue. Drain and rinse the chitterlings in cold water until the water runs clean. In a large pot, place the chitterlings, add cold water to cover, add ½ cup of the vinegar, and soak for 1 hour or up to 24 hours, refrigerated.

2. Drain the chitterlings, place in a large pot, add water to cover, and bring to a boil over high heat. Reduce heat to medium-low and simmer slowly, removing juices as they accumulate (see Note).

3. Stir in the remaining vinegar, the salt, potatoes, onions, garlic, bay leaves, thyme, and crushed red pepper. Bring to a boil, reduce the heat, and cover, stirring occasionally to prevent sticking. Allow the chitterlings to simmer for 3½ to 4 hours, until tender. Remove the bay leaves and adjust seasoning with salt, pepper, and hot sauce. Serve immediately.

    Note: Cooking chitterlings usually produces a large amount of liquid. I prefer to remove as much liquid as possible while cooking and return the liquid only as needed.

Fancy Dressed Chitterlings

10 pounds chitterlings, drained
½ cup cider vinegar
2 to 3 shallots, sliced
½ cup white wine

½ cup chicken stock or broth
Seasoned salt and freshly ground black
    pepper to taste

1. Follow steps 1 and 2 of above recipe, reserving a small amount of the cooking fat.
2. In a large skillet or Dutch oven, sauté the sliced shallots in a small amount of chitterling fat over medium heat. Add the cooked chitterlings, turn up the heat, and stir well. Add the white wine, chicken stock, seasoned salt, and pepper to the pot. Simmer for about 12 minutes, tossing the chitterlings frequently with tongs. Serve immediately.

Seared Filet Mignon with Peppercorn Pan Sauce

YIELDS 4 SERVINGS

Tender beef steaks glazed with a dark, shiny peppercorn sauce make an elegant, special-occasion dish. A mix of black, green, white, and even pink or red peppercorns works well for this dish, but if a blend is not available, all black peppercorns or a mix of any variety of peppercorns works just as well.

4 filet mignon steaks, 4 to 6 ounces each
1 teaspoon kosher salt
½ teaspoon freshly ground black pepper
1 tablespoon canola oil
5 tablespoons butter, divided
1 tablespoon minced shallots

¼ cup red wine
¾ cup beef stock or broth
1 tablespoon Dijon mustard
2 tablespoons cracked peppercorn medley
of black, green, and white peppercorns

1. Preheat oven to 200°F and place an ovenproof platter in the oven. Season the steaks with the salt and pepper. Let sit at room temperature for about 15 minutes.
2. In a large sauté pan, heat the oil and 1 tablespoon of the butter over medium-high heat until hot and bubbly. Add the steaks and cook for 4 minutes per side for medium rare, or longer until desired doneness. When cooked, place the steaks on the warm platter in the oven while the sauce is prepared.
3. In the same skillet, lower heat to medium. Add the shallots and cook, stirring frequently, for about 2 minutes, until softened. Add the red wine, scraping the browned bits off the bottom of the pan. Allow the wine to cook and reduce for about 2 minutes. Stir in the beef stock, mustard, and peppercorns. Raise heat to bring the sauce to a boil, and cook for about 5 minutes, until sauce is reduced by half. Slowly whisk in the remaining 4 tablespoons of butter, one tablespoon at a time, to blend.
4. When the sauce is thickened to gravy consistency, taste to adjust seasonings. Pour the sauce over the steaks and serve immediately.

Ham Steak with Redeye Gravy

This recipe can be made with leftover ham or bone-in or boneless ham steak; applewood smoked ham is a great choice. I add cream to the gravy to mellow out the strong flavors; it is perfect served over grits or polenta anytime of the day.

One 1½-pound bone-in or boneless cooked ham steak, about 1 inch thick

2 tablespoons unsalted butter, as needed

⅛ to ¼ teaspoon finely grated bittersweet or semisweet chocolate, optional

¼ teaspoon ground cinnamon

1 to 2 teaspoons instant coffee granules, or to taste

1½ cups very hot water

1 to 3 tablespoons heavy cream, or more to taste

1. Trim off fat from the ham; dice the fat and set aside the ham steak.
2. In a large skillet, cook the fat over low heat until it renders 1 tablespoon of drippings, then discard the solids. Alternatively, if the ham is particularly lean, melt 2 tablespoons butter in the pan.
3. In a small bowl, combine the dark chocolate if using and the cinnamon; rub the mixture onto both sides of the ham steak.
4. Add the ham to the skillet, and cook over medium heat for approximately 2 minutes on each side, until browned and warmed through. Transfer the ham to a plate and cover loosely with foil to keep warm.
5. In a measuring cup, dissolve the instant coffee in the very hot water. Add the coffee to the skillet, raise heat to medium-high, and boil for about 5 minutes, scraping up the browned bits from the bottom of the pan. Stir in the heavy cream and cook, stirring frequently, until the sauce thickens to gravy consistency. Pour the gravy over the ham and serve immediately.

Grilled Pork Tenderloin

Pork tenderloin is a great cut of meat, as it is inexpensive, highly versatile, and succulent. With no bone and little fat, there is no waste, and it is delicious when barbecued.

2 pork tenderloins (about 1 pound each),
*   trimmed of fat*
1 teaspoon salt
½ teaspoon freshly ground black pepper

Barbecue sauce of choice (see recipes
*   in Chapter 10, or store-bought),*
for serving

1. Preheat an outdoor gas or charcoal grill or indoor grill to medium heat. Season the pork with the salt and pepper. Place the pork on the grill, cover, and cook, turning once during cooking, for 20 to 30 minutes, or until internal temperature reaches 155°F to 160°F on a meat thermometer.
2. Remove the pork to a platter and cover loosely with foil to keep warm. Allow to rest for 10 minutes before slicing, to retain juices. Serve with your favorite barbecue sauce passed on the side.

Barbecued Pork Tenderloin

This is essentially the same recipe as above, but the pork is basted with barbecue sauce while cooking. Prepare one of the flavorful homemade barbecue sauces from this book, such as B's Sweet Maple Barbecue Sauce (page 231), Bourbon Brown Sugar Barbecue Sauce (page 232), Low-Sugar Maple Barbecue Sauce (page 233), or Pomegranate Barbecue Sauce (page 234), or use a store-bought sauce for quicker preparation.

1 cup barbecue sauce of choice (see recipes in Chapter 10, or store-bought), plus additional sauce for serving

2 pork tenderloins (about 1 pound each), trimmed of fat
1 teaspoon salt
½ teaspoon freshly ground black pepper

1. Prepare barbecue sauce of choice, and pour 1 cup of the sauce into a small bowl.
2. Preheat an outdoor gas or charcoal grill or indoor grill to medium. Season the pork with salt and pepper. Place the pork on the grill, cover, and cook, basting it with the barbecue sauce every 10 minutes, for 20 to 30 minutes, or until the internal temperature reaches 155°F to 160°F on a meat thermometer. Discard leftover basting sauce. Remove the pork to a platter and cover loosely with foil to keep warm. Allow to rest for 10 minutes before slicing, to retain juices. Serve the sliced pork with additional barbecue sauce passed on the side.

Jerk-Spiced Beef Tenderloin

YIELDS 6 SERVINGS

I've been cooking with jerk seasoning for years. My family and friends love the flavors! Begin marinating the beef at least 8 hours before roasting. This tenderloin can be served warm or at room temperature at any time of the day. Add more seasoning if your guests like it hot!

¼ cup extra virgin olive oil
1¾ tablespoons dried jerk seasoning
2 teaspoons balsamic vinegar
2 small bay leaves, crumbled finely
1½ large cloves garlic, minced

One 1½-pound beef tenderloin roast,
preferably thick end
Salt and freshly ground black pepper
to taste

1. In a small bowl, whisk the olive oil, jerk seasoning, vinegar, bay leaves, and garlic. Pierce the beef tenderloin all over with a fork. Place the tenderloin in a 1-gallon resealable plastic bag; add the marinade and seal the bag tightly. Turn the bag to distribute marinade evenly over meat. Refrigerate for at least 8 hours and up to 1 day, turning occasionally.
2. Preheat oven to 400°F. Remove the beef from the marinade and pat dry. Place the beef on a rimmed baking sheet. Sprinkle generously with salt and pepper. Roast until a meat thermometer inserted into the tenderloin registers 130°F for rare, about 30 minutes, or longer until desired doneness. Remove pan from oven; allow the beef to rest for 10 minutes to retain juices. Slice the beef crosswise into ½-inch-thick slices and serve immediately.

Lamb Shanks

Lamb shanks come in a variety of sizes. Smaller ones, known as foreshanks, are the leanest cut, and are close to a pound; larger ones will need a bit more cooking to become tender. Lamb often has a strong flavor, which is mellowed out quite well with the herbs and spices in this recipe.

4 lamb shanks, about 1 pound each	1 small bay leaf
Salt and freshly ground black pepper to taste	One 14½-ounce can diced tomatoes
2 tablespoons olive oil	1 cup white wine
1 large onion, coarsely chopped	1 cup chicken, beef, or vegetable stock or
3 cloves garlic, minced	broth
1 tablespoon chopped fresh rosemary	1 large fennel bulb, cut into 1-inch pieces
2 tablespoons chopped fennel sprigs,	3 medium carrots, peeled and cut into
optional	1-inch pieces
2 to 3 strips orange zest, white pith removed	¼ cup chopped fresh parsley

1. Trim excess fat from the lamb shanks and discard the fat. Generously season the shanks with salt and pepper. In a large heavy stockpot or Dutch oven, heat the oil over medium-high heat. Working in two batches, cook the lamb shanks for about 10 minutes, until well browned on all sides. Transfer them to a large bowl or plate.

2. Pour off all but 2 tablespoons of fat from the pan and set over medium heat. Add the onion and cook, stirring frequently, for about 10 minutes, until golden. Add the garlic, rosemary, chopped fennel sprigs (if using), orange zest, and bay leaf to the pot and cook, stirring frequently, for 1 minute. Stir in the tomatoes with their juice, the wine, and broth, scraping up any browned bits from the bottom of the pan.

3. Return the lamb to the pot and bring to a boil. Reduce heat to low, cover, and simmer gently for 1½ hours, turning and repositioning the shanks occasionally so they braise evenly. Add the fennel bulb and carrots to the pot and turn the lamb one last time. Simmer for about 30 minutes more, until the lamb and vegetables are just tender.

4. Using a slotted spoon, transfer the lamb and vegetables to a serving platter and cover loosely with foil to keep warm. Skim off any fat from the pan juices. Boil the juices over medium-high heat for about 5 minutes, until slightly reduced. Discard the bay leaf. Stir in the parsley and season with salt and pepper. Spoon the sauce over the lamb and vegetables, and serve immediately.

Madeira-Braised Leg of Spring Lamb

Leg of lamb is a traditional holiday roast generally served in the spring, giving it the name "spring lamb." Try this recipe for boneless leg of spring lamb braised with Madeira, a flavorful Portuguese wine; if fresh sage, thyme, rosemary, and mint are available, nothing beats the flavor combination!

One 4- to 5-pound boneless leg of spring lamb, rolled and tied	2 tablespoons chopped fresh herbs (a combination of sage, thyme, and rosemary), or 1½ teaspoons mixed dried herbs
Salt and freshly ground black pepper to taste	
2 tablespoons butter	2 tablespoons all-purpose flour
2 onions, quartered	1½ cups beef stock or broth
4 carrots, peeled and cut into 2-inch pieces	¾ cup Madeira wine
4 cloves garlic, coarsely chopped	¼ cup chopped fresh mint

1. Season the lamb with salt and pepper. In a large heavy pot, heat the butter over medium-high heat. Sear the lamb for about 15 minutes, until well browned on all sides. Transfer the lamb to a large plate.
2. Pour off all but 2 tablespoons of fat from the pan and set over medium heat. Add the onions and carrots and cook, stirring frequently, for about 12 minutes, until the vegetables are soft and well browned.
3. Add the garlic, herbs, and flour to the pan and cook, stirring frequently, for 1 minute. Stir in the broth and Madeira, scraping up any browned bits from the bottom of the pan.
4. Return the lamb to the pot and bring to a boil. Reduce heat to low, cover, and simmer gently, turning the lamb occasionally to braise evenly, for about 2½ to 3 hours, until tender. Transfer the lamb to a platter and cover loosely with foil to keep warm.
5. Strain the juices from the vegetables into a medium saucepan, pressing down on the vegetables to release their juices, and then discard the solids.
6. Skim off any fat from the juices in the saucepan. Bring the juices to a boil and cook for about 5 to 10 minutes, until the sauce is slightly thickened and glossy. Stir in the chopped mint and season with salt and pepper. Pour the sauce into a gravy boat.
7. Remove the strings from the lamb, cut into ½-inch-thick slices, and serve immediately with the sauce passed on the side.

Roasted Leg of Venison with Cherry Sauce

When marinating the venison with the butter mixture up to 24 hours before roasting, the herbs won't infuse as well with the solidified butter, but the flavors will definitely develop and infuse the meat. I also like roasting the leg with the solidified butter, as it keeps the seasonings from immediately sliding off. If you do this, it's best to simply pepper the roast beforehand, save the salt for just before roasting, and spread the butter over the entire leg (not just the top).

One 6- to 8-pound bone-in venison roast
Salt and freshly ground black pepper to
    taste
8 tablespoons (1 stick) butter, at room
    temperature
4 cloves garlic, minced
3 tablespoons chopped fresh parsley
1 teaspoon dried thyme
1 teaspoon dried oregano

2 large onions, chopped
3 celery stalks, sliced
2½ cups dry red wine
2 cups beef or chicken stock or broth
¾ cup dried cherries
1 tablespoon honey
¾ teaspoon balsamic vinegar
One 2-inch strip lemon zest

1. Generously season the venison roast with salt and ground black pepper. Cover the venison and refrigerate for up to 24 hours.
2. Remove the venison from the refrigerator and bring to room temperature. Place the venison on a rack in a roasting pan.
3. In a small bowl, combine the butter, garlic, parsley, thyme, and oregano.
4. Preheat oven to 450°F. Spread the butter mixture evenly over the top of the venison. Roast for 20 minutes, then reduce the oven temperature to 325°F and add the onion, celery, and wine to the pan. Roast, basting occasionally with the pan juices, until a meat thermometer inserted in the thickest part of the roast registers 120°F to 130°F for rare to medium rare, about 13 minutes per pound, or longer until desired doneness.
5. Remove the roast to a platter and cover loosely with foil to keep warm. Set the roasting pan over high heat. Add the broth to the pan and boil, scraping up any browned bits, until the sauce is reduced to about 3 cups.
6. Strain the sauce into a medium saucepan, pressing down on the vegetables to release their juices,

and then discard the solids. Set the saucepan over high heat and add the cherries, honey, vinegar, and lemon zest. Boil for 2 to 3 minutes, until the cherries are plump and the sauce is slightly thickened. Season with salt and ground black pepper and pour the sauce into a gravy boat.

7. Slice the roast and serve with the sauce passed on the side.

Pecan Roasted Rack of Lamb

These elegant, delicious lamb chops can be served as hors d'oeuvres or as a main course. Ask your butcher to "french" the lamb, which means cutting the meat away from the end of a rib or chop so that part of the bone is exposed. The meat looks more elegant, and it facilitates holding the rib chop if you choose to pick it up to eat it, which is perfectly acceptable etiquette. A very large pan—such as a 14-inch sauté pan—is needed to sear both racks simultaneously. Otherwise, you may need to sear the racks of lamb one at a time.

Two 1¼- to 1½-pound racks of lamb,
for a total of 16 chops (8 per rack)
Salt and freshly ground black pepper
to taste
3 large sprigs fresh rosemary, stems
removed and leaves chopped fine
2 tablespoons olive oil

1 tablespoon dark brown sugar
2 tablespoons pomegranate molasses
(see Note)
½ cup finely chopped pecans
1 cup water, or beef or chicken stock
or broth
½ cup ruby port

1. Preheat oven to 375°F. Trim the lamb of excess fat. Season the racks of lamb well with salt, pepper, and rosemary.
2. In a very large skillet, heat the olive oil over medium-high heat. Sear the racks of lamb fat-side-down (with bones curving upward) for 3 minutes, then turn and sear other side for 3 minutes. Remove the lamb from the skillet and place on a rack in a large roasting pan.
3. In a small bowl, stir the brown sugar into the pomegranate molasses and brush on the lamb. Sprinkle the lamb with the chopped pecans. Roast the lamb in the oven until the internal temperature with a meat thermometer registers 130°F for medium rare, about 15 to 20 minutes, or longer until desired doneness. Remove the lamb from the oven and allow to rest for 5 minutes to retain juices.
4. Meanwhile, over medium-high heat, deglaze the skillet with the cup of water or stock and the ruby port, scraping up any browned bits from the bottom of the pan. Allow the sauce to heat thoroughly, cook down slightly, and thicken.
5. Carve the roast, serving 4 lamb chops per person on each plate with the sauce spooned over the top.

Note: Pomegranate molasses is a specialty ingredient that can be found in gourmet stores, or can be made easily at home (see Box).

How to Make Homemade Pomegranate Molasses

1 cup pomegranate juice
¾ cup sugar

2 teaspoons lemon juice

1. In a small saucepan, heat the pomegranate juice over medium-high heat. Stir in the sugar and lemon juice until dissolved.
2. Reduce the heat and simmer, stirring frequently, until the liquid is reduced to ½ cup, about 20 minutes. Remove from the heat and cool to room temperature.
3. Place in a resealable container and refrigerate until ready to use.

Pork Chops with Glazed Sweet Potatoes and Butternut Squash

YIELDS 4 SERVINGS

If you are preparing this meal to impress, be sure to purchase one-pound bone-in pork chops. Brining the chops in advance of cooking results in a juicy, flavorful chop that won't dry out during cooking. The sweet potatoes and squash can be prepared in advance by parboiling them (see Box) a day or two ahead. You can also use bourbon instead of rum for the sauce.

2 cups sugar, divided
⅔ cup plus 2½ tablespoons kosher salt
10 cups warm water
4 bone-in loin pork chops (about 1 pound
    each, 1½ to 2 inches thick)
½ teaspoon freshly ground nutmeg
1 teaspoon ground cinnamon
2 tablespoons cornstarch
¼ teaspoon salt
½ cup frozen orange juice concentrate,
    thawed
1 cup cold water
¼ cup rum
7 tablespoons butter, divided

1 large sweet potato, parboiled, peeled,
    and cut into 1-inch cubes (about
    1 pound uncooked, unpeeled)
½ of an average butternut squash (about a
    1-pound uncooked, unpeeled squash),
    peeled, cut into 1-inch cubes,
    and parboiled
⅓ cup raisins or Craisins
1 tablespoon vegetable oil
Freshly ground black pepper to taste
6 slices bacon, cut into 1-inch pieces
One 11-ounce can mandarin oranges
    in light syrup, drained

1. To brine the pork chops, in a large bowl combine 1¼ cups of the sugar, the kosher salt, and 10 cups warm water; stir to dissolve the sugar and salt. Add the pork chops to the brine mixture, cover, and refrigerate at least 12 hours, turning once or twice while brining.
2. In a large saucepan, stir together the nutmeg, cinnamon, cornstarch, ¾ cup of the sugar, and ¼ teaspoon salt. Over medium heat, whisk in the orange juice, 1 cup cold water, and the rum; blend ingredients well. Add 6 tablespoons of the butter, stirring until melted. Cook, stirring frequently, for about 5 to 7 minutes, until the sauce has thickened. Add the sweet potatoes, squash, and raisins to the sauce; toss gently to coat well. Set aside.
3. Preheat oven to 375°F. Remove the pork from the brine and pat dry with paper towels. Discard the brining liquid. Sprinkle the pork with pepper, if desired.

4. In a large skillet, melt the remaining 1 tablespoon butter and the vegetable oil over medium-high heat. Sear the pork on both sides, 1 to 2 minutes per side, in batches if the pan is too crowded. Place the seared pork in a large baking pan. Spoon the potato and sauce mixture on top.
5. In the same skillet, add the bacon pieces and cook over medium-high heat for about 4 to 5 minutes, turning, until brown and crisp. Crumble the bacon and set aside.
6. Place the baking pan with the pork in oven and bake for 50 to 55 minutes, or until pork juices run clear and the meat is no longer pink along the bone when pierced with a sharp knife. Sprinkle the mandarin oranges on top, then bake for 2 minutes longer until oranges are heated through. Garnish with the crumbled bacon. Serve immediately.

How to Parboil Vegetables

When dense vegetables such as potatoes or winter squash are baked in a casserole, it's best to parboil them first to ensure they cook thoroughly during baking. Parboil sweet potatoes whole, with skin on, in boiling salted water just until fork tender. Butternut squash is available year round; peel the squash and cut it into cubes, place in a saucepan with water to cover, then boil for about 5 to 8 minutes, just until fork tender. Parboiled vegetables can be prepared a day or two in advance; cover and refrigerate until using.

Roast Fresh Pork Shoulder

YIELDS 6 TO 8 SERVINGS

Purchase a fresh pork shoulder with the skin for this recipe, which calls for a flavorful paste-like marinade rubbed over the entire shoulder and under the skin. The slow roasting brings out the flavors of the herbs and spices, while the meats remains moist, tender, and delicious.

4 cloves garlic	2 teaspoons freshly ground black pepper
1 medium onion, quartered	2 tablespoons peanut, vegetable,
2 tablespoons fresh oregano leaves,	or canola oil
or 1 tablespoon dried oregano	2 tablespoons cider vinegar
1 tablespoon salt	One 4- to 7-pound pork shoulder, skin on

1. In a food processor fitted with the metal blade, combine the garlic, onion, oregano, salt, and pepper. Drizzle in the oil, scraping down the sides as necessary. Add the vinegar and process until combined. Rub the mixture well over the pork shoulder and under the skin. Cover the pork and refrigerate for at least 8 hours and up to 24 hours.
2. Preheat oven to 350°F. Remove the pork shoulder from the refrigerator and place on a rack in a large roasting pan. Roast the pork for about 3 hours, turning every 30 minutes or so and basting with the pan juices, until the skin is crisp and the internal temperature reaches between 150°F and 160°F on a meat thermometer. Allow the meat to rest for 10 to 15 minutes to retain juices before slicing.
3. While the meat is resting, place the roasting pan over medium-high heat and deglaze the pan with 2 cups of water. Bring to a boil, stirring to loosen up the browned bits on the bottom of the pan. Reduce heat to simmer and cook for about 10 minutes, until the sauce is slightly thickened. Strain the sauce and pour into a gravy boat.
4. Slice the pork and serve with the sauce passed on the side.

Root Beer Barbecued Pulled Pork

When I was young, one of my all-time favorite beverages was my family's homemade root beer. After tasting a pulled pork sandwich in North Carolina, I was inspired to create this recipe using lots of spices, root beer, and barbecue sauce. My friends and family approve!

2 pounds fresh boneless pork butt

1 teaspoon freshly ground black pepper,
   more to taste

1 teaspoon kosher salt

1 teaspoon ground cumin

1 teaspoon dried thyme

1 teaspoon dried sage

1 teaspoon chili powder

1 teaspoon sweet paprika

1 teaspoon dry mustard

1 teaspoon garlic powder

2 tablespoons vegetable oil

1¼ cups root beer

1¼ cups barbecue sauce

1. Preheat oven to 325°F. Trim the excess fat from the pork butt. In a small bowl, mix together the pepper, kosher salt, cumin, thyme, sage, chili powder, paprika, mustard, and garlic powder. Rub the pork with an even coating of the seasoning mix.

2. In a heavy ovenproof pot or small Dutch oven (the pork should fit snugly in the pan), heat the oil. Sear the meat over medium heat, browning well on all sides, about 4 minutes per side. Add the root beer (the liquid should come about ⅓ of the way up the meat), and cover the pot with a lid.

3. Place the pot in the oven and bake for 1 hour, then turn the meat over. Cover and continue baking until the meat is tender enough to shred, about 1 more hour.

4. Remove the pot from the oven. In a large bowl, shred the pork using 2 forks (you should have about 4 cups of shredded meat). Skim the fat from the pan juices, and stir in the pork and barbecue sauce. Place the pan uncovered in the oven, and bake for about 30 minutes, until the juices thicken. Serve immediately.

Apple Mint Jelly–Marinated Lamb Chops

Who doesn't love succulent baby lamb chops? I serve them often at my cocktail parties. In this recipe I use Crosse & Blackwell mint-flavored apple jelly, fresh rosemary, and a squeeze of lime to create a flavorful marinade. The combination of watermelon and mint make for a cool, refreshing side to these sweet, savory lamb chops.

One 12-ounce jar mint-flavored apple jelly
¼ cup finely chopped garlic (about 10 cloves)
¼ cup finely chopped fresh rosemary
¼ cup freshly squeezed lime juice
3 tablespoons balsamic vinegar

1¼ teaspoons coarsely ground black pepper
1¼ teaspoons salt
16 rib lamb chops (about 2 ounces each)
Watermelon Mint Salad (see recipe on page 120), for serving

1. In a small saucepan, melt the jelly over medium heat; stirring well until liquefied. Remove from heat.
2. Stir the garlic, rosemary, lime juice, vinegar, pepper, and salt into the melted jelly. Pour the marinade mixture into a 1-gallon resealable plastic bag. Add the lamb to the marinade; seal the bag tightly and toss to coat the lamb well. Refrigerate laying bag flat on a shelf, allowing the lamb to marinate overnight, or at least 12 hours.
3. Line a broiler pan with foil. Remove the lamb from the marinade, reserving the marinade. Place the lamb on the prepared broiler pan so the clean bone ends are facing in the same direction. Meanwhile, pour the reserved marinade into a small saucepan. Simmer over medium heat for about 20 to 25 minutes, until the sauce is thickened.
4. Preheat oven to broil. Place the lamb in the broiler and cook for about 3 to 4 minutes per side for medium rare, or longer to desired doneness. (You may want to cover the clean bone ends of the lamb chops lightly with foil halfway through cooking to prevent burning.) Drizzle the sauce over the lamb and serve immediately, with Watermelon Mint Salad on the side.

Venison Roulade with Dried Fruit Stuffing

When I have dinner parties, I prepare food to impress. It's not often that venison, which can be any one of several varieties of deer, is on the menu. Have the butcher butterfly the venison loin (one less thing for you to do!). The fruit stuffing has lots of flavor and looks beautiful when the roulade is sliced and served.

4 tablespoons butter

1 small onion, diced

1 stalk celery, diced

1¼ cups dried chopped fruit of choice
(such as cherries, apricots, or raisins)

⅔ cup freshly squeezed orange juice

1½ teaspoons finely grated orange zest

½ teaspoon ground cinnamon

¼ teaspoon ground ginger

3 tablespoons bourbon

Salt and freshly ground black pepper
to taste

3 slices stale cinnamon-raisin bread,
cut into ½-inch cubes (about 1½ cups)

½ cup chopped toasted pecans

3 tablespoons orange marmalade

1 tablespoon brown sugar

1 teaspoon honey mustard

½ venison loin (about 2 to 2 ½ pounds),
trimmed and cut in a tri-fold butterfly

1. In a large skillet over medium heat, melt the butter. Add the onion and celery, and cook, stirring occasionally, for about 5 minutes, until tender but not browned. Add the dried fruit, orange juice, orange zest, cinnamon, and ginger. Cook, stirring frequently, over medium-low heat for about 4 minutes, until the fruit is tender and the orange juice is reduced to about 3 tablespoons.

2. Remove pan from heat and stir in the bourbon, salt, and pepper. Add the cubed bread and pecans. Toss gently until the ingredients are blended and the bread is moistened. Set aside to cool.

3. Preheat oven to 450°F. In a small bowl, stir together the marmalade, brown sugar, and honey mustard. Set aside.

4. Position the butterflied venison loin cut-side-down on a work surface. Slightly flatten the loin (it will be about 9 x 11 inches); season with salt and pepper. Spread the cooled stuffing mixture over the meat. Beginning with the short end, roll up the loin and tie with kitchen twine or secure with metal skewers.

5. Line a rimmed baking sheet with foil. Place the venison roulade on the prepared pan and roast for 15 minutes. Spoon the glaze over the top of the roulade and continue roasting for 10 to 20 minutes

longer, until the outside is a rich brown and a meat thermometer inserted near the center reads 135°F to 140°F for medium rare, or 140°F to 145°F for medium. Remove the roulade from the oven and allow to rest for 10 minutes before removing twine or skewers. Cut the roulade into ½-inch slices and serve immediately.

(left to right) Sugarcane-Skewered Chicken
with Sweet and Spicy Ginger Pineapple Dipping Sauce (page 39),
Glazed Duck Breasts with Sweet Potato–
Scallion Pancakes and Peanut Dipping Sauce (page 162),
Fried Green Tomatoes with Roasted
Red Pepper Aioli (page 34)

Root Beer Barbecued
Pulled Pork Sliders (page 42)

Braise of Black-Eyed Peas
and Greens Soup (page 68)

Pain Perdu Served
with Home-Style Cane Syrup
(page 18)

Bourbon Street Bread Pudding
with Sweet Bourbon Sauce
(page 255)

Grilled Chicken and Strawberry Salad
with Toasted Sugared Pecans and
Strawberry Vinaigrette (page 106)

Kentucky Burgoo (page 83)

Pan-Fried Trout,
Southern-Style (page 196)

Roast Turducken Roulade (page 174)

*Sweet Maple
Barbecue Chicken
(page 153)*

Down-Home Cornbread (page 52)

*Seafood Salad
with Collard Greens Slaw
(page 114)*

Glazed Duck Breasts with Sweet Potato–
Scallion Pancakes and Peanut Dipping Sauce
(page 162)

Beer-Braised Rabbit (page 125)

(left to right) Bourbon Street Bread Pudding
with Sweet Bourbon Sauce (page 255),
Coconut-Pecan Cupcakes (page 264),
Chocolate Pecan Pie (page 258)

Chapter 7

Poultry

Fried chicken is one of the most famous dishes in America. It was first brought to the American South by Scottish immigrants, who had long had the tradition of deep-frying. Enslaved Africans working in plantation kitchens gave fried chicken flavor with various seasonings and spices. Chicken became a staple for slaves, because unlike other meats, chickens were affordable to raise. Sunday chicken dinners have been a mainstay for Southern families.

The first thing I learned how to prepare in my mother's kitchen was fried chicken. We ate a lot of fried chicken and never got tired of it. Mom's recipe was very simple—no tricks or secret ingredients. I brought Mom's recipe to New York with me years ago. She'd be tickled to know how much of a hit it was and still is. It's so easy to make and very easy to enjoy.

These days we're watching what we eat and how it's prepared. Many people are cutting down on fried foods, including my husband Dan and me. You'll find, as we did, that the Oven-Baked Herbed Chicken is just as satisfying as fried chicken, with the bonus of less fat and a tangy flavor. This is a great alternative for fried chicken lovers who don't want to fry. But if you get that urge, try my recipe for Marinated Fried Chicken. Smothered Chicken with Onion Gravy is another soul-satisfying dish that knows no regional boundaries.

Cornish game hens aren't hens and they're not game. They're young, small domestic chickens that have a slightly stronger flavor than large chickens. I've included a couple of recipes for Cornish hens because they're easy to prepare and lend elegance to a meal. In the summertime I like to butterfly Cornish hens and marinate them in a curry-ginger yogurt for a few hours, then grill them over charcoal. I prepare stuffed hens with Cranberry-Chestnut Stuffing for special occasions, depending on who's coming for dinner.

Now, when I want to serve something other than chicken, I'll do duck or pheasant, especially for special occasions. Bourbon is considered Southern nectar; even if you're not a bourbon drinker, you'll like the way it enhances the taste of Roasted Pheasant with Spicy Peach Bourbon Dressing.

A roast turkey can't get more Southern than when it's served with a Cornbread Oyster Dressing. The texture and taste of this dressing is melt-in-your-mouth good. I've also included a recipe for a roast capon, turkey's juicier cousin. Whatever the bird, I like rich dressings. I don't have them all the time, but for holidays and special occasions, I like to splurge. You'll find many recipes for dressings in this book; you choose how fancy or simple you want to go.

I think one of the most fascinating and elaborate poultry dishes is the Turducken. Traditionally, it's a boned turkey stuffed with a boned duck that's stuffed with a boned chicken. Each layer has its own stuffing. I prefer making my recipe for a Roast Turducken Roulade. It takes about eight hours to make and never ceases to amaze our family and friends. Turducken is so special, it gets its own section in this book.

If you're for the birds like I am, you won't be disappointed by any of these recipes.

Sweet Maple Barbecue Chicken

YIELDS 8 SERVINGS

This recipe makes a large quantity of barbecue chicken, enough for eight hungry adults with plenty of leftovers. Medium heat and frequent turning ensure that the chicken is tender on the inside, while the sauce cooks gently on the outside. Take a bit of New England to your next barbecue, a decidedly non–New England invention.

> 8 pounds frying chicken, cut into pieces
> Salt and freshly ground black pepper
>   to taste
>
> 2 cups B's Sweet Maple Barbecue Sauce
>   (see recipe on page 231)

1. Rinse the chicken pieces and pat dry with paper towels. Liberally season with salt and pepper on both sides.
2. Prepare the grill (charcoal or gas) according to the manufacturer's instructions for medium heat.
3. Have 1½ cups of the Sweet Maple Barbecue Sauce ready in a separate bowl.
4. Place the chicken skin-side-down on the grill, and cook for 10 minutes. Turn and cook other side for 10 minutes.
5. Brush each piece of chicken with the barbecue sauce, turn, and grill for 10 to 15 more minutes, turning frequently to avoid burning, and brushing with barbecue sauce on each turn, until chicken is cooked through (when juices run clear when flesh is pierced with a sharp knife). The total cooking time will be about 35 to 45 minutes, depending on the size of the pieces.
6. Serve warm or at room temperature with additional barbecue sauce on the side.

Cornish Hens with Cranberry-Chestnut Stuffing

I didn't grow up on Cornish hens, and it wasn't until I moved to New York as an adult that I tasted my first hen. I love the versatility of cooking them, either grilling or, when they are whole, roasting. This recipe, stuffed with a delicious Cranberry-Chestnut Stuffing, is a wonderful fall dish! I love to prepare it when entertaining guests, serving either a half or whole hen per person depending on how many appetizers and sides accompany the meal.

4 Cornish hens (about 1½ pounds each)
Cranberry-Chestnut Stuffing (recipe
  follows)
5 tablespoons unsalted butter, softened
Freshly ground black pepper to taste,
  plus ¼ teaspoon for gravy

4 tablespoons chopped fresh rosemary,
  or 2 tablespoons dried
1 cup low-sodium chicken stock or broth
1 cup dry white wine
Salt to taste, plus ½ teaspoon for gravy

1. Preheat oven to 450°F. Remove the giblets from the hens, rinse them with cold water, and pat dry with paper towels. Stuff each bird with ¾ cup Cranberry-Chestnut Stuffing.
2. In a large roasting pan, set the hens, breast-side-up. Spread 1 tablespoon of the butter over each one, and modestly season with salt and pepper. Sprinkle 1 tablespoon of the rosemary on each bird.
3. Roast the hens for 20 minutes to brown.
4. Reduce the oven temperature to 350°F and continue roasting for 30 minutes, or until juices run clear when the flesh is pierced near the bone with a sharp knife.
5. Transfer the hens to a serving platter. Keep warm while making the gravy.
6. Skim most of the fat from the roasting pan and stir in the stock, wine, ½ teaspoon salt, and ¼ teaspoon pepper. Stir to scrape up all the browned bits on the bottom of the pan. Bring to a boil, reduce the heat, and simmer for 3 to 5 minutes.
7. Taste the gravy for seasoning. Strain it through a fine sieve to remove bits, and finish by stirring in the remaining tablespoon of butter.
8. Serve the hens whole or halved, pouring gravy over them or serving it separately.

Cranberry-Chestnut Stuffing

YIELDS 3 CUPS

Cranberries and chestnuts really say fall to me. And unlike most nuts, chestnuts are nearly fat-free. They have a sweet, buttery flavor that comes to life with the addition of a few herbs and Craisins and the added richness of the wild rice blend.

2 tablespoons butter
½ cup diced onion
½ cup diced celery
¾ cup (3½ ounces) canned or bagged
    chopped chestnuts
1 teaspoon minced fresh rosemary,
    or ½ teaspoon dried
1 teaspoon minced fresh thyme,
    or ½ teaspoon dried

¼ teaspoon salt
2 to 3 tablespoons Craisins
¼ cup low-sodium chicken stock or broth,
    or more as needed
½ cup cooked wild rice blend
1½ cups dried bread cubes
Salt and freshly ground black pepper
    to taste

1. In a large saucepan, melt the butter and sauté the onion and celery until translucent. Add the chestnuts, rosemary, thyme, and salt, and sauté for about 30 seconds. Add the Craisins and ¼ cup stock and mix well.
2. Remove from heat and fold in the rice and bread cubes. Add more stock as needed—the mixture should be moist, but not wet. Season with salt and pepper.
3. To serve as a side dish, preheat oven to 350°F, place the stuffing in a buttered 7-quart covered casserole or soufflé dish, and bake for 40 to 50 minutes. Remove cover for the last 10 minutes for a toasty crust.

Grilled Cornish Hens with Pomegranate Barbecue Sauce

The combination of nonfat yogurt and all of the spices infuses a bounty of flavors into these tender birds. Serve warm off the grill or picnic style at room temperature.

1 cup chopped onion

1 cup nonfat yogurt

2 tablespoons curry powder

2 tablespoons vegetable oil

1 tablespoon grated gingerroot

2 cloves garlic, minced

¼ teaspoon freshly ground black pepper

¼ teaspoon cayenne pepper

¼ teaspoon salt

4 Cornish hens (about 1½ pounds each), butterflied (see Box)

Pomegranate Barbecue Sauce (see recipe on page 234)

1. In a gallon-size plastic food storage bag, mix the onion, yogurt, curry powder, vegetable oil, ginger, garlic, black pepper, cayenne, and salt.
2. Add the hens and turn to coat. Refrigerate for at least 4 hours or up to 12 hours, turning occasionally.
3. Prepare an outdoor grill with medium-hot coals, or preheat a gas grill or broiler to medium. Remove the hens from the bag; discard the marinade.
4. Oil the grill or broiler rack. Grill or broil the hens 4 to 6 inches from heat for 35 minutes, turning 4 times during cooking, until hens are lightly charred and juices run clear when flesh is pierced near the bone with a sharp knife. Serve warm or at room temperature.

How to Butterfly a Cornish Hen

To butterfly a Cornish hen means to remove the backbone. Place the hen back-side-up on a cutting board. Using a sharp knife or kitchen shears, cut closely along one side of the backbone from bottom to top, then repeat on the other side of the backbone. Remove and discard the backbone. Turn the hen breast-side-up so the drumsticks point out. Using the palm of your hand, press down firmly on the breast to flatten the hen and turn the wings under.

Roasted Capon with Sausage-Apple-Pear Dressing and Lillet Sauce

YIELDS 4 TO 6 SERVINGS

Capons are roosters that have been castrated at a very young age. They are moist, flavorful, and very tender, since the flesh starts out tender and the higher fat content acts as a natural basting agent. A high-quality capon has a dramatically different flavor than traditional roast chicken, though if you can't find capons you can substitute a large roasting chicken. Like a formal ball gown, this is a special-occasion recipe; there is nothing everyday about the combination of chicken and apple-pear-sausage dressing with crystallized ginger, fresh herbs, and Lillet or port. Just the right amount of decadence, of which our first gourmand, Thomas Jefferson, would have highly approved!

One 6- to 8-pound capon or roasting chicken
Salt and freshly ground pepper to taste

Sausage-Apple-Pear Dressing (recipe follows)
Melted butter for basting
Lillet Sauce (recipe follows)

1. Preheat oven to 450°F.
2. Rinse the capon under cold water and dry thoroughly inside and out. Season the inside of the bird with salt and pepper. Stuff the chicken's body and neck cavity loosely with the Sausage-Apple-Pear Dressing.
3. Using kitchen twine, tie the legs of the capon together. Brush the skin with melted butter and sprinkle generously with salt and pepper.
4. Place the capon breast-side-up on a rack in a roasting pan. Turn the oven down to 350°F and immediately place the capon in the oven. Roast for approximately 20 minutes per pound, or until the skin is golden brown, the juices run clear when the flesh is pierced with a sharp knife at the thigh, and the internal temperature of the stuffing is 165°F when checked with an instant-read thermometer. During roasting, baste the chicken frequently with pan drippings and melted butter.
5. Spoon the extra dressing that does not fit in the bird into a buttered casserole dish. Cover with foil and bake for 35 to 40 minutes.
6. When the capon is cooked, remove it from the roasting pan to a large platter. Remove the roasting rack from the pan. Let the capon rest at least 20 minutes before carving while making the Lillet Sauce.

Sausage-Apple-Pear Dressing

YIELDS 8 CUPS

5 dried apricots, diced

2 tablespoons Lillet or white port

2 tablespoons butter, divided

3 precooked chicken-and-apple sausage
    links, chopped

1 cup chopped onion

3 ribs (about 1 cup) celery, chopped

½ tablespoon minced garlic

1½ tablespoons crystallized ginger, finely
    diced

Salt and freshly ground black pepper to
    taste

1 Braeburn apple, cored, peeled, and diced

1 firm Anjou pear, cored, peeled,
    and diced

1½ tablespoons chopped fresh sage

1 tablespoon chopped fresh parsley

1 tablespoon chopped fresh thyme

1 cup cooked wild rice

½ cup cooked wheat berries

¾ cup chopped pecans

2 cups dried bread cubes

¼ cup low-sodium chicken stock or broth,
    or more as needed

1. In a small bowl, place the dried apricots. Pour the Lillet or white port over the apricots and set aside to plump the fruit.
2. In a large saucepan, heat 1 tablespoon of the butter over medium heat. Stir in the chopped sausage, onion, and celery and cook for about 8 minutes, until soft. Stir in the garlic and ginger, and season with salt and pepper.
3. Add the remaining tablespoon of butter and stir in the apples and pears. Cook for 5 minutes. Add the apricots along with their soaking liquid, stirring and scraping any browned bits off the bottom of the pan. Simmer for 3 more minutes.
4. Pour the mixture into a large bowl. Stir in the sage, parsley, thyme, rice, wheat berries, pecans, bread cubes, and ¼ cup chicken broth. If the mixture seems dry, add a little more chicken broth a few tablespoons at a time to just moisten, but do not let dressing get too wet or it will be soggy.
5. Use the dressing to stuff the capon, or preheat oven to 350°F, place the dressing in a buttered casserole dish, cover, and bake for 30 to 40 minutes. Serve hot.

Lillet Sauce

Lillet is a French aperitif made from a blend of wines and fruit liqueurs. White port is a dry to semi-sweet aperitif; both work equally well in this recipe, which will yield plenty of leftover sauce.

½ cup Lillet or white port
1 cup low-sodium chicken stock or broth
½ cup pear nectar or apple juice

1 teaspoon pear-infused vinegar or apple
   cider vinegar
2 tablespoons butter, cut into bits
Salt and freshly ground black pepper to taste

1. Place the roasting pan from the cooked capon over 2 burners and turn the heat to medium-high. Add the Lillet or white port and stir, scraping the bottom of the roasting pan to release the browned bits with a wooden spoon.
2. Stir in the chicken stock, pear nectar or apple juice, and vinegar, combining well.
3. Strain to remove any solids, skim off the fat, and pour the sauce into a small clean saucepan. Bring to a boil, then lower heat to a simmer and allow the sauce to reduce by half, about 2 minutes. Slowly whisk in the butter, a piece at a time, to enrich the flavor. Season with salt and pepper.
4. Pour the sauce into a gravy boat and serve alongside the roasted capon.

Marinated Fried Chicken

YIELDS 6 SERVINGS

I like my chicken tender and full of flavor. The herbs and spices in the marinade give the chicken a down-home, finger-lickin' good taste!

2 frying chickens, cut into 8 pieces each
2 cups buttermilk
2 tablespoons low-sodium soy sauce
⅓ cup Dijon mustard
1 teaspoon chopped fresh rosemary

1 teaspoon seasoned salt
½ teaspoon freshly ground black pepper
2 cups all-purpose flour
2 cups vegetable or canola oil, for frying

1. Rinse the chicken in cool water and pat dry with paper towels.
2. In a large bowl, blend the buttermilk, soy sauce, mustard, rosemary, seasoned salt, and pepper. Add the chicken pieces and turn to coat them evenly. Cover the bowl and let chicken marinate for 2 to 3 hours or overnight in the refrigerator.
3. Remove the chicken from the marinade and let it drain. In a shallow dish, place the flour. Roll each piece of chicken in flour and transfer to a baking sheet. Set aside to allow to rest for about 30 minutes.
4. Preheat oven to 350°F. In a cast-iron or other deep-sided, heavy skillet, heat about ½ inch of vegetable oil over medium heat. When the oil is hot but not smoking, add the chicken pieces a few at a time so as not to crowd the pan. Fry, turning to cook all sides, until the coating is well browned, for a total of 6 to 8 minutes (chicken will not be fully cooked through). Add more oil to the pan as necessary, allowing it to get hot before frying more chicken.
5. As the chicken is browned, transfer to a baking sheet. Bake the chicken pieces in the oven for 30 to 40 minutes, until they are fully cooked and the juices run clear when the flesh is pierced at the bone with a sharp knife.
6. Drain the chicken briefly on paper towels and serve immediately or at room temperature.

Oven-Baked Herbed Chicken

YIELDS 6 SERVINGS

Fried chicken is a Southern classic, and no picnic would be complete without it. This oven-baked chicken is a healthier variation on the original but lacks none of the taste. Thick and creamy, buttermilk is lower in fat and calories than regular milk, because the fat from buttermilk has already been removed to make butter, yet it adds a delicious flavor.

3 whole skinless, bone-in chicken breasts
2 cups low-fat buttermilk
1 tablespoon reduced-sodium soy sauce
½ teaspoon garlic powder
½ teaspoon onion powder
¼ teaspoon poultry seasoning

Nonstick cooking spray
¾ cup plain breadcrumbs
½ teaspoon seasoned pepper
½ teaspoon paprika
½ teaspoon dried thyme
Salt and freshly ground pepper to taste

1. Cut each chicken breast in half, diagonally. Place in a large bowl or resealable gallon-size plastic bag and set aside.
2. In another bowl, whisk together the buttermilk, soy sauce, garlic powder, onion powder, and poultry seasoning, then pour the mixture over the chicken, cover, and refrigerate. After 4 hours, remove the chicken from the buttermilk marinade.
3. Preheat oven to 375°F. Spray a baking sheet with cooking spray.
4. In a large bowl, combine the breadcrumbs, seasoned pepper, paprika, and thyme. Roll the chicken pieces in the mixture, tossing to coat well.
5. Place the chicken bone-side-down on the prepared baking sheet. Lightly coat the chicken with cooking spray. Bake for 30 to 35 minutes, or until juices run clear when pierced at the bone with a sharp knife. Season with salt and pepper. Serve hot or at room temperature.

Glazed Duck Breasts with Sweet Potato–Scallion Pancakes and Peanut Dipping Sauce

YIELDS 4 SERVINGS

For this recipe, I use skinless duck breast; duck is a rich dark meat with delicious flavor. It works well as an entrée or an appetizer, depending on how you want to serve it. I like to pair it with the Peanut Dipping Sauce, making it a great combination of savory and sweet.

⅓ cup orange marmalade (or substitute with Simply Fruit or reduced-sugar orange marmalade)

2 tablespoons ketchup

1 tablespoon molasses

1 teaspoon soy sauce (regular or low-sodium)

1 teaspoon orange zest

¼ cup freshly squeezed orange juice

4 boneless, skinless duck breasts (see Note)

Nonstick cooking spray

Salt and freshly ground pepper to taste

Sweet Potato–Scallion Pancakes (recipe follows)

Chopped scallions, minced parsley, and toasted sesame seeds, for garnish if desired

Peanut Dipping Sauce (recipe follows)

1. To make the glaze, in a small bowl, place the marmalade, ketchup, molasses, soy sauce, orange zest, and juice, and whisk together until combined. (This step can be done up to 3 days ahead, with the glaze covered with plastic wrap and refrigerated.) Reserve ¼ cup glaze for assembly of duck in the pancake.

2. To grill the duck breasts, preheat a grill pan over medium heat and spray with nonstick cooking spray. Season the breasts with salt and pepper. Place the breasts on the pan and grill for 3 to 4 minutes, then brush them liberally with glaze. Cook for 2 more minutes, then turn the breasts over. Brush the newly exposed side of breasts with half the remaining glaze and cook for 5 to 6 minutes more, depending on desired doneness (duck is best served medium-rare to medium). Allow the breasts to rest for 5 minutes to retain juices, then thinly slice the meat on the bias and serve with Sweet Potato–Scallion Pancakes and Peanut Dipping Sauce.

3. To assemble, place a cooked Sweet Potato–Scallion Pancake plain-side-up (the other side is the presentation side, which shows the scallions and parsley) on a plate. Place a few slices of glazed

duck down the center of the pancake. Drizzle a teaspoon of reserved glaze on top and wrap envelope style, or in the shape of a cone. (For appetizers, place 2 pieces of duck on mini-pancakes and drizzle with ½ teaspoon glaze.)

4. Garnish with additional scallions, parsley, and sesame seeds, if desired. Serve with Peanut Dipping Sauce.

Note: Duck breasts can often be found in the frozen foods section of the grocery store. Other resources for duck breasts include Grimaud Farms, 800-466-9955 or grimaudfarms.com, and D'Artagnan Company, 800-327-8246 or dartagnan.com.

Sweet Potato–Scallion Pancakes

YIELDS 12 PANCAKES

Once cooked, these thin, orange-glazed pancakes will show flecks of scallion and parsley on one side for a beautiful presentation. Stacking cooked pancakes with sheets of parchment—readily found in the food wrap aisle of the grocery store—will keep them from sticking together.

½ cup precooked mashed sweet potatoes,
   or 1 small sweet potato, peeled, cubed
   into 1-inch pieces, and boiled
   for 12 minutes until tender
2 large eggs (or substitute with ½ cup Egg
   Beaters)
2 cups water
2 teaspoons sesame oil

1 cup all-purpose flour
½ teaspoon kosher salt
⅔ cup finely chopped scallion, white
   and green parts
⅓ cup finely chopped flat-leaf parsley
   (or substitute with cilantro)
2 teaspoons sesame seeds, toasted
Nonstick cooking spray

1. In the bowl of a blender or food processor, place the mashed sweet potatoes, eggs, water, sesame oil, flour, and salt, and blend until smooth, about 2 minutes. Pour the batter into a large measuring cup (so it's easy to pour) and add the scallions, parsley, and sesame seeds. Stir well to combine.

2. For entrée-size pancakes, prepare an 8-inch nonstick pan by spraying with nonstick cooking spray and placing over medium-high heat.

3. Pour ¼ cup of the batter into the pan, tilting the pan in all directions to coat the entire bottom with a thin layer of batter. Cook for about 2 minutes, until the batter is set and lightly golden brown around the edges. Using a large spatula, gently flip the pancake and cook the other side for about 1 minute, until lightly golden.

4. Remove pancake to a parchment-lined tray and continue making pancakes with the remaining batter, layering parchment between finished pancakes so they do not stick together. Repeat the process until all of the batter is used and you have 12 pancakes. Keep the pancakes warm after cooking by covering with foil. (To serve later, cover pancakes with plastic wrap and refrigerate for up to 3 days. Reheat pancakes in a preheated 350°F oven for 15 minutes before serving.)

Peanut Dipping Sauce

YIELDS ¾ CUP

⅓ cup smooth peanut butter
¼ cup soy sauce (regular or low-sodium)
¼ cup rice vinegar
1 teaspoon sesame oil

1 teaspoon hot chili paste, or more to taste
3 teaspoons granulated sugar
2 teaspoons sesame seeds, toasted

In a small bowl, place all of the ingredients. Using a whisk, slowly stir the mixture together until the peanut butter is dissolved and the sauce is smooth. Cover with plastic wrap and refrigerate up to 3 days before serving. Stir well to combine just before serving.

Appetizer-Size Sweet Potato–Scallion Pancakes

For appetizer-size pancakes, follow the same directions in step 3, above, using 1 tablespoon of batter per pancake. This will make 36 2-inch pancakes.

Roasted Pheasant with Spicy Peach Bourbon Dressing

YIELDS 4 TO 6 SERVINGS

I like to serve pheasant for special occasions. Most pheasants are farm raised and have a mild, delicate flavor, while wild pheasant has a gamey flavor. Because pheasants are lean game birds, I like to use a barding technique to infuse moisture and flavor into the meat, which is simply laying bacon or pancetta over the entire skin and tying it in place with kitchen twine. Or, you can just brush the birds with butter and sprinkle with salt and pepper; this method is easier and the bird will brown beautifully! Brining the pheasant results in a moist, delicious bird, and the hibiscus, juniper berries, and Chinese five-spice powder add even more flavor; you can find dried hibiscus at specialty food stores and Trader Joe's, or order from amazon.com.

1½ cups kosher salt	1 gallon water
¾ cup sugar	2 pheasants, about 3 pounds each
5 dried hibiscus flowers	Spicy Peach Bourbon Dressing (recipe
12 smashed juniper berries	follows)
5 bay leaves	2 teaspoons freshly ground black pepper
1 tablespoon Chinese five-spice powder	16 to 20 slices bacon or pancetta
1 cup boiling water	Bourbon Sauce (recipe follows)

1. In a large stockpot, add the salt, sugar, hibiscus flowers, juniper berries, bay leaves, five-spice powder, and 1 cup boiling water. Stir until the salt and sugar are dissolved, then let cool.
2. When cooled, add 1 gallon of water. Submerge the pheasants in the liquid, cover, and refrigerate for 3 to 4 hours.
3. Preheat oven to 450°F. Remove the pheasants from the brine, rinse, and dry well with paper towels. Sprinkle the cavities with the freshly ground black pepper, and fill with about 1½ cups Spicy Peach Bourbon Dressing per bird.
4. Place the extra dressing in a buttered casserole dish. Cover and bake for 35 to 40 minutes.
5. Meanwhile, tie the pheasant legs tightly together with kitchen twine, then lay the bacon or pancetta over the skin, covering the pheasants entirely, and tie on well with kitchen twine.
6. Roast the pheasants for 25 minutes, then lower oven to 375°F and bake for another 25 to 30 minutes, until the internal temperature registers 155°F on an instant-read thermometer. Remove birds from roasting pan and let rest.

7. Prepare the Bourbon Sauce, and serve immediately with the roasted pheasant and Spicy Peach Bourbon Dressing.

Spicy Peach Bourbon Dressing

YIELDS 8 CUPS

This spicy dressing gets a triple kick from the habanero pepper, ginger, and tasso, a highly seasoned, intensely flavored smoked ham that's often used in Cajun cuisine. It can be found in specialty stores or ordered by mail from cajungrocer.com.

5 dried apricots, diced
2 tablespoons bourbon
3 ounces tasso ham, diced
1 tablespoon butter
½ large Vidalia onion, diced
3 ribs (about 1 cup) celery, diced
½ teaspoon minced garlic
1½ tablespoons finely diced crystallized
   ginger
1 small habanero chile pepper, seeded and
   minced
⅛ teaspoon salt

⅛ teaspoon freshly ground black pepper
1 tablespoon chopped fresh parsley
1 tablespoon chopped fresh thyme
1 tablespoon chopped fresh sage
2 peaches, peeled, pitted, and diced
1 cup cooked wild rice
½ cup cooked wheat berries
¾ cup chopped pecans
2 cups dried bread cubes
¼ cup low-sodium chicken stock or broth,
   or more as needed

1. In a small bowl, plump the apricots in the bourbon.
2. In a large saucepan, sauté the tasso ham over medium heat for a minute or two until some of the fat is released, then add the butter, onion, and celery and cook until soft. Stir in the garlic, ginger, habanero, salt, and pepper.
3. Pour the plumped apricots and bourbon into the pan, stirring to deglaze pan. Simmer for a minute or two, until some of the alcohol has evaporated, and turn off heat.
4. Mix in the herbs, peaches, wild rice, wheat berries, pecans, bread cubes, and chicken broth. If the mixture seems dry, add a little more chicken broth a few tablespoons at a time to just moisten, but do not let the dressing get too wet or it will be soggy.

5. Use the dressing to stuff the pheasants, or preheat oven to 350°F, place the dressing in a buttered casserole dish, cover, and bake for 30 to 40 minutes. Serve hot.

Bourbon Sauce

YIELDS ABOUT ½ CUP

½ cup bourbon
½ cup peach nectar
1½ cups chicken stock or broth

1 tablespoon butter
Salt and freshly ground pepper to taste

1. Place the roasting pan from the pheasant over medium-high heat and add the bourbon, peach nectar, and chicken stock. Cook, stirring well to scrape the bottom of the pan and release the browned bits. Allow the sauce to reduce by half, then strain and skim off the fat.
2. In a small clean saucepan, pour the sauce, stir in the butter, and season with salt and pepper. Cook for about 2 minutes.
3. Pour the sauce into a gravy boat and serve alongside the roasted pheasant.

Roast Turkey with Cornbread Oyster Dressing

Growing up, Thanksgiving was a big deal in our house. All the family members would converge upon our home to celebrate with Mom's Thanksgiving Day feast. It's my favorite holiday, because it reminds me of Mom and bridges differences of religion and ethnicity—and the turkey is king! I'm well known for my Jerk Turkey, but for this book I decided to change it up a bit with more of a traditional Southern turkey with rich Cornbread Oyster Dressing.

1 whole turkey, 10 to 12 pounds
Salt and freshly ground black pepper to taste
Cornbread Oyster Dressing (see recipe on
  page 54)

4 tablespoons softened butter, more
  if needed
3 cups chicken stock or broth
1 to 2 tablespoons cornstarch

1. Preheat oven to 350°F.
2. Remove and reserve the giblets (neck, gizzard, and heart) from the turkey.
3. Rinse the turkey and pat dry with paper towels inside and out; season well with salt and pepper.
4. Loosely fill the chest and neck cavity with the Cornbread Oyster Dressing. Place the extra dressing in a buttered casserole dish, cover, and bake for 35 to 40 minutes.
5. Rub the turkey skin with the butter. Place the bird on a rack in a roasting pan, add about ¼ inch of water to the pan, and cover the bird loosely with foil.
6. Roast the turkey until the meat registers 180°F on an instant-read thermometer in the thickest portion of the thigh and the center of the stuffing registers 165°F (about 15 minutes per pound, or approximately 3 hours). Check frequently during cooking, adding more water to the pan if it begins to dry out.
7. While the bird is roasting, in a medium saucepan, simmer the reserved giblets in the chicken stock over low heat for 1 hour, then strain and set aside.
8. When the bird is done, remove it from the pan and let it rest for 15 minutes.
9. To prepare the gravy, pour the roasting pan drippings into a clean saucepan. Place the roasting pan over medium heat, add some of the giblet broth, and stir well to bring up the browned bits clinging to the bottom. Add this to the saucepan with the drippings. Skim as much fat as possible from the surface of the drippings mixture. Add the remaining giblet broth to the saucepan and

bring to a simmer over medium heat. Stir the cornstarch into a little cold water to dissolve, then slowly add it to the gravy, stirring well and continuing to simmer for about 5 minutes, until the gravy thickens. Adjust the seasonings to taste and strain the gravy.

10. Remove the stuffing from the cavity of the turkey and place it in a warmed casserole dish. Carve the turkey and serve with the Cornbread Oyster Dressing and pan gravy served alongside.

Smothered Chicken with Onion Gravy

YIELDS 4 TO 6 SERVINGS

When the word "smothered" is used to describe a cooking technique, I know I'm about to have a "take me back to Grandma" experience, with the right recipe and cook to be sure.

2 cups buttermilk
1 teaspoon dried sage
1 teaspoon seasoned salt
1 whole chicken, cut into pieces
2 teaspoons salt
¾ teaspoon freshly ground black pepper
2 tablespoons butter

2 tablespoons vegetable oil, or more as needed
¾ cup plus 3 tablespoons all-purpose flour
2 cups sliced yellow onion
1 cup chopped celery
3 cloves garlic, minced
3 cups chicken stock or broth
¼ teaspoon cayenne pepper

1. In a gallon-size resealable plastic bag or large bowl, mix together the buttermilk, sage, and seasoned salt. Add the chicken pieces, cover, and marinate for at least 1 hour, but no longer than 4 hours.
2. Remove the chicken from the marinade, wipe off any excess liquid with a paper towel, and discard leftover marinade.
3. Season the chicken with 1 teaspoon of the salt and ½ teaspoon of the black pepper. In a large skillet, melt the butter and oil over medium-high heat.
4. In a shallow dish, place ¾ cup of the flour. Dredge the chicken in the flour, then place in the skillet, in batches if necessary, to brown the chicken on all sides.
5. Set the chicken aside and drain the skillet, reserving about 1 tablespoon of cooking oil. (If all the oil has been absorbed, add 1 tablespoon vegetable oil to the skillet.)
6. Reduce skillet heat to medium-low and stir in the onion, celery, and garlic. Cook for 5 minutes, stirring often, until the onion is softened.
7. Stir in the remaining 3 tablespoons flour and cook for 5 minutes more.
8. Add the chicken broth, cayenne pepper, remaining 1 teaspoon salt, and remaining ¼ teaspoon black pepper. Stir well and bring just to a boil, then reduce heat to low.
9. Allow the gravy to thicken slightly. Return the chicken to the skillet, cover, and continue cooking for 30 minutes, or until chicken juices run clear when pierced with a sharp knife and the gravy has thickened. Serve immediately.

Fall Holiday Turducken

When I was planning to open our restaurant in Washington, D.C.'s Union Station, I knew I wanted the menu to be a combination of Cajun, Creole, and Southern cuisine. I had met the world-famous Cajun chef Paul Prudhomme several times. So, when I started thinking about a chef, I asked Paul for recommendations. He told me, in glowing terms, about a talented young cook who was working for him named Robert Holmes. Chef Paul felt this would be a great opportunity, and Robert became our first chef at B. Smith's Union Station restaurant. He came with Paul's blessings and a recipe for turducken, which I found to be fascinating—a boned turkey, stuffed with a boned duck, stuffed with a boned chicken, and each layer had its own dressing!

I'd always roasted turkeys following traditional, familiar recipes. I liked the idea of something as different as a turducken, but I didn't like the idea of all of that work. Of course you can order a turducken fully prepared, but that's not my style. When I decided to write this book, I was inspired to try something new, something unconventional. So I came up with my own version of turducken, a huge roulade composed of the poultry breasts which, when layered with different dressings, makes a stunning presentation when sliced and served.

Because of all the steps and ingredients it takes to prepare turducken, many cooks like to share the experience with friends and family, making it a party in itself. When it comes to my kitchen, though, I'm territorial. I enjoy doing it all. Whether you're like me or not, preparing a whole turducken or my Roast Turducken Roulade will test your organizational skills. That's why along with the recipes for the roulade and the dressings—Cornbread Andouille, Whole-Grain Giblet, and Shrimp Dressing—and for Sweet Potato or Pan Gravy, I've also included a timeline and a shopping list.

A lot goes into making this roulade, but it promises to give a lot back to you and your guests in terms of its rich, exciting flavors. Once at the table, what I love is watching everyone's eyes widen as the roulade is sliced, revealing the different layers of meat and their dressings.

Turducken Tools and Timetable

As with any complicated recipe, it helps ease the process to begin a week ahead of time to make sure you have all the tools and ingredients you'll need and complete any steps that can be done in advance. Many of the steps in this recipe can be simplified by ordering ahead and having your butcher prepare the boned poultry for you. In addition, you have the option to purchase some pre-prepared ingredients, such as cornbread, whole-grain croutons, bottled clam juice, chicken stock, and precooked andouille sausage, to help you speed up the process.

Preparation Tools Checklist

Plastic wrap

Paper towels

Cooking twine and needle (for trussing)

Metal turkey skewers (for closing
    the turducken)

Heavy-duty aluminum foil

11-gallon heavy-duty resealable plastic bags

Kitchen twine and needle (for trussing),
    or metal skewers

Roasting pan and rack

Cutting board

Meat mallet (for pounding poultry flat)

Electric carving knife

1 Week Ahead

1. Order the poultry and giblets from the butcher if you are not boning and trimming them yourself. Be sure to order *boned* turkey, duck, and chicken breast, and request that the butcher save and package your bones, because they are an important ingredient for the poultry stock. *If you are boning your poultry yourself, please refer to recipe for recommended guidelines (for weight) when ordering poultry.*

2. You will need to order trimmed chicken giblets from the butcher if you don't wish to prepare them yourself; otherwise, trimming instructions are found within the recipe (see Whole-Grain Giblet Dressing recipe, page 179). Some markets don't carry andouille sausage. Be sure to check with the butcher at the market and order it, if necessary, or purchase it by mail from cajunsausage.com or cajungrocer.com.

3. Order ½ pound of raw shrimp from your supermarket or fishmonger; you will need them for your Shrimp Dressing (see recipe on page 180). Schedule the order to be picked up 3 days prior to the day you are roasting and serving the turducken.

3 Days Ahead

1. Review the recipes and create a shopping list with all the necessary ingredients and preparation tools.
2. Go grocery shopping, purchasing everything you need to prepare the turducken and dressings.
3. Pick up the poultry and seafood order.
4. Bake homemade cornbread (if not using store-bought) for the Cornbread Andouille Dressing.

2 Days Ahead

1. Bone the poultry if you are doing it yourself. Reserve the bones for the poultry stock. Cover all and refrigerate until use.
2. Trim the giblets if you are doing it yourself. Cover with plastic wrap and refrigerate until use.
3. Make the poultry stock; cover and refrigerate until use.
4. Make the shrimp stock; cover and refrigerate until use.
5. Cut the cornbread and whole-grain bread into cubes, cover, and set aside until use.

1 Day Ahead

1. Prepare Cornbread Andouille Dressing, Whole-Grain Giblet Dressing, and Shrimp Dressing (see recipes on pages 178–80); cover with plastic wrap and refrigerate until use.
2. Prepare the brine (see recipe on page 174) and brine the poultry; cover and refrigerate overnight.
3. Chop all fresh vegetables and herbs for dressings; cover and refrigerate until use.

Day of Assembling, Roasting, and Serving

1. Remove the poultry from the brine solution, rinse with cold water, and pat dry with paper towels.
2. Prepare, assemble, and cook the Roast Turducken Roulade (see recipe) at least 4 hours before you wish to serve it.
3. While the turducken is resting (after completion of roasting and before carving), prepare the Sweet Potato Gravy and/or the Pan Gravy (see recipes on page 177).

Roast Turducken Roulade

This is a recipe that gives back over and over. Like that wonderful Nat King Cole song "Unforgettable," once you hear it, you never forget it. With turducken, once you taste my take on this traditional New Orleans recipe, you'll never forget the unique combinations of textures and flavors.

To Brine the Poultry

The weights given below are for boned poultry. If you are boning the poultry yourself, you will need to add ½ pound when ordering to allow for the bones. So you will need a 2½-pound chicken breast, a 2½-pound duck breast, and a 4½-pound turkey breast.

2 quarts water, or equal amounts store-bought chicken stock
1 gallon (4 quarts) water
½ cup kosher salt
½ cup granulated sugar
1 teaspoon cayenne pepper
1 tablespoon dried thyme
1 teaspoon coarsely ground black pepper

4 bay leaves
One 4-pound fresh turkey breast, boned (reserve bones for stock; see Note below)
One 2-pound skinless chicken breast, boned (reserve bones for stock)
One 2-pound skinless duck breast, boned (reserve bones for stock)

1. To prepare the poultry brine, in a large bowl, place the water, salt, sugar, cayenne, thyme, black pepper, and bay leaves; stir well to combine and dissolve the salt and sugar.
2. Pour the brining liquid into an 11-gallon heavy-duty resealable plastic bag. Add the turkey, duck, and chicken breasts to the brine. Squeeze the air out of the bag and seal closed.
3. Place the bag (seal-side-up) on a large baking sheet; refrigerate overnight or up to 24 hours. Occasionally massage the outside of the bag while carefully rotating the poultry to infuse flavors.
4. Before assembling Turducken, remove the poultry from the solution, rinse, and dry thoroughly with paper towels.

Note: If purchasing a Butterball-brand turkey breast, do not brine it with the duck and chicken, as Butterballs are injected with up to 15 percent of a solution of turkey broth, salt, sodium phosphate, sugar, and flavor. You will need to marinate only the duck and chicken, so reduce the brining solution by half.

To Assemble Turducken Roulade

1 recipe Cornbread Andouille Dressing, for turkey (recipe follows)
1 recipe Whole-Grain Giblet Dressing, for duck (recipe follows)

1 recipe Shrimp Dressing, for chicken (recipe follows)
1 tablespoon butter, margarine, or olive oil
Salt and freshly ground pepper to taste

1. Remove the prepared Cornbread Andouille Dressing, Whole-Grain Giblet Dressing, and Shrimp Dressing from the refrigerator and bring to room temperature.
2. Prepare kitchen counter or a large cutting board by lining the surface with plastic wrap. Place an 11-gallon heavy-duty resealable plastic bag on center of prepared area. Place the turkey breast skin-side-down inside the bag. Release air from bag and seal closed. Gently pound the turkey breast with a meat mallet to uniformly flatten to about ¾ inch thick (the breast should measure about 15 x12 inches in size when flattened in order to accommodate the other ingredients that will be stuffed into it). Set aside.
3. Repeat the process above, placing the duck breast and the chicken breast in separate heavy-duty resealable plastic bags, and flatten each to about ½ inch thick. Set aside.
4. Stuff and assemble the turducken following these steps:

   Step A: Starting with the prepared turkey breast skin-side-down on the prepared counter, spread the Cornbread Andouille Dressing over the surface of the turkey, leaving a 2-inch border. Set aside.
   Step B: Place the flattened duck breast skin-side-down on the counter and spread the Whole-Grain Giblet Dressing over the surface of the duck, leaving a 2-inch border. Set aside.
   Step C: Place the flattened chicken breast skin-side-down on the counter and spread the Shrimp Dressing over the surface of the chicken, leaving a 2-inch border. Roll the chicken up, enclosing the dressing inside to form a neat, tight roll.
   Step D: Place the prepared chicken roll, open-side-down, in the center of the prepared duck breast. Fold the sides of the prepared duck over the chicken to enclose chicken. Place the duck roll, open-side-down, in the center of the prepared turkey breast; fold the long sides of the turkey over the duck to enclose. Gently bring the edges of the turkey together to form a seam.
   Step E: Close the edges of the turkey roll by sewing both sides of the meat and skin together with

a needle laced with kitchen twine. You can also secure it with metal skewers, making sure all edges of the turkey are closed shut. (Do this step carefully to protect the dressing from oozing out during the roasting process.)

Step F: Rub the turkey skin with the butter to coat the entire surface of the roll. Season with salt and pepper just before roasting.

To Roast Turducken Roulade

You may find that the top of the roll cracks while cooking during the last hour. This is due to the expansion of the dressings, and is normal.

1 assembled Turducken Roulade

½ cup Poultry Stock (see recipe on page 96) or chicken stock or broth, or more as needed

1. Place oven rack in lower third of oven. Preheat oven to 450°F. Place the turducken seam-side-down on a rack that has been placed inside a large roasting pan.
2. Lower the temperature to 350°F. Bake for 1 hour; add ½ cup Poultry Stock to bottom of roasting pan to loosen pan drippings for basting. Continue to roast for an additional 2½ hours, basting frequently with pan drippings; if necessary, add small amounts of stock to the bottom of the roasting pan to loosen pan drippings from time to time.
3. Roast the turducken for a total of 3½ hours, or until a meat thermometer placed in the center registers 180°F and the turducken is golden brown. If the roll starts to brown too quickly, place a sheet of aluminum foil over surface.
4. Carefully remove pan from oven, place Turducken Roulade on a cutting board, tent with aluminum foil, and allow to rest for 30 minutes. Use the roasting pan with pan drippings to make the Sweet Potato Gravy or Pan Gravy (recipes follow).

To Carve and Serve Roasted Turducken Roulade

1. After the turducken has rested and gravy has been prepared, using an electric knife or carving knife, slice the roll into ½-inch pieces.
2. Using a large spatula, carefully move each entire slice onto a plate or serving platter, working slowly to prevent the roulade from unraveling and to preserve the formation of the layers of poultry and dressings.
3. Serve immediately, with Sweet Potato Gravy and/or Pan Gravy (recipes follow) passed alongside.

Sweet Potato Gravy

1 large sweet potato, peeled and cut into 1-inch cubes

3 cups Poultry Stock (see recipe on page 96), or chicken stock or broth, divided

1 clove garlic, minced

One 1-inch piece fresh ginger, peeled and grated

⅛ teaspoon cayenne pepper

Pan drippings from Roasted Turducken Roulade

1 cup half-and-half

¼ cup cornstarch dissolved in ¼ cup water, optional to thicken gravy

Salt and freshly ground black pepper to taste

1. In a large saucepan, place the sweet potatoes, 2 cups of the stock, the garlic, ginger, and cayenne pepper and bring to a boil over high heat. Reduce heat to a simmer and cook for 10 to 15 minutes, or until the sweet potatoes are cooked through.
2. Remove pan from heat and allow the mixture to cool. Purée the mixture by using a potato masher, immersion blender, stand blender, or food processor.
3. Skim off the fat from the drippings in the Turducken Roulade roasting pan. Add the sweet potato mixture to roasting pan and place over medium-high heat.
4. Add the remaining 1 cup stock and the half-and-half, and stir to combine while scraping the bottom of the roasting pan to loosen browned bits.
5. Cook the mixture for 5 minutes, and if needed, stir in the cornstarch mixture until desired thickness is achieved. Season with salt and pepper. Serve hot in a gravy boat alongside the Roasted Turducken Roulade.

Pan Gravy

Turkey giblets are not required for this recipe, though they do give an additional depth of flavor to the gravy.

3 cups combined pan drippings and
    Poultry Stock (see recipe on page 96),
    or chicken stock or broth
¼ cup all-purpose flour

½ cup water
Cooked chopped turkey giblets, if desired
Salt and freshly ground black pepper
    to taste

1. Using the drippings from the Turducken Roulade roasting pan, skim off all but 4 tablespoons of the fat in the pan. Place the pan over high heat.
2. Add the Poultry Stock and bring to a boil, scraping the bottom to loosen browned bits. Reduce the heat to simmer.
3. In a small bowl, mix the flour and water together and whisk into the gravy to blend well. Add the giblets if desired and simmer for 5 more minutes. Season with salt and pepper. Serve hot in a gravy boat alongside the Roasted Turducken Roulade.

Cornbread Andouille Dressing

YIELDS ABOUT 2½ CUPS

2 tablespoons butter, margarine, or olive
    oil
1 cup ¼-inch-diced turkey andouille
    sausage or smoked ham
½ cup finely diced onion
¼ cup finely diced celery (including some
    leaves)
¼ cup finely diced red or green bell pepper
1½ cups homemade or store-bought
    cornbread, cut into 1-inch cubes

2 teaspoons poultry seasoning or Bell's
    Seasoning
1 teaspoon finely chopped fresh thyme
    leaves, or ½ teaspoon dried
Salt and freshly ground black pepper
    to taste
1 large egg, slightly beaten
1 cup Poultry Stock (see recipe on page
    96) or chicken stock or broth,
    or as needed

1. In a large skillet, melt the butter over medium heat, add the sausage, and cook for about 2 minutes, until the sausage is cooked through. Add the onion, celery, and bell pepper. Sauté the mixture until the vegetables are tender but not browned, about 2 minutes. Remove from heat; cool for 5 minutes.

2. In a large bowl, place the cornbread cubes, poultry seasoning, thyme, salt, and pepper, and toss to combine.
3. Add the cooled sausage/vegetable mixture and egg to the cornbread; gently stir to combine.
4. Add the stock, a little at a time, until the mixture becomes moist but not wet. Cover with plastic wrap, and refrigerate until ready to use.

Whole-Grain Giblet Dressing

YIELDS ABOUT 1½ CUPS

This dressing gets its flavor from chicken giblets. Chicken gizzards have a chewy connective outer layer; it is best to trim them with a sharp knife to release the tender meat inside. To save time, have your butcher prepare them for you.

2 tablespoons butter, margarine, or olive oil
½ pound chicken giblets, trimmed
*   of connective tissue and cartilage,*
*   to equal 1 cup*
½ cup finely chopped onion
½ cup finely chopped celery (including
*   some leaves)*
1 clove garlic, minced
2 to 3 slices whole-grain bread, crusts
*   removed, cut into 1-inch cubes*
*   to equal 1 cup cubes, or 1 cup*
*   prepared whole-grain croutons*

2 teaspoons finely chopped fresh sage,
*   or ½ teaspoon dried sage*
1 teaspoon finely chopped fresh thyme
*   leaves, or ½ teaspoon dried thyme*
Salt and freshly ground black pepper to
*   taste*
1 large egg, slightly beaten
½ cup Poultry Stock (see recipe on page
*   96), or chicken stock or broth,*
*   or as needed*

1. In a large skillet, melt the butter over medium heat; add the giblets and cook for 2 minutes. Add the onion, celery, and garlic and sauté the mixture for about 2 minutes, until the vegetables are tender but not browned.
2. Remove from heat; cool for 5 minutes.
3. In a medium-size bowl, place the bread cubes. Add the sage, thyme, salt, and pepper, and toss to combine.

4. Add the cooled giblet/vegetable mixture and egg to the bread, gently stirring to combine. Add the stock, a little at a time, until the mixture becomes moist but not wet. Cover with plastic wrap, and refrigerate until ready to use.

Shrimp Dressing

YIELDS ABOUT 2 CUPS

2 tablespoons butter, margarine, or olive oil, divided

½ pound whole raw shrimp, shelled, deveined, and diced into ½-inch cubes to equal about 1 cup (reserve shells for Shrimp Stock if making)

½ cup finely diced onion

¼ cup finely chopped celery (including leaves)

¼ cup finely chopped red bell pepper

1 clove garlic, minced

1 cup fine plain breadcrumbs

1 teaspoon finely chopped fresh oregano, or ½ teaspoon dried oregano

1 teaspoon finely chopped fresh basil, or ½ teaspoon dried basil

1 tablespoon finely chopped fresh parsley, or ½ teaspoon dried parsley

¼ teaspoon Cajun or Creole seasoning

½ teaspoon celery seed

1 large egg, slightly beaten

⅓ cup Shrimp Stock (see recipe on page 95) or bottled clam juice, or as needed

1. In a large skillet, melt 1 tablespoon of the butter over medium heat. Add the shrimp and cook just until they turn pink, less than 1 minute. Remove the shrimp from the skillet and set aside.
2. Add the remaining tablespoon of butter, the onion, celery, bell pepper, and garlic to the skillet and sauté for about 2 minutes, until the vegetables are tender but not browned. Remove from heat and let cool for 5 minutes.
3. In a medium bowl, place the breadcrumbs, oregano, basil, parsley, Cajun or Creole seasoning, and celery seed. Toss to combine.
4. Add the cooled shrimp and vegetable mixture and the egg to the breadcrumbs, and stir to combine. Add the Shrimp Stock or clam juice, a little at a time, until the mixture becomes moist but not wet.
5. Cover with plastic wrap and refrigerate until ready to use.

Spiced Braised Quail with Mushrooms

Quail are delicate farm-raised birds. The hint of jerk seasoning and lime add just enough spiced flavor. I like to use a mix of sliced sautéed cremini, shiitake, and portobello mushrooms flavored with dry vermouth for the sauce. This is one of my favorite creamy dishes.

8 *whole quail*	*2 tablespoons olive oil*
2 teaspoons lime juice	*6 cups sliced mixed mushrooms*
2 teaspoons salt, divided	*1 cup dry vermouth*
1 teaspoon freshly ground black pepper	*⅓ cup light cream*
2 teaspoons dried jerk seasoning	*2 tablespoons chopped fresh parsley,*
2 tablespoons butter	*divided*

1. Using kitchen shears or a sharp knife, split each quail down the backbone. Press down on the quail with the palm of your hand to flatten. Sprinkle each quail on both sides with the lime juice, ¼ teaspoon of the salt, the black pepper, and jerk seasoning. Set aside.
2. In a large nonstick skillet, melt the butter and olive oil over medium-high heat, add the mushrooms, and sauté for 4 to 6 minutes, stirring frequently, until the mushrooms are light brown. Remove the mushrooms from the pan and set aside.
3. Place the quail breast-side-down in the pan and cook over medium-high heat (in batches if necessary) for about 6 minutes, until browned. Turn the quail over and cook for 4 to 6 minutes more, until browned. Remove quail from pan, cover to keep warm, and set aside.
4. Reduce heat to medium and add the vermouth to the pan, stirring well to scrape up the browned bits. Add the cream and stir well to combine. Add the mushrooms and 1 tablespoon of the parsley.
5. Reduce heat to low and place the quail on top of the mushrooms. Cover pan and simmer for 30 minutes. Garnish with the remaining parsley and serve immediately.

Chapter 8

Seafood

When I started writing the introduction to this seafood chapter, I drew a stick figure of myself in fishing gear off to catch the evening meal. I quickly came to my senses; I'm in the restaurant business and the fish is delivered daily—no need for me to go and catch my own! Fishing is such a time-honored tradition in the South; everywhere you go on the coast the catch of the day is fresh, and you often see the fishermen out crabbing or trawling for shrimp. Whether it's a fresh catch of blue crabs in Maryland, shellfish in the Low Country, alligator in New Orleans, or mahi mahi in Florida, the South is bountiful when it comes to seafood. However, the frozen but tasty cornmeal-crusted whiting my mom prepared when I was growing up in landlocked western Pennsylvania could stand up to any I have had while traveling. If I'm cooking at home these days, I enjoy shopping at my favorite specialty fish markets in New York City and in the Hamptons on Long Island. It's fun just seeing what's available and being creative with the catch of the day!

Our seasonal restaurant in Sag Harbor is in a marina and specializes in seafood. We look forward to summertime and all the lobster and other seafood we can eat. It's a great thing, since nutritionists recommend eating three or more servings of fish per week. Dan and I like to get to the restaurant as much as possible to enjoy the gorgeous weather and the fresh seafood. Even with the restaurants, I still enjoy cooking and entertaining at home as well. I love getting outside and grilling, and in Sag Harbor, with the fresh catch and the vegetables from my garden, it's hard to find better ingredients to work with!

As well as inspiration from the restaurants, and some of my old favorites, the seafood recipes in this book are influenced by our travels and taste, and range from quick and easy to elaborate. My chefs like to prepare deep-fried or pan-fried soft-shell crab, but I think you'll like my recipe for quick and easy Butter-Spiced Grilled Soft-Shell Crab. I don't quite remember in which of the Brennan's restaurants we first tasted New Orleans Barbecued Shrimp, but I do remember deciding then and there that at some point I would create my own version at home. And of course taking a cue from Chef Paul Prudhomme, there is a recipe for Blackened Tilapia. And I had to include a recipe for frog legs, marinated in herbs and grilled and served with Spicy Herb-Caper Butter Sauce; these are a favorite in New Orleans and will become one of your favorites, too.

The Oyster Pie is a hit at our dinner parties, with its creamy texture, flavored with seafood sausage topped with puffed pastry. I've also included two recipes that are extremely popular seafood entrées at our restaurant, Southern Spiced Catfish Roulade with Black-Eyed Pea Gravy and the ultra-popular Swamp Thang—shrimp, scallops, and crawfish in a Dijon mustard sauce served over a bed of collard greens and garnished with Deep-Fried Julienne Vegetables, a dish that really has it all!

Butter-Spiced Grilled Soft-Shell Crab	185
Grouper with Persimmon Salsa	186
New Orleans Barbecued Shrimp	188
Blackened Tilapia	189
Grilled Mahi Mahi with Coconut Curry Sauce	191
Herb-Marinated Grilled Frog Legs with Spicy Herb-Caper Butter Sauce	193
Oyster Pie	195
Pan-Fried Trout, Southern-Style	196
Bacon-Wrapped Scallops with Chive Oil	197
Southern Spiced Catfish Roulade with Black-Eyed Pea Gravy	199
Swamp Thang with Deep-Fried Julienne Vegetables	200

Butter-Spiced Grilled Soft-Shell Crab

YIELDS 4 SERVINGS

Fresh soft-shell crabs are truly a delicacy, and one of my all-time favorite treats. My chefs at the restaurants usually serve them deep-fried or pan-fried, but I love them simply grilled. Grilling seems to bring out their delicate flavor. Crabs should be alive when you buy them; cook them right away or refrigerate.

8 large soft-shell crabs	½ teaspoon Old Bay Seasoning
¼ teaspoon salt	8 tablespoons (1 stick) unsalted butter,
½ teaspoon freshly ground black pepper	melted
¼ teaspoon garlic powder	Lemon wedges, for garnish

1. To prepare the soft-shell crabs for cooking, cut off the eyes, lift the apron, and remove the gills. Rinse well and blot dry with paper towels.
2. Preheat an outdoor charcoal or gas grill to high, according to the manufacturer's instructions. In a small bowl, mix together the salt, pepper, garlic powder, Old Bay Seasoning, and melted butter. Brush the crabs with the butter mixture.
3. Grill the crabs over high heat, turning occasionally, for about 4 to 5 minutes, until bright red and crisp. Remove the crabs from the grill and serve immediately with lemon wedges.

Grouper with Persimmon Salsa

Grouper is firm-textured warm-water fish. The sweet chilled Persimmon Salsa complements the taste of the warm, cooked firm-textured grouper. If you can't find grouper, a good substitute with the right amount of flavor and texture is red snapper. For this quick and easy recipe, you can either pan sauté the fillets or cook them in a grill pan, though when the weather permits, try grilling the fish on an outdoor grill.

Four 6- to 8-ounce grouper fillets
½ teaspoon salt
¼ teaspoon freshly ground black pepper

2 tablespoons butter or vegetable oil
Persimmon Salsa (recipe follows),
    for serving

1. Rinse the grouper fillets and pat dry with paper towels. Sprinkle with salt and pepper, cover, and set aside.
2. In a large skillet or grill pan, melt the butter over medium-high heat. Sauté the fillets for about 3 minutes on each side, or until fish flakes easily when tested with a fork. Using a slotted spatula, transfer the fillets to a serving platter. Serve immediately with Persimmon Salsa.

Persimmon Salsa

For this recipe I've used Fuyu persimmons, which are smaller and sweeter than the Hachiya variety of persimmons (which is tart until very soft and ripe) and are edible while still firm. If not available, substitute fresh papaya or mango.

1 cup fresh cubed Fuyu persimmon (peeled and cut into ½-inch cubes)
½ cup diced fresh pineapple
¼ cup finely diced red bell pepper
1 scallion, finely chopped

2 tablespoons chopped fresh cilantro
Juice of 1 lime
Salt and freshly ground black pepper to taste

In a small bowl, combine all the ingredients. Cover the bowl and refrigerate before serving with the cooked grouper.

New Orleans Barbecued Shrimp

It seems like most restaurants in New Orleans serve their own version of barbecued shrimp, and what surprised me was that none of these dishes are actually grilled with a barbecue sauce. Some are oven-baked, and others—my version included—are prepared in a skillet. For my recipe, I've given the shrimp lots of flavor with herbs, spices, and beer—serve them with crusty French bread to soak up every last drop of sauce!

4 tablespoons unsalted butter
6 cloves garlic, minced
2 teaspoons Worcestershire sauce
1 teaspoon Creole seasoning
1 teaspoon dried thyme leaves
1 teaspoon dried oregano
½ teaspoon smoked paprika

½ cup beer
1 pound medium to large shrimp, peeled
    and deveined, tails left on
2 tablespoons chopped fresh parsley,
    for garnish
4 lemon wedges, for garnish

1. In a large skillet, melt the butter over low heat. Add the garlic and cook very gently over low heat, stirring frequently, for 5 minutes. Add the Worcestershire sauce, Creole seasoning, thyme, oregano, and paprika. Increase heat to medium and cook for 2 minutes, allowing the butter to bubble, the garlic to cook further, and the spices to blend together.
2. Pour the beer into the garlic mixture and stir well to combine. Add the shrimp and sauté for 2 to 3 minutes, just until they turn pink and start to curl slightly. Using a slotted spoon, remove the shrimp to a warm platter.
3. Turn the heat up to medium-high and cook the sauce for about 5 minutes, until thickened. Pour the sauce over the shrimp and garnish with the chopped parsley. Serve with the lemon wedges.

Blackened Tilapia

YIELDS 4 SERVINGS

When I first cooked blackened tilapia in my apartment, the kitchen filled with smoke and of course the smoke alarm went crazy, even though I had the vent on. Fast forward to today and I'm still using my cast-iron skillet, but I open up the kitchen window very wide, close both doors, and cook the fish as quickly as possible!

Four 6- to 8-ounce tilapia fillets, or other
    firm-fleshed fish of choice
½ cup Worcestershire sauce

2 tablespoons Blackened Seasoning (recipe
    follows)
Vegetable oil, for frying

1. Preheat oven to 200°F. Rinse the tilapia fillets and pat dry with paper towels. In a shallow baking dish, place the fillets and pour the Worcestershire sauce over them. Refrigerate for 30 minutes, turning a couple of times. Remove the fish from the refrigerator and bring to room temperature. Sprinkle both sides with the Blackened Seasoning.
2. Heat a cast-iron skillet over medium-high heat until it is very hot. Coat the surface of the skillet with vegetable oil. Place two fillets in the skillet and cook for about 2 minutes on each side, or until fish flakes easily when tested with a fork. Place the fillets in the oven to keep warm.
3. Carefully wipe the skillet clean, add more oil, and reheat until very hot. Cook the remaining fillets for 2 minutes on each side, or until fish flakes easily when tested with a fork. Serve the fish immediately.

Blackened Seasoning

YIELDS ⅓ CUP

Noted New Orleans chef Paul Prudhomme makes a wonderful blackened seasoning widely available in grocery stores, but I prefer to make my own because I have all of the ingredients on hand, plus I can tweak the recipe to add more or less heat. And yes, when I'm in Sag Harbor, I prepare this blackened fish in my iron skillet placed on the burner of our outdoor gas grill.

2 teaspoons hot paprika

2 teaspoons salt

2 teaspoons freshly ground black pepper

2½ teaspoons garlic powder

2½ teaspoons onion powder

1½ teaspoons cayenne pepper

2 teaspoons dried thyme

2 teaspoons dried oregano

In a small bowl, mix all the ingredients together well. Store in an airtight container at room temperature until ready to use.

Grilled Mahi Mahi with Coconut Curry Sauce

YIELDS 4 SERVINGS

Mahi mahi is also known as common dolphin, which is caught offshore in the Atlantic from New Jersey to the Florida Keys. For this recipe, broil or use a grill pan or an outdoor grill to cook the fish. The sauce can be made in advance and reheated before serving.

Four 6- to 8-ounce mahi mahi fillets
1 tablespoon olive oil
Salt and freshly ground black pepper to taste

Coconut Curry Sauce (recipe follows),
*   for serving*

1. Rinse the mahi mahi fillets and dry with paper towels. Brush each fillet with olive oil, then season with salt and pepper.
2. Preheat a broiler, grill pan, or outdoor gas or charcoal grill according to the manufacturer's instructions.
3. Grill the fillets over medium heat, turning once until the fish flakes, about 6 to 8 minutes. Serve immediately with Coconut Curry Sauce.

Coconut Curry Sauce

YIELDS 1 CUP

The Southern cook enjoys many cultural influences. Coconut and curry are a classic Caribbean combination, and they come together here in a knockout blend that transforms grilled mahi mahi or tuna.

One 13.5-ounce can lite coconut milk
½ cup fish stock or clam juice
1 clove garlic, minced
1½ teaspoons chopped fresh ginger
½ cup minced scallion

1 teaspoon curry powder, or to taste
¼ teaspoon red pepper flakes
2 teaspoons soy sauce
Brown sugar to taste

1. In a medium saucepan, combine the coconut milk, fish stock, ginger, scallion, curry powder, and red pepper flakes. Bring to a boil over medium heat. Reduce the heat and simmer for 15 minutes, stirring occasionally.

2. Remove the pan from the heat and strain the sauce through a fine-mesh sieve, pressing as much of the sauce through as possible. Discard the solids; return the sauce to a clean saucepan. Add the soy sauce and brown sugar. Keep warm over low heat until serving. The Coconut Curry Sauce can be prepared ahead and refrigerated in a tightly sealed container for up to 3 days before serving.

Herb-Marinated Grilled Frog Legs
with Spicy Herb-Caper Butter Sauce

YIELDS 6 SERVINGS

The legs of large frogs taste like chicken wings or lobster. In this recipe I use a white wine garlic marinade with herbs, then grill them.

⅔ cup white wine

¼ cup olive oil

1 small onion, diced

3 cloves garlic, minced

Juice of ½ lemon

1 tablespoon chopped fresh thyme,
    or 1 teaspoon dried thyme

1 tablespoon chopped fresh rosemary,
    or 1 teaspoon dried rosemary, crushed

1 teaspoon salt

¼ teaspoon freshly ground black pepper

24 pairs frog legs

Vegetable oil or nonstick cooking spray

Salt and freshly ground black pepper
    to taste

Spicy Herb-Caper Butter Sauce (recipe
    follows), for serving

1. To make the marinade, in a medium bowl, combine the white wine, olive oil, onion, garlic, lemon juice, thyme, rosemary, salt, and pepper.
2. Wash the frog legs under cold water and pat dry with a paper towel. Place them in a shallow dish or a 1-gallon resealable plastic bag. Add the marinade, tossing gently to coat the frog legs fully. Cover the dish or close the resealable plastic bag and refrigerate overnight, turning occasionally.
3. Heat a grill pan over medium-high heat, or prepare a charcoal or gas grill according to the manufacturer's instructions. Lightly brush the cooking grate with vegetable oil, or very liberally coat the frog legs with oil or spray with nonstick cooking spray on both sides.
4. Salt and pepper the frog legs on both sides. Grill them for 2 to 2½ minutes per side, turning clockwise ¼ turn on each side. Serve immediately with Spicy Herb-Caper Butter Sauce.

Spicy Herb-Caper Butter Sauce

In this sauce, vermouth adds that slight bit of sweetness for balance, though you can substitute white wine.

1 cup vermouth or white wine	3 tablespoons chopped fresh parsley
2 cups chicken stock	½ teaspoon hot sauce, optional
4 tablespoons softened butter, divided	2 to 3 tablespoons capers
1½ tablespoons all-purpose flour	½ teaspoon salt
2 cloves garlic, minced	¼ teaspoon freshly ground black pepper
1 tablespoon chopped fresh lemon thyme,	Juice from ½ lemon, freshly squeezed
or 1 teaspoon dried thyme	

1. In a medium saucepan, pour the vermouth and stock and bring to a boil over medium-high heat.
2. In a small bowl, blend 1½ tablespoons of the butter with the flour until smooth. Whisk the butter mixture into the hot broth, lower the heat, and simmer until the mixture is reduced by half, or until it thickens to desired consistency.
3. Add the garlic, herbs, hot sauce if desired, capers, salt, pepper, and lemon juice to the pan and simmer for an additional minute or two. Whisk in the remaining 2½ tablespoons butter. Serve immediately over Herb-Marinated Grilled Frog Legs.

Oyster Pie

At our seasonal marina restaurant in Sag Harbor, which is open from May through mid-October, oysters are very popular. Whether they are served raw on the half shell or fried, they remain a crowd pleaser. At home, I think of oysters as more of a special-occasion food, especially during the holidays. This oyster pie is one of my favorite recipes. I love the creamy texture and the flavor the seafood sausage adds to the pie; the puff pastry gives it a touch of elegance.

3 dozen freshly shucked oysters with liquid
3 tablespoons butter
6 ounces seafood sausage
¼ cup finely chopped onions
3 tablespoons all-purpose flour
1½ cups heavy cream
½ teaspoon salt

½ teaspoon Old Bay Seasoning
¼ teaspoon cayenne pepper
⅓ cup thinly sliced scallions
¼ cup chopped fresh parsley
1 sheet (half of a 17-ounce package)
  frozen prepared puff pastry, thawed
  according to package directions

1. Preheat oven to 375°F. Drain the oysters, reserving ½ cup of their liquid (also known as liquor); dry the oysters on paper towels.
2. In a large skillet, heat the butter over medium heat. Add the seafood sausage and cook, turning often, for 4 to 5 minutes, until lightly browned on all sides. Remove the sausage from the pan and set aside. When cool enough to handle, cut the sausage into ½-inch pieces.
3. Add the chopped onions to the skillet and sauté over medium heat for about 5 minutes, until soft and translucent but not browned. Add the flour to the skillet; cook, stirring frequently, for 2 to 3 minutes. Remove skillet from heat and stir in the heavy cream and reserved oyster liquor; cook, stirring frequently, for about 3 to 4 minutes, until thickened.
4. Add the salt, Old Bay Seasoning, and cayenne to the pan. Remove from heat and add the oysters, seafood sausage, scallions, and parsley. Pour the mixture into a 9-inch pie dish.
5. Cut a 9-inch circle from the puff pastry and place it on top of the oyster mixture in the pie dish; cut a small hole in the middle of the pastry to allow steam to escape. Discard pastry scraps.
6. Place the pie dish on a baking sheet to catch any drips and bake for 25 to 30 minutes, or until the pastry is golden brown and the filling is bubbling. Serve immediately.

Pan-Fried Trout, Southern-Style

I created this recipe to serve two, though the recipe can easily be doubled and the first batch kept warm in a 200°F oven while the second batch cooks. If desired, the dish can be made with trout fillets instead of the whole boneless variety; just reduce the cooking time until the fish flakes easily when tested with a fork. If cooking the trout butterflied, each fish may need to be cooked separately depending on the size of the skillet.

2 whole 10-ounce trout, boned and
    butterflied
Salt and freshly ground black pepper
    to taste
¾ cup cornmeal
2 teaspoons Old Bay Seasoning

4 bacon slices
2 tablespoons butter
¼ cup finely chopped fresh parsley,
    for garnish
Lemon wedges, for garnish

1. Rinse the trout and pat dry with paper towels. Season inside and out with salt and pepper.
2. On a large plate, combine the cornmeal and Old Bay Seasoning. Set aside.
3. In a large cast-iron or other heavy skillet, cook the bacon slices over medium heat for about 5 minutes, until crisp. Transfer the bacon to a paper towel–lined plate and cover loosely with foil.
4. Pour off all but 2 tablespoons of the bacon fat from the skillet. Add the butter to the skillet and melt over medium-high heat. Dredge the seasoned trout in the cornmeal to coat completely, then place in the skillet. Cook for about 3 minutes, until well browned.
5. Carefully turn the trout and continue cooking until well browned and cooked through, about 3 to 5 minutes depending on the thickness of the fish. Transfer the fish to serving plates.
6. Crumble the bacon and sprinkle it over the trout along with the chopped parsley. Serve immediately with lemon wedges.

Bacon-Wrapped Scallops with Chive Oil

YIELDS 4 SERVINGS

There are two kinds of scallops: large sea scallops and tiny bay or Cape Cod scallops; this recipe calls for the large ones. Fresh scallops are preferable to frozen. If using frozen scallops, cook them while they are still partially frozen so they do not overcook. Scallops cook fast, so be careful not to overcook.

16 large sea scallops
2 tablespoons olive oil
2 tablespoons lemon juice
¼ teaspoon white pepper

8 slices bacon (½ slice bacon per scallop)
Chive Oil (recipe follows), for serving
Lemon wedges, for garnish

1. In a medium bowl, combine the scallops with the olive oil, lemon juice, and white pepper. Mix well, cover, and allow to marinate at room temperature for 30 minutes, turning once or twice during marinating.
2. Cut each bacon slice crosswise in half, making 2 pieces from each slice of bacon. Remove the scallops from the marinade and wrap each in a piece of bacon. Secure each bacon-wrapped scallop with a toothpick, or skewer them on metal skewers or presoaked bamboo skewers. (If using large skewers and placing more than 1 scallop per skewer, allow space between scallops to cook on all sides.)
3. Preheat oven to broil. Arrange the scallops on a baking sheet and broil, watching closely, for 6 minutes, then turn and continue to broil until the scallops are opaque and the bacon cooks evenly. To serve, drizzle Bacon-Wrapped Scallops with Chive Oil and garnish with lemon wedges.

Chive Oil

YIELDS ABOUT ½ CUP

¼ cup sliced fresh chives
½ cup extra virgin olive oil

Salt and freshly ground black pepper to taste
Salt-free Cajun seasoning, optional

1. In the bowl of a food processor fitted with the metal blade, place the chives. Turn the processor on, and slowly add the olive oil through the feed tube in a thin stream. Season with salt and pepper and salt-free Cajun seasoning, if desired.
2. Strain the Chive Oil through a fine-mesh sieve into a bowl, and then transfer to a tightly lidded glass jar or decorative bottle. Chive Oil will keep in the pantry up to 2 weeks.

Southern Spiced Catfish Roulade with Black-Eyed Pea Gravy

For this dish, the catfish is cut lengthwise and carefully rolled into a spiral, then dipped into milk and dredged in a seasoned cornmeal mixture. The presentation of this roulade is perfect for elegant dinner parties, and it can be served with or without Black-Eyed Pea Gravy.

Four 8-ounce catfish fillets	*½ cup all-purpose flour*
2 teaspoons salt	*¾ cup whole milk*
2 teaspoons Creole seasoning	*6 tablespoons unsalted butter*
1 teaspoon Hungarian hot paprika	*Lemon wedges, for garnish*
½ teaspoon freshly ground black pepper	*Black-Eyed Pea Gravy (see recipe on page*
½ cup yellow cornmeal	*229), for serving*

1. Rinse the catfish fillets and pat dry with paper towels. Cut each fillet lengthwise, keeping the halves attached at the tail end. Arrange each fillet into one long strip with the flat surface facing down.
2. In a small bowl, combine 1 teaspoon of the salt, 1 teaspoon of the Creole seasoning, ½ teaspoon of the paprika, and ¼ teaspoon of the black pepper. Sprinkle the fillets with the seasoning mix.
3. Carefully roll each fillet up into a tight spiral and secure with a presoaked 6-inch bamboo skewer.
4. In a shallow dish, combine the cornmeal, flour, remaining salt, Creole seasoning, paprika, and pepper.
5. In another shallow dish, pour the milk. Dip each fillet into the milk and then in the cornmeal mixture, coating well and shaking off any excess. Arrange the coated fillets in a single layer on a baking sheet, cover with plastic wrap, and refrigerate for 4 hours.
6. Preheat oven to 200°F. In a medium skillet, melt 4 tablespoons of the butter over medium heat. Place 2 fillets in the pan, then cook for 6 to 7 minutes on each side, until the coating is golden brown and the fish is cooked through. Drain the fish on paper towels, then carefully remove the wooden skewers and place the fish in the oven to keep warm.
7. Add the remaining 2 tablespoons of butter to the pan and cook the remaining fillets. Transfer the fillets to a warm serving platter, garnish with lemon wedges, and serve immediately with Black-Eyed Pea Gravy.

Swamp Thang with Deep-Fried Julienne Vegetables

Swamp Thang was created at our Union Station restaurant in Washington, D.C. Shrimp, scallops, and crawfish are combined in a creamy, light Dijon mustard sauce and served over a bed of Southern-style collard greens. The dish is topped with Deep-Fried Julienne Vegetables. Of course it was put on the New York City restaurant menu by popular demand!

3 tablespoons butter
1 cup finely diced onion
⅔ cup finely diced green bell pepper
⅔ cup finely diced celery
2 cloves garlic, minced
1 cup white wine
1 teaspoon dried thyme
1 bay leaf
2 cups shrimp or fish stock or broth
1 tablespoon lemon juice
1 tablespoon Worcestershire sauce
1 cup heavy cream
2 tablespoons grainy Dijon mustard

½ teaspoon Old Bay Seasoning
1 pound medium shrimp, shelled
    and deveined
1 pound medium scallops
1 pound peeled crawfish tails, defrosted
    frozen if fresh is not available
Salt and freshly ground black pepper
    to taste
Southern-Style Collard Greens (see recipe
    on page 217)
Deep-Fried Julienne Vegetables (recipe
    follows)

1. In a large nonstick skillet, heat the butter over medium heat. Add the onion, bell pepper, celery, and garlic; sauté for about 5 minutes, until soft but not browned. Stir in the wine, thyme, and bay leaf; simmer for 2 minutes. Add the shrimp stock, lemon juice, and Worcestershire sauce to the pan and bring to a boil.
2. Stir in the heavy cream, mustard, and Old Bay Seasoning. Reduce heat to medium-low; add the shrimp, scallops, and crawfish. Cook the shrimp for about 3 to 5 minutes, until pink. Season with salt and pepper. Discard the bay leaf.
3. Serve the seafood mixture immediately over a bed of Southern-Style Collard Greens, and garnish with Deep-Fried Julienne Vegetables.

Deep-Fried Julienne Vegetables

1 cup ¼-inch-julienne zucchini
1 cup ¼-inch-julienne yellow squash
1 cup ¼-inch julienne carrot
1½ cups whole milk

Vegetable oil for deep frying
1 cup all-purpose flour
½ teaspoon salt
¼ teaspoon freshly ground black pepper

1. In a 1-gallon resealable plastic bag, combine the zucchini, yellow squash, carrot, and milk; seal the bag and refrigerate for 1 hour.
2. Preheat oven to 200°F. In a deep skillet, pour enough oil to reach a depth of 1 inch; heat over medium-high heat to 350°F.
3. Meanwhile, in a shallow dish, combine the flour, salt, and pepper. Drain the vegetables and toss in the seasoned flour. Transfer the vegetables to a large sieve and shake off excess flour. Working in batches, deep-fry large handfuls of vegetables in hot oil for 2 to 3 minutes, or until golden brown. Using a wire skimmer or slotted spoon, remove the vegetables from the oil and drain on paper towels; keep warm in the oven until serving.

Chapter 9

Sides

To me, sides are accessories; they should complement and embellish a meal. I can't think of another American cuisine that has the wonderful array of side dishes that Southern cuisine offers from all its different regions. Southern cooks have a knack for taking one ingredient and cooking it in a number of ways alone or as part of a dish. For example, okra can be stewed, grilled, steamed, or blanched; a corn pudding can be sweet or savory; a cup of rice can be dirty or hoppin' with beans.

A genuine Southern meal always comes with plenty of sides. Colonists in the South showed off their wealth at meal times with an abundance of food for their guests. There may have been three different main-course meat dishes and triple or more the amount of sides. That's called Southern hospitality, and it still rules to this day at a Southern table. There's plenty to choose from, and no one leaves the table hungry.

My mother prepared side dishes as if she'd lived her whole life in the Deep South. She made the best collard greens. Try the Southern-Style Collard Greens recipe and you'll taste what I mean. As good as my mom's greens were, she didn't have to force us to eat our vegetables! What I love most about vegetables is that they can be prepared so many ways. I like to sauté chopped mustards, collards, kale, and garlic. However, if I'm having guests who want a take-me-back-to-mama experience, I serve them greens Southern style. Most people are so busy they don't have the time to come home from work and make a pot of greens the old-fashioned way. The Winter Greens recipe calls for collard, kale, and turnip greens, but you can substitute your favorite greens. For seasoning, I prefer smoked turkey to bacon or salt pork (no one seems to be missing them).

My mother and father canned vegetables from the garden, so we ate everything all year round. These days everything seems to grow year round, and of course you can buy frozen or canned foods. I prefer fresh and always recommend it before anything else. You can prepare Maque Choux, a traditional corn dish from Louisiana, with frozen corn, but it won't give you that delicious milk that only fresh corn yields. Tomatoes grow all year round, but to me, there's nothing like the tomatoes we buy from farm stands on Long Island during the summer. Stewed Okra, Corn, and Tomatoes is great prepared with all fresh vegetables, but if you don't have them, canned works well, too.

My family loves puddings, sweet or savory. The Tomato Bread Pudding and the corn puddings can go either way. They add a nice texture and color to a meal. I can't remember a Thanksgiving without a corn pudding.

Many of my friends have either cut down on eating meat or have stopped altogether. You never know when a newly minted vegetarian or vegan is going to show up. No need to panic if there are several sides that'll ensure something for everybody. The Herbed Quinoa Pilaf is high in protein and pairs well with many of the sides in this chapter. In Louisiana, Brabant potatoes are deep-fried. In my kitchen, they're oven-roasted until they're a golden brown.

One thing's for sure about the richness of Southern cooking: there are many sides to this great story.

Oven-Roasted Brabant Potatoes

I first tasted Brabant potatoes during one of those huge New Orleans brunches. Back then, the potatoes were fried and very tasty, but I think this recipe will spark folks to convert and come on over to this oven-roasted version. They're tossed with olive oil, baked to a golden brown, then perfectly seasoned to serve with fish, poultry, or meat, morning, noon, or night!

1½ pounds red-skinned potatoes, quartered
2 tablespoons olive oil
1 teaspoon salt, divided
½ teaspoon freshly ground black pepper
2 tablespoons butter

2 cloves garlic, chopped
1 teaspoon Worcestershire sauce
½ teaspoon Creole seasoning
¼ cup chopped flat-leaf parsley
2 scallions, white and green parts thinly sliced

1. Preheat oven to 400°F. In a large bowl, toss the quartered potatoes with the olive oil, ½ teaspoon of the salt, and the black pepper. Spread on a large rimmed baking sheet, turning a cut side of each potato down on the sheet.
2. Place in the oven and roast for 25 minutes, then stir the potatoes and continue to roast for 5 to 10 minutes more, until they are golden brown.
3. While the potatoes are roasting, in a small saucepan, melt the butter over medium-low heat. Stir in the garlic and allow to cook over very low heat for about 3 minutes, until fragrant. Add the Worcestershire sauce, Creole seasoning, and remaining ½ teaspoon salt.
4. When the potatoes are cooked, place them in a large serving bowl or on a large platter. Pour the butter mixture evenly over the potatoes. Sprinkle with the parsley and scallions, and stir gently to coat the potatoes fully. Serve immediately.

Broccoli and Broccoli Rabe with Roasted Red Peppers

YIELDS 6 SERVINGS

I love mixing mild-flavored broccoli with its bitter but zesty-flavored cousin, broccoli rabe. The red bell peppers can be roasted and the broccoli blanched a day ahead, leaving just the sautéing to do before serving. This dish is equally delicious served right off the stove or at room temperature. Double the recipe and serve on a large platter, buffet style!

2 medium red bell peppers
1½ pounds broccoli, stems trimmed,
   crowns cut into small florets
1 pound broccoli rabe (about 1 large
   bunch), tough stems trimmed,
   tops and leaves coarsely chopped

⅓ cup extra virgin olive oil
3 large cloves garlic, thinly sliced
Salt and freshly ground black pepper
   to taste

1. To roast the bell peppers, char the whole peppers directly over a gas flame or in the broiler until blackened on all sides. Enclose the peppers in a paper bag for 10 minutes. Peel and seed the peppers, then cut into ¼-inch-wide strips. (Roasted peppers can be prepared 1 day ahead. Cover and refrigerate until using.)
2. Working in batches, in large heavy pot of boiling salted water, cook the broccoli and broccoli rabe until just crisp-tender, about 3 minutes per batch.
3. Using a large slotted spoon or wire skimmer, transfer the vegetables to a bowl of ice water to cool and retain the bright green color. Drain well. (Blanched broccoli and and broccoli rabe can be prepared 1 day ahead. Wrap them in paper towels; enclose in a 1-gallon resealable plastic bag and refrigerate.)
4. Discard the broccoli cooking liquid and heat the olive oil in the same large pot over medium-high heat. Add the garlic; cook, stirring frequently, for about 1 minute, until golden. Add the blanched broccoli and broccoli rabe to the pot; toss until coated with garlic oil and heated through, about 5 minutes.
5. Add the roasted red pepper strips to the pan; toss well to blend. Season with salt and pepper. Transfer the vegetables to a serving platter. Serve warm or at room temperature.

Brussels Sprouts with Toasted Pecans

YIELDS 4 SERVINGS

Here is a recipe for Brussels sprouts with brown sugar and pecans, which add sweetness and crunch, that will turn the taste buds of the most fervent sprout hater into "I'll have an extra helping, please."

¼ cup chopped pecans

1 pound Brussels sprouts, halved

2 tablespoons butter

¾ teaspoon seasoned salt

1 tablespoon brown sugar

¼ teaspoon freshly ground black pepper

1. In a large skillet, toast the pecans over medium heat for about 8 minutes, until fragrant and lightly browned. Remove from pan and set aside.
2. Meanwhile, remove any wilted outer leaves from the Brussels sprouts and cut off the stems. Soak the sprouts in cold water and drain well.
3. Using the same skillet, melt the butter over medium heat until bubbly. Add the Brussels sprouts and seasoned salt. Stir and cook, tossing frequently, for about 8 to 10 minutes, until barely tender.
4. Add the brown sugar, pepper, and reserved pecans to the skillet. Toss the Brussels sprouts to coat and cook, stirring frequently, for about 2 more minutes, until the sugar is melted and the Brussels sprouts are coated in the melted sugar and pecans. Transfer to a warm serving bowl and serve immediately.

Cinnamon-Spiced Carrots

This is a quick and easy recipe, and cutting the carrots into matchstick-size pieces makes the dish look sophisticated, with just the right amount of sass from the honey, cider, and cinnamon.

2 tablespoons unsalted butter
1 pound fresh carrots, peeled and cut into
   matchstick-size pieces
1½ teaspoons ground cinnamon

⅓ cup apple cider or juice
2 tablespoons honey, or less to taste
½ teaspoon fine sea salt
½ teaspoon freshly ground black pepper

1. In a large nonstick skillet, melt the butter over medium heat. Add the carrots, cinnamon, and apple cider. Bring to a boil, cover, and steam for about 5 minutes, until the carrots are just tender but not overcooked.
2. Remove the cover, add the honey, salt, and pepper, and continue to cook over medium-high heat for about 2 minutes more, stirring frequently, until the carrots are nicely glazed and tender but still al dente. Transfer the carrots to a warm serving dish and serve immediately.

Dijon Mashed Potatoes

YIELDS 4 SERVINGS

Everyone loves mashed potatoes, a true comfort food. The addition of rich, creamy buttermilk and Dijon mustard has everyone going back for seconds. Garnish with chopped fresh parsley, delicate chives, or scallions.

2 pounds (about 4 to 5 medium) russet potatoes, peeled and cut into cubes
½ cup buttermilk
2 tablespoons butter

2 to 3 tablespoons Dijon mustard, or more to taste
Salt and freshly ground black pepper to taste
Chopped fresh parsley, chives, or scallions, for garnish

1. In a medium saucepan, place the cubed potatoes. Cover with cold water and bring to a boil. Cook for about 20 minutes, until the potatoes are tender.
2. Drain the potatoes and place back in the pan or in a large bowl. Add the buttermilk, butter, and mustard, and mash until creamy. Season with salt and pepper. Serve immediately, garnished with parsley, chives, or scallions.

Herbed Quinoa Pilaf

The Incas called quinoa "the mother grain." Today, this ancient South American grain is being heralded as the super-grain of the future. Quinoa is sold at natural food stores and some supermarkets. It has a nutty flavor and is a good source of protein. Dressed up with olive oil and lemon juice, then tossed with toasted pine nuts, dried cranberries, chopped red onions, and basil, it's a tasty and unusual side dish or addition to your buffet spread!

2 cups (about 9 ounces) quinoa
4½ cups water
⅛ teaspoon salt
3 tablespoons extra virgin olive oil
1 tablespoon freshly squeezed lemon juice
¾ cup pine nuts, lightly toasted

¼ cup chopped dried cranberries
3 tablespoons finely chopped red onion
Salt and freshly ground black pepper
    to taste
½ cup chopped fresh basil

1. Place the quinoa in a large strainer. Rinse under cold running water until the water runs clear. Transfer the quinoa to a large saucepan, and add the water and salt. Bring to a boil, then reduce heat to medium-low, cover, and simmer for about 15 to 20 minutes, until the water is absorbed and the quinoa is tender.
2. Transfer the quinoa to a large bowl and fluff with a fork. Stir in the olive oil and lemon juice. Let cool to room temperature.
3. Mix the pine nuts, cranberries, and red onion into the quinoa. Season with salt and pepper. (Recipe can be prepared up to this point 6 hours ahead. Cover and chill until serving.) Mix in the fresh basil, and serve at room temperature.

Hoppin' John

Eating Hoppin' John on New Year's Day is a Southern tradition thought to bring good luck. The black-eyed peas in this dish signify coins. Add a side of collards, the color of dollar bills, and you've got a great meal and hopefully a year of prosperity.

This recipe easily can be reduced by half, and every cook prepares it differently. In the past, I've used salt pork and smoked turkey to flavor this dish. Lately, I like the flavor of Applegate Farms certified organic Spicy Andouille Chicken and Turkey Sausage in this recipe, and my family and friends have yet to ask, "Where's the pork?"

2 cups dried black-eyed peas, rinsed and
   drained
2 tablespoons vegetable oil
1 pound andouille chicken or turkey
   sausage, diced
1 large onion, chopped
1 cup chopped green bell pepper
2 cloves garlic, minced

4 cups chicken stock or broth
2 bay leaves
½ teaspoon dried thyme
1 teaspoon seasoned salt
1 teaspoon red pepper flakes
2 cups uncooked long-grain white rice
Salt and freshly ground black pepper to taste
Chopped fresh parsley, for garnish

1. The day before serving, place the black-eyed peas in a large bowl. Cover with water and let soak overnight. Drain and rinse thoroughly. Or, to quick-soak the peas, place them in a large pot or Dutch oven, cover with water, and bring to a boil over high heat. Remove from the heat, cover tightly, and let stand for 1 hour, then drain.

2. In a large pot or Dutch oven, heat the vegetable oil over medium heat and sauté the sausage, onion, bell pepper, and garlic, for about 5 minutes, stirring frequently, until the vegetables are softened.

3. Add the chicken stock, bay leaves, thyme, seasoned salt, and red pepper flakes to the pot. Bring to a boil over high heat. Reduce heat to low, cover, and simmer for about 1 hour, until the black-eyed peas are tender.

4. Add the rice to the pot, raise the heat, and bring to a boil. Reduce heat to medium, cover, and continue cooking for 15 to 20 minutes, until the rice is cooked.

5. Remove the bay leaves and place Hoppin' John in a warm serving dish. Season with salt and pepper, sprinkle with chopped parsley, and serve immediately.

Macaroni and a Plethora of Cheeses

This is not your everyday mac and cheese. Serve this on special occasions when you want to impress your guests. It's prepared with a plethora of cheeses, each one adding distinctive flavors, and finished with a soul-satisfying breadcrumb topping if you prefer it baked as a casserole, or it can simply be served hot off the stove without the topping.

1 pound corkscrew pasta (rotini
    or cavatappi, see box)
1 tablespoon olive oil
4 tablespoons unsalted butter, divided,
    plus more for greasing pan
1 medium onion, finely chopped
½ cup white wine
2½ cups heavy cream

2½ cups grated cheddar cheese, divided
¾ cup grated Monterey jack cheese
¾ cup grated mozzarella cheese
¾ cup grated Swiss cheese
½ cup finely grated Parmigiano-Reggiano
Salt and freshly ground black pepper
    to taste
½ cup plain breadcrumbs, optional

1. If baking the macaroni, preheat oven to 375°F and butter a 2-quart baking dish or a 13 x 9 x 2-inch baking pan.
2. Cook the pasta according to package directions. Drain the pasta, place in a large bowl, and toss with the olive oil.
3. In a large pot, melt 2 tablespoons of the butter over medium-high heat. Add the onion and cook, stirring frequently for 2 to 3 minutes, until soft and golden. Add the wine and allow to reduce by half, about 3 minutes. Add the heavy cream and allow to reduce slightly, for 2 to 3 minutes.
4. Stir in 1½ cups of the cheddar, the Monterey jack, mozzarella, Swiss, and Parmigiano cheese, and remove pot from heat. Add the cooked pasta to the pot and stir well to combine. Season with salt and pepper. Serve immediately, or for baked macaroni, pour the coated pasta evenly into the prepared baking dish.
5. To make the topping, melt the remaining 2 tablespoons butter. In a small bowl, mix the breadcrumbs with the melted butter. Evenly sprinkle the top of the pasta with the remaining 1 cup cheddar, then the buttered breadcrumbs. Sprinkle the top with salt and pepper.
6. Bake the macaroni for 25 to 30 minutes, until the breadcrumbs are golden brown and the cheddar is melted.

Cavatappi Pasta

In the New York restaurant, we use cavatappi, which has a corkscrew shape and slight ridges that help the sauce adhere to the noodle.

Parsnip Purée

Parsnips are a root vegetable that is available year round. With a hint of sweetness and a pinch of spice, parsnips can be boiled, steamed, roasted, braised, or mashed. This parsnip purée is a wonderful alternative to mashed potatoes.

*2 pounds parsnips, peeled and cut into
  ½-inch-thick slices
4 tablespoons unsalted butter
2 to 3 tablespoons chicken stock or broth*

*1 teaspoon salt, or more to taste
¼ teaspoon freshly ground white pepper,
  or more to taste
Chopped fresh chives, optional for garnish*

1. In a large pot, cover the parsnips with cold water. Place over high heat, cover, and bring to a boil. Reduce heat and gently simmer the parsnips for about 15 minutes, until tender.
2. Drain the parsnips and return them to the pot. Cook over low heat, shaking, until most of the water has evaporated.
3. In a food processor fitted with the metal blade or using a potato masher, purée the hot parsnips with the butter and chicken stock until smooth. Season with the salt and white pepper and serve immediately, garnished with chopped chives if desired.

Red Beans and Rice

Louis Armstrong signed autographs with the sentiment "Red Beans and Ricely Yours." This should give you a sense of the significance this dish has for Southerners. Traditionally it was made on Mondays, which was wash day. Women could keep an eye on a pot on the stove while getting their laundry done. Most recipes for red beans and rice use the leftover ham bones from Sunday supper, which add a great layer of flavor. For a fresh twist on the classic dish, carrots add color to the beans. If desired, substitute chopped andouille sausage for part or all of the ham, or use half sausage and half ham. I like to serve mine with a bottle of hot sauce on the side for anyone wanting a little extra kick!

2 tablespoons olive oil
1 cup chopped onions
2 cloves garlic, minced
¾ cup chopped celery
¾ cup chopped carrots
1 cup chopped red or green bell pepper
1 fresh jalapeño pepper, seeded and
   chopped
8 ounces (about 2 cups) chopped ham
2 teaspoons hot paprika
1 teaspoon dried thyme
1 teaspoon dried basil
1 teaspoon dried oregano

¾ teaspoon ground cumin
¾ teaspoon salt
4 cups chicken stock or broth
Two 15-ounce cans red kidney beans,
   drained, or 3 cups cooked red kidney
   beans
One 15-ounce can whole tomatoes,
   drained and chopped
½ cup uncooked long-grain white rice
Salt and freshly ground black pepper
   to taste
Chopped scallions, optional for garnish

1. In a Dutch oven or large skillet, heat the olive oil over medium heat. Sauté the onion and garlic for about 3 minutes, until softened.
2. Add the celery, carrots, bell pepper, jalapeño, ham, paprika, thyme, basil, oregano, cumin, and salt to the pot. Cook, stirring frequently, for about 5 minutes.
3. Stir in the chicken broth, kidney beans, and tomatoes. Bring to a boil, reduce the heat, and simmer partially covered for 45 minutes.
4. Stir the rice into the pot. Cover and cook for 10 minutes. Stir again, replace the cover, and cook

for another 10 minutes, or until the rice is soft and the liquid is absorbed. (The rice might have a tendency to stick to the bottom of the pot, so be sure to stir a few times while cooking the beans and rice together.) Season with salt and pepper, and serve immediately garnished with scallions, if desired.

Southern-Style Collard Greens

YIELDS 8 SERVINGS

Collard greens are one of the oldest members of the cabbage family. This recipe is reminiscent of my mother's. She seemed to let her greens simmer away for hours! I make mine with ham hocks, which help tenderize the greens and add flavor, along with a little brown sugar to take away any bitterness. A lot of Southern families serve their greens with a side of bread to dip in the cooking broth, known as pot-likker. The broth is packed with vitamins and refers to the leftover "liquor" in the pot, after your greens have cooked. It not only tastes good—it's really good for you!

4 smoked ham hocks
1 large onion, thinly sliced
3 bay leaves
4 pounds collard greens
Chicken stock or broth, or water, as needed

1 tablespoon brown sugar
2 teaspoons red pepper flakes
1 teaspoon salt
1 teaspoon freshly ground black pepper

1. Rinse the ham hocks and score the skin in several places. In a heavy 8- to 10-quart pot, combine the hocks, onion, and bay leaves with enough water to cover. Bring to a boil, reduce heat, cover, and simmer for 1½ to 2 hours, until the hocks are falling apart.
2. Remove the ham hocks from the cooking liquid and reserve the meat, discarding the bones, skin, and fat. Strain the cooking liquid, skim off the fat, and return it to the pot. (To skim as much fat as possible, see Box.)
3. While the ham hocks are cooking, remove the stems from the collard greens and roughly chop; set aside.
4. Add enough chicken stock or water to the cooking liquid to make 6 cups. Add the chopped collard greens, brown sugar, red pepper flakes, salt, black pepper, and reserved ham. Bring to a simmer over medium-low heat and cook for 45 minutes to 1 hour, until the greens are very tender. Serve immediately.

Defatting Ham Hocks

Since ham hocks tend to be a bit fatty, you can prepare them ahead to remove as much fat as possible. Once you have finished cooking them off, remove the pot from the heat, allow it to cool to room temperature, then cover and place the pot in the refrigerator. Allow the hock mixture to chill for at least an hour or overnight so the fat comes to the top. Skim off all excess fat before proceeding with the recipe.

Winter Greens

YIELDS 8 SERVINGS

One side dish that takes its place at most Southern dinner tables is a "mess o' greens," which refers to the large quantity most families cook up. This recipe calls for a combination of collard, kale, and turnip greens, which are available year round. Smoked turkey gives them a nice layer of flavor. I like to serve this recipe around the holidays, because it's easy to prepare and a real crowd pleaser!

¼ cup olive oil

1 large onion, thinly sliced

3 cloves garlic, sliced

8 cups chicken or turkey stock or broth

3 bay leaves

2 teaspoons red pepper flakes

2 teaspoons dried thyme

6 pounds collard, kale, and turnip greens, cleaned and chopped

3 cups chopped smoked turkey

Salt and freshly ground black pepper to taste

1. In a large heavy pot, heat the olive oil over medium heat. Sauté the onion and garlic for about 3 to 4 minutes, until softened. Add the chicken or turkey stock, bay leaves, red pepper flakes, and thyme. Simmer for 12 minutes.
2. Add the greens and smoked turkey to the pot. Simmer uncovered until the greens are tender. Remove the bay leaves, season with salt and pepper, and serve immediately.

Savory Corn Pudding

YIELDS 6 TO 8 SERVINGS

This is a savory pudding with fresh chives, though feel free to add a combination of your favorite herbs. When possible, use fresh corn kernels cut off the cob. Using a knife, scrape the cob after removing the kernels to get all the pulp and milk to add their creamy flavor to the dish.

3 cups fresh or frozen corn kernels
3 large eggs, beaten
1½ cups heavy cream
2 tablespoons sugar

½ teaspoon kosher salt
⅛ teaspoon freshly ground white pepper
⅓ cup chopped fresh chives

1. Preheat oven to 350°F. In a large bowl, combine the corn, eggs, heavy cream, sugar, salt, white pepper, and chives, and stir to mix thoroughly. Pour into a buttered 8-inch glass baking dish.
2. Bake the corn pudding for 45 to 48 minutes, until the edges are browned and the pudding is slightly puffed, the center jiggles like gelatin when the pan is nudged, or the tip of a knife comes out clean from the center. Serve immediately.

Removing Corn from the Cob

When cooking recipes with corn, nothing beats the flavor and texture of fresh corn from the cob. To remove corn kernels from the cob quickly and easily, use a bowl or Bundt pan to catch all the corn and its flavorful milk. Place the cob in the center to give you a little support and leverage, and using a sharp knife, slice down the sides of the cob to remove the kernels. Then, scrape the dull edge of the knife down the cob to extract as much pulp and juice as possible. The kernels and milk will collect neatly in the bowl.

Sweet Bourbon Corn Pudding

This continues to be one of my family's favorite recipes. The casserole is great served at the dinner table, and it's a big hit when I serve it buffet style. If you prefer not to use bourbon in this recipe, replace it with 2 tablespoons of water to dissolve the cornstarch.

2 large eggs
¾ cup evaporated milk
2 cups canned cream-style corn
2 cups fresh corn kernels; or canned corn, drained; or frozen corn, thawed and drained
2 tablespoons unsalted butter, melted

3 tablespoons dark brown sugar
3 tablespoons cornstarch mixed with 2 tablespoons bourbon
½ teaspoon ground nutmeg
¼ teaspoon salt
⅛ teaspoon ground white pepper

1. Preheat oven to 350°F. Butter an 8-inch square or 6-cup baking dish.
2. In a large bowl, whisk the eggs and the evaporated milk together. Stir in the cream-style corn, corn kernels, melted butter, brown sugar, cornstarch mixture, nutmeg, salt, and white pepper. Stir well to combine.
3. Pour the mixture into the prepared baking dish. Bake for 45 to 48 minutes, or until slightly browned and the tip of a small knife inserted in the center comes out clean. Serve immediately.

Tomato Bread Pudding

Bread puddings are versatile enough to be made into desserts, or sweet or savory side dishes. This one is perfect to serve as a side with any meal, or on a buffet for a weekend brunch. I like to use fresh tomatoes when in season, but there are a number of good canned varieties on the market that also work well. For a special occasion, try using a combination of garden-fresh heirloom tomatoes—they look beautiful, and taste even better!

One 28-ounce can plum tomatoes with
  juices, or 3½ cups stewed fresh
  tomatoes (see Box)
1¼ cups chicken stock or broth
¼ cup packed dark brown sugar
¼ teaspoon ground cinnamon
1 teaspoon dry mustard
¼ teaspoon garlic powder, or 2 cloves fresh
  minced garlic

Salt and freshly ground black pepper
  to taste
3 to 4 leaves fresh basil, roughly chopped,
  plus more for garnish if desired,
  or 1 tablespoon dried basil
3 tablespoons unsalted butter, melted
8 slices best-quality crusty white or whole-
  wheat bread, crusts removed, cut into
  ¾-inch cubes, approximately 8 cups

1. Preheat oven to 375°F. In a medium saucepan, place the tomatoes with their juices, crushing them with your fingers as you place them in the pan. Add the stock, brown sugar, cinnamon, mustard, garlic, salt, and pepper. Bring to a boil over medium-high heat, then reduce heat to medium and cook until the mixture has thickened and the sugar has dissolved, about 10 to 15 minutes. Adjust the seasoning, then fold in the basil.
2. Brush the inside of an 11 x 7-inch baking dish with some of the melted butter. Arrange the bread cubes in the dish in an even layer and drizzle with the remaining butter. Pour the tomato mixture over the bread, and gently stir so the tomato is evenly incorporated into the bread.
3. Place the dish on the center rack of the oven and bake for about 45 minutes, until the pudding is golden and firm to the touch.
4. Remove the baking dish from the oven. Allow the pudding to cool for about 10 minutes and then serve immediately or at room temperature, garnished with fresh basil if desired. Or allow pudding to cool completely, cover, and refrigerate overnight, then bring it to room temperature and reheat before serving.

Using Fresh Tomatoes Instead of Canned

When in season, especially in the summertime, fresh heirloom or plum tomatoes can be substituted for canned tomatoes in dishes that call for them. Simply remove the stems, and peel and seed the whole tomatoes. Place the tomatoes in a heavy saucepan over medium heat and let simmer for 20 to 25 minutes, stirring occasionally, until tender. Allow to cool before proceeding with recipe, or store in a tightly covered container in the refrigerator for up to 5 days.

Maque Choux

This is a vegetarian version of Maque Choux, but it can be prepared with bacon or ham. Whenever possible, use fresh corn off the cob for this recipe. Be sure to scrape the cob after cutting off the kernels, adding the pulp and milk to the mix. If using frozen corn, add a tablespoon or more of heavy cream to add richness.

2 tablespoons unsalted butter or vegetable oil

1 cup chopped onion

½ cup chopped green bell pepper

4 cups fresh or frozen corn kernels

Fresh chopped basil or thyme, to taste

2 cups chopped plum tomatoes

½ cup vegetable or chicken stock or broth

¼ teaspoon ground white pepper

¼ teaspoon cayenne pepper

Salt and freshly ground black pepper to taste

½ cup sliced scallions, for garnish

1. In a large skillet, melt the butter over medium-high heat. Add the onion and bell pepper and sauté for 4 to 5 minutes, until softened.

2. Stir in the corn, basil, tomatoes, stock, white pepper, and cayenne. Reduce the heat to medium and cook for 10 minutes, stirring occasionally, until the vegetables are cooked. Season with salt and pepper and serve immediately, garnished with the scallions.

Stewed Okra, Corn, and Tomatoes

This stew is easy to make and takes very little time to prepare, so I like to put it on the menu when I'm shopping for fresh produce and find fresh okra, corn on the cob, and large ripe tomatoes. Garnish with crumbled bacon and serve with warm cornbread fresh from the oven.

1 pound fresh okra

4 strips smoked bacon, diced

2 cloves garlic, sliced

1 medium onion, sliced

1 cup chopped green bell pepper

2 cups fresh corn, or frozen corn, thawed and drained

1 bay leaf

3 large tomatoes, peeled, seeded, and chopped

½ cup vegetable broth or stock, or water

Salt and freshly ground black pepper to taste

1. Rinse the okra, trim away the stems, and slice each pod crosswise into about ½-inch pieces. Set aside.
2. In a large skillet or large pot over medium-high heat, fry the bacon for about 5 to 6 minutes, until crisp and brown. Using a slotted spoon, remove the bacon from the skillet, leaving the bacon fat in the pan. Drain the cooked bacon on paper towels and set aside.
3. Add the garlic, onion, and bell pepper to the skillet and reduce the heat to medium. Sauté, stirring frequently, for about 2 to 3 minutes, until the vegetables are soft.
4. Add the okra, corn, and bay leaf to the skillet. Cover the skillet and reduce the heat to low. Cook gently, stirring from time to time, for about 3 to 4 minutes.
5. Add the tomatoes and vegetable broth or water to the skillet. Cook for about 10 minutes, or longer if you prefer the okra to be softer. Remove the bay leaf, and season with salt and pepper. Serve immediately, garnished with reserved crumbled bacon pieces.

Succotash

Succotash is a quick and easy dish to prepare. Fresh vegetables are my favorite for this recipe, but frozen or canned will do. If fresh lima beans are not available, use frozen lima beans that have been thawed, and cut the cooking time to 10 minutes. Use this as a basic recipe and get creative: add chopped kale, green peas, or beans, spice it up with Cajun or Creole seasoning, and/or garnish with a crumble of ham or bacon.

2 cups fresh lima beans, skin removed by blanching and transferring to cold water

4 ears fresh sweet corn

½ cup heavy cream

2 tablespoons butter

⅓ cup finely chopped scallions

Salt and freshly ground black pepper to taste

Chopped fresh parsley, for garnish

1. In a large saucepan, place the skinned lima beans in just enough salted water to prevent sticking; bring to a boil. Reduce the heat to low, cover, and simmer for about 25 minutes, until almost tender. Check frequently and add more water as needed. Drain if necessary before proceeding.
2. Using a sharp knife, cut the corn kernels from the cob, and scrape the cobs with the dull edge of the knife to extract the milk. Add the corn and its juices to the lima beans and stir in the heavy cream. Simmer over low heat for 5 minutes. Add the butter, scallions, salt, and pepper, stirring well to combine. Heat the Succotash thoroughly and serve immediately, garnished with fresh parsley.

Chapter 10

Sauces and Condiments

Historically, barbecue sauce has been so inventive that early cookbooks didn't even include recipes for them. No other sauce can stir up a debate amongst the best of friends or family like barbecue. Don't even think about thinking that you have the secret to the best barbecue sauce. Everyone, even the least experienced of cooks, turns into a barbecue expert and believes his or her recipe or store-bought brand is the very best.

I've never claimed to be the Queen of Barbecue Sauce, so I've added just a few of my favorite recipes to this chapter. For my friends with health issues who require low-sugar foods, the Low-Sugar Maple Barbecue Sauce is sweetened with Splenda and sugar-free maple syrup. Please note, if I'm ever passing through your town and you would like me to try your sauce, don't worry about me trying to steal the recipe, I just want to taste it, no matter how much sugar you use.

As with barbecue sauce, there's much discussion about gravies. I've always been impressed with how Southerners can whip up rich, delicious gravy like it's nothing. My first adventures with gravy in my mother's kitchen were lumpy, but I learned. I like rich, velvety gravies. There's something about gravies: more than being gravies, they're a state of mind. Many of the gravies in this book are pan gravies prepared from the natural pan juices and drippings from cooked meats, poultry, and seafood.

Much as I appreciate basic gravies, I love coming up with variations on the theme. I like black-eyed peas and their "Southernness," so I've created a Black-Eyed Pea Gravy. Its texture and Creole seasoning really wake up and complement a meal.

Sauces should be hearty and full of flavor, too, at least in my book. I also like to take the familiar and create something new in a sauce. Fruit sauces with mango or pineapple are perfect with poultry, a wonderful combination of sweet and savory flavors.

One recipe that's very special to me is Watermelon Rind Pickles. We used to pickle watermelon rinds. When they were ready, we ate them out of the jar like pickles. I've spiced up my mom's recipe with cloves, allspice, and cinnamon. When they're ready, we don't pop them in our mouths—we eat them on a plate with meat or fish. They turn a simple meal special in one bite.

We've all heard about fried green tomatoes, but try the Green Tomato Relish; it's pretty and tasty. There's something to say when a meal you've spent time preparing has just the right finish or touch. It deserves it and so do your guests. Right, Dan?

Black-Eyed Pea Gravy

When I started making black-eyed pea gravy, it was one of those times I just wanted to be creative with leftovers. I literally used what I found in the fridge. When you read the recipe, you'll see both chicken and clam stock. These days, I tailor the recipe, using clam or seafood stock to pair with catfish, or just chicken stock if I'm serving poultry. Vegetable broth works just fine, too. You can't go wrong with black-eyed peas paired with Southern spices!

1 tablespoon vegetable oil
½ cup chopped shallots
3 tablespoons red wine
¾ teaspoon Hungarian hot paprika
¾ teaspoon Creole seasoning
1 cup chicken stock or broth
¼ cup clam juice, or chicken or vegetable
*   stock or broth*

One 15-ounce can black-eyed peas,
*   drained and rinsed*
2 bay leaves
Salt and freshly ground black pepper to
*   taste*
1 tablespoon chopped parsley, for garnish

1. In a medium sauté pan, heat the oil and cook the shallots over medium heat until soft but not brown, 3 to 4 minutes. Add the red wine, paprika, and Creole seasoning. Simmer a few minutes until the wine has evaporated. Stir in the chicken stock, clam juice, black-eyed peas, and bay leaves. Simmer 7 to 8 minutes, until the black-eyed peas are very soft.
2. With a wooden spoon, mash some of the peas to thicken the gravy; continue cooking 1 to 2 minutes.
3. Remove bay leaves, and adjust seasoning to taste. Serve immediately, garnished with chopped parsley.

Red Pepper Black-Eyed Pea Gravy

For a delicious variation, try adding roasted red peppers to your Black-Eyed Pea Gravy. In a food processor fitted with the metal blade, purée 2 roasted red peppers with ¼ cup of the chicken stock from the Black-Eyed Pea Gravy recipe above. Proceed with the recipe, adding the red pepper purée to the pan after mashing the black-eyed peas in Step 2, and continue cooking the gravy for 5 minutes before serving per recipe instructions.

B's Sweet Maple Barbecue Sauce

"The Queen of Barbecue" is not the title for me! That's a competition I'll pass on. Everyone has their personal favorite barbecue sauce, whether it's a store-bought brand or a recipe created in a home kitchen. This is one of my quick and easy recipes, sweetened with maple syrup and orange juice and the perfect blend of spices to sauce up meat, poultry, or seafood. Give a quick brush to vegetables while on the grill to wake up the flavors!

2 tablespoons butter
1 medium onion, finely chopped
2 cloves garlic, minced
2 cups ketchup
1 cup maple syrup
½ cup orange juice
½ cup cider vinegar

¼ cup Worcestershire sauce
2 tablespoons lemon juice
2 slices fresh lemon
2 tablespoons dry mustard
1 teaspoon salt
½ teaspoon red pepper flakes
½ teaspoon paprika

1. In a large saucepan, melt the butter over medium heat. Add the onion and garlic, and cook, stirring frequently, until softened, about 5 minutes.
2. Add the ketchup, maple syrup, orange juice, vinegar, Worcestershire sauce, lemon juice, lemon slices, dry mustard, salt, red pepper flakes, and paprika to the pan. Stir well to combine, and simmer, stirring occasionally, for 30 minutes. Remove the lemon slices.
3. Serve warm, or place in a tightly sealed container and store in the refrigerator for up to 2 weeks.

Bourbon Brown Sugar Barbecue Sauce

YIELDS 2⅔ CUPS

We love bourbon in our house. The bottle on the bar is never full, as I love to use it in recipes, and it seems to be a popular beverage with guests. Mixing two great things, brown sugar and bourbon, this sauce is certain to lift your spirits!

¼ cup vegetable oil

2 tablespoons butter

1 large sweet onion (such as Vidalia),
    finely chopped

1 cup ketchup

¾ cup bourbon

½ cup brown sugar

2 tablespoons Worcestershire sauce

2 tablespoons cider vinegar

2 tablespoons molasses

½ teaspoon salt

⅛ teaspoon cayenne pepper

1. Heat oil and butter in a small saucepan over medium heat. Add the onion and cook, stirring frequently, for 8 to 10 minutes, until light golden brown.
2. Stir in the ketchup, bourbon, brown sugar, Worcestershire sauce, vinegar, molasses, salt, and cayenne pepper, and mix well. Bring to a simmer and allow to cook until thickened, about 20 minutes.
3. Serve warm, or place in a tightly sealed container and store in the refrigerator for up to 2 weeks.

Low-Sugar Maple Barbecue Sauce

I frequently prepare recipes for friends and family who have diabetes. My goal is to make great food for *everyone* to enjoy, without knowing it's low-sugar or not!

1 cup low-sodium chicken or vegetable
    stock or broth
½ cup finely chopped onion
⅓ cup finely chopped celery
1 garlic clove, minced
1 bay leaf
2 teaspoons dry mustard
½ teaspoon celery seed

1½ cups ketchup
½ cup sugar-free maple syrup
½ cup Splenda Brown Sugar Blend
1 tablespoon Worcestershire sauce
½ teaspoon salt
½ teaspoon freshly ground black pepper
½ teaspoon paprika
½ teaspoon hot sauce, or more to taste

1. Place the broth, onion, celery, garlic, and bay leaf in a medium saucepan over medium heat. Cover pan and simmer until the vegetables are softened, about 10 minutes.
2. Add the mustard, celery seed, ketchup, maple syrup, brown sugar, and Worcestershire sauce to the pan. Stir well and simmer, uncovered, stirring often, until the sauce is slightly thickened, about 20 minutes.
3. Discard the bay leaf, and stir in the salt, pepper, paprika, and hot sauce. Serve sauce warm or place in a tightly sealed container and refrigerate for up to 2 weeks.

Pomegranate Barbecue Sauce

Ginger and pomegranate molasses provide exotic flavors to this thick, dark sauce, which is delicious served with grilled pork, lamb, or salmon. Pomegranate molasses is available at Middle Eastern food markets and some specialty food stores.

2 tablespoons butter
1 cup chopped onion
1 tablespoon minced garlic
1 tablespoon grated ginger
3 tablespoons firmly packed brown sugar

3 tablespoons pomegranate molasses,
   store-bought or homemade (see recipe
   on page 143)
¼ cup cider vinegar
1 cup ketchup
Salt and freshly ground pepper to taste

1. In a medium nonstick saucepan, melt the butter over medium heat. Add the onion and garlic, and sauté until soft, about 5 minutes.
2. Add the ginger, brown sugar, pomegranate molasses, and vinegar to the pan. Stir well and cook for 5 minutes.
3. Add the ketchup to the pan, stir well to combine, lower heat, and simmer the sauce for 12 to 15 minutes, until thickened. Season with salt and pepper. Serve warm or place in a tightly sealed container and refrigerate for up to 2 weeks.

Coconut Curry Sauce

YIELDS ABOUT 1¼ CUPS

Coconut and curry are a classic Caribbean combination, and they come together here in a knockout blend that transforms any seafood or poultry dish!

1¼ cups canned lite coconut milk
1 garlic clove, minced
2 tablespoon chopped fresh ginger

½ cup minced scallions
1 tablespoon curry powder
½ teaspoon red pepper flakes

1. Combine the coconut milk, garlic, ginger, scallions, curry powder, and red pepper flakes in a medium saucepan and bring to a boil over medium heat. Reduce heat to low and simmer for 15 minutes, stirring occasionally.
2. Remove pan from heat and strain the sauce through a fine sieve into a clean saucepan, pressing down on the solids to extract as much of the sauce as possible. Discard solids. Serve sauce immediately, or keep warm over low heat until serving.

Sweet and Spicy Ginger Pineapple Dipping Sauce

YIELDS 1½ CUPS

Pineapple and ginger are a great combination. This sauce is slightly sweetened with brown sugar and the pineapple preserves, and the red pepper adds just the right amount of heat. This recipe was created as a dipping sauce for the Sugarcane-Skewered Chicken (page 39).

1 cup freshly grated pineapple,
    or one 8-ounce can crushed pineapple
½ cup pineapple preserves
1 tablespoon light brown sugar

One 1-inch piece of fresh ginger, peeled
    and grated
¼ teaspoon red pepper flakes
¼ teaspoon salt

1. In a medium saucepan, place all the ingredients; stir to combine. Bring the mixture to a boil on medium-high heat and cook, stirring constantly, for 2 minutes.
2. Remove from heat, cool to room temperature, and place in a bowl or resealable container. Cover and refrigerate until serving.

Green Tomato Relish

Unripe green tomatoes resemble fully ripened red tomatoes. They are firm and slightly tart. You can often find green tomatoes at your local farmers' market, or you can use homegrown. This tasty green tomato relish will keep in the refrigerator for two weeks. Its bright flavor goes well with everything from chicken and fish to beef or pork.

1 tablespoon olive oil	¾ teaspoon salt
2 shallots, diced	¼ cup brown sugar
1 teaspoon yellow mustard seeds	2 tablespoons cider vinegar
¼ teaspoon red pepper flakes	4 green tomatoes, cored and chopped
¼ teaspoon ground allspice	

1. Heat oil in a sauté pan over medium heat. Add the shallots, mustard seeds, red pepper flakes, allspice, and salt. Cook for 3 minutes, stirring frequently. Reduce heat to medium-low and continue cooking for 5 more minutes, stirring frequently, until shallots are soft.
2. Add the brown sugar, vinegar, and tomatoes to the pan and cook for 20 minutes, stirring occasionally, until tomatoes are soft.
3. Remove pan from heat, allow to cool, and serve at room temperature, or place in a tightly sealed container and refrigerate for up to 2 weeks.

Guinness Tartar Sauce

YIELDS ABOUT 1 1/4 CUPS

The Guinness Stout adds a unique flavor without overpowering the sauce. Full of flavor, it shouts, "Bring on the seafood, poultry, or meat—I got something for ya!"

1/2 cup mayonnaise
1/2 cup sour cream
3 tablespoons Guinness Stout
2 tablespoons chopped dill pickles or
    dill pickle relish
2 tablespoons capers, drained

2 tablespoons minced scallion, white and
    green parts
1 tablespoon minced fresh tarragon,
    or 1 teaspoon dried
2 dashes hot pepper sauce

Mix mayonnaise, sour cream, Guinness stout, dill pickles, capers, scallion, tarragon, and hot pepper sauce together in a small bowl and stir until well blended. Cover and store in the refrigerator until serving. To thin the sauce, stir in a tablespoon of Guinness to desired consistency.

Roasted Red Pepper Aioli

This recipe works well with homemade roasted peppers (see Box) or with jarred red peppers. If using jarred roasted red peppers, be sure to drain the peppers well to remove excess moisture before proceeding with the recipe.

1 large clove garlic	*1 tablespoon olive oil*
½ cup chopped roasted red peppers	*¼ teaspoon salt*
⅓ cup mayonnaise, or light canola mayo	*Pinch of freshly ground black pepper*

1. Place the garlic in the bowl of a food processor fitted with a metal blade and pulse to chop. Add the red pepper and process until the garlic and peppers are well blended. Add the mayonnaise, olive oil, salt, and pepper and process mixture until smooth.
2. Place aioli into a tightly sealed container and refrigerate until ready to use. It will keep refrigerated for up to 1 week.

How to Make Roasted Peppers

Homemade roasted peppers are easy to prepare. Simply hold a fresh bell pepper with tongs over the flame of a gas burner or on an outdoor grill, turning frequently, until skin is scorched and blistered. Immediately place scorched pepper in a paper bag, roll top of bag closed, and allow pepper to cool to room temperature. Remove pepper from bag, then peel, core, and remove seeds and membranes from the flesh. Use immediately for recipes, or store up to 1 week in a tightly covered container in the refrigerator.

Watermelon Rind Pickles

I've always loved watermelon, but this recipe made with the rind takes me over the top. Make a batch of these Watermelon Rind Pickles and you will see what I mean. They are very sweet, so a little goes a long way! They are a wonderful sweet condiment for meat or fish or poultry. Plus, the jars make for a memorable hostess gift prepared with love!

4 pounds watermelon rind
1 quart plus 2 cups cold water, divided,
*   plus more for boiling*
4 tablespoons salt
Ten 2-inch cinnamon sticks

2 tablespoons whole allspice
2 tablespoons whole cloves
2 cups cider vinegar
4½ cups sugar

1. Peel green skin from the watermelon rind and cut the peeled rind into 1-inch squares. Combine 1 quart cold water and the salt in a large plastic or other nonreactive bowl, stirring until salt is dissolved. Add the rind to the bowl. Cover and refrigerate overnight.

2. Drain rind in a colander, and rinse well with cold water. Place rind in a large stockpot or Dutch oven, and cover with fresh cold water. Bring to a boil over medium-high heat, then lower heat and simmer about 1½ hours, or until rind is tender. Drain rind in a colander.

3. Tie cinnamon sticks, allspice, and cloves in a piece of cheesecloth to make a spice bag. In the same stockpot, combine the vinegar, remaining 2 cups water, and the sugar over medium-high heat, bring to a boil, reduce heat to a simmer and cook until the sugar dissolves, about 6 minutes. Add the spice bag and the cooked watermelon rind to the pot. Simmer gently over medium-low heat for 2 hours. The rind will turn translucent and the syrup will thicken and turn a tea-like color. Remove and discard spice bag.

4. Sterilize five 8-ounce canning jars. Pack the rind into the jars and fill with the hot syrup to cover rind. Seal with a boiling-water canning bath. Store canned Watermelon Rind Pickles for up to 3 months in the pantry. Alternatively, store pickles in a tightly sealed glass or plastic container for up to 2 weeks in the refrigerator.

Sweet Bourbon Sauce

You can't get more Southern than bourbon—from Bourbon County, Kentucky, where the spirit got its name, to Bourbon Street, Louisiana, one of the most recognized street names in the South. It's no surprise that in 2007, the U.S. Senate passed a resolution declaring September 2007 National Bourbon History Month. It is estimated that 95% of the world's bourbon is distilled and aged in Kentucky, with few refinements since the eighteenth century. I can't get enough of it in my recipes, and it doesn't get easier than this sauce; the combination of the sweetened condensed milk with Kentucky bourbon gives any dessert a nice kick!

One 14-ounce can sweetened condensed milk

3 to 4 tablespoons bourbon, or to taste

1. Place the sweetened condensed milk into a 2-cup measuring pitcher with a pouring spout. Microwave on high power in 30-second increments, stirring between heating, until warm.
2. Add the bourbon, stir to combine, and serve warm over your favorite dessert.

Spicy Herb-Caper Butter Sauce

I originally created this flavorful sauce to serve with fresh marinated grilled frog legs. Try serving it over grilled seafood or pan-fried fish. In this sauce, vermouth adds that slight bit of sweet for balance, though you can use white wine in place of the vermouth.

1 cup vermouth or white wine	3 tablespoons chopped fresh parsley
2 cups chicken stock	2 to 3 tablespoons capers
4 tablespoons softened butter, divided	Juice from ½ lemon, freshly squeezed
1½ tablespoons all-purpose flour	½ teaspoon hot sauce, optional
2 cloves garlic, minced	½ teaspoon salt
1 tablespoon chopped fresh lemon thyme, or 1 teaspoon dried thyme	¼ teaspoon freshly ground black pepper

1. Place the vermouth and chicken stock in a medium saucepan, and bring to a boil over medium-high heat.
2. In a small bowl, blend 1½ tablespoons of the butter with the flour until smooth. Whisk the butter mixture into the hot broth, lower the heat, and simmer until the mixture is reduced by half, or until it thickens to desired consistency.
3. Add the garlic, thyme, parsley, capers, lemon juice, hot sauce if desired, salt, and pepper to the pan, and simmer for 1 to 2 minutes more. Whisk in the remaining 2½ tablespoons butter. Serve immediately.

Chapter 11

Desserts

If Native Americans brought the vegetables, grits, and meats to the Southern table, Europeans brought the sweets; most foods made with dairy products are attributed to them. Thomas Jefferson was known for his sweet tooth, cultivated during his European travels. He brought back recipes to Monticello for cakes, custards, and jellies.

Southern desserts may come out of the kitchen, but they taste like they were made in heaven. And no matter how heavy the meal, there's always room for something sweet. It's nothing for a hearty Southern meal to end with a variety of cakes, pies, cookies, puddings, and cobblers.

I never was a big dessert eater, but I've always enjoyed making and serving them. The nods and smiles of approval are priceless. I've taken culinary license with some all-time favorite desserts and put a new, fun spin on them. Try the easy-to-make Bourbon Street Bread Pudding or the Chocolate Pecan Pie with Sweet Bourbon Whipped Cream.

My mom grew rhubarb and made pies with it but used cups of sugar to sweeten its tartness. I think fresh, rich, succulent strawberries can take the place of some of the sugar needed in this recipe. If you are pie-crust challenged, don't let that stop you from baking pies. Pillsbury has excellent pie crusts.

Red Velvet Cake is always welcomed at the dessert table. Once upon a time, it got its red color from boiled beets. Food color and cocoa are how it's done these days. Along with the classic Red Velvet Cake recipe, I've added a new version: Red Velvet Cake Roll with Peanut Butter Frosting drizzled with melted chocolate. It won't stay on the dessert table for long. Coconut-Pecan Cupcakes were inspired by the triple-layer Coconut-Pecan Cake—they have a great mouth sensation. First you bite into softness, and then comes the surprise of a crunchy pecan center.

The Blackberry-Cardamom Cobbler is luscious with its warm, sweet, gingerlike flavor. Deep-Dish Apple Pie is always a hit. Or take it to the rich, decadent Walnut Molasses Tart.

Grits for dessert, anyone? I like taking something as basic and familiar and loved as grits and finding a place for them in another part of a meal. In this case, it's Candy Apple Grits Crème Brûlée.

When you taste Dan's Chocolate Chip Cookies, don't thank me, thank him. He loves his cookies. I wanted to find a way to let him have his cookies and eat them, too, with healthy substitutions.

Instead of sugar, I used Splenda. For eggs, I suggest an egg substitute. Dan finds semisweet chocolate chunks instead of chocolate chips sweet enough.

Desserts don't have to take hours and don't have to be complicated. Pumpkin Spice Mousse can be prepared in advance. The Bananas Foster Sundaes are quick and easy, plus there is a Lite version. The peach turnovers are as simple to make as they are delicious.

I think I can safely say that no one looks forward to any other course the way they look forward to dessert. Have you ever heard anyone say, "Wait until you taste the salad"?

Almond Peach Turnovers

YIELDS 8 SERVINGS

Peach turnovers made with puff pastry are a versatile, easy-to-make treat. Serve them for breakfast, brunch, or tea, as a snack, and of course, for dessert! I love the flavor the almond paste adds and the pretty garnish of sliced almonds and a dusting of confectioners' sugar. These turnovers are best served the day they are made.

1 pound (4 to 5) fresh ripe peaches, or one 16-ounce bag sliced frozen peaches
¼ cup granulated sugar
⅛ teaspoon salt
One 17.3-ounce package of 2 (9 x 9 x ½-inch) prepared puff pastry sheets, thawed according to package directions

¼ cup pure almond paste (see Note)
1 large egg, lightly beaten with 1 teaspoon water
¼ cup sliced almonds
¼ cup sifted confectioners' sugar

1. To peel the fresh peaches, drop them whole into a pot of boiling water; boil for 2 to 3 minutes. Using a slotted spoon, remove the peaches, and when cool enough to handle, peel off the skin. (If using frozen sliced peaches, thaw according to package directions.) Divide the peaches in half. Chop half of the peaches into ½-inch cubes, and finely chop the remaining half.
2. In a large skillet, place all the chopped peaches, the granulated sugar, and salt, and stir to combine. Cook the mixture over medium heat for about 2 to 3 minutes, until the sugar melts and the peaches give up their juices. Lower the heat and cook for 3 to 4 more minutes (or longer if peaches are juicy), stirring often, until the mixture thickens. Pour the mixture into a bowl, cover, and refrigerate for 15 minutes.
3. Place parchment paper on two large baking sheets and set aside. To assemble the turnovers, unfold one sheet of puff pastry onto a lightly floured counter and using a rolling pin, gently roll the pastry into a 10-inch square. Using a pizza cutter or sharp knife, cut the pastry into four 5-inch squares.
4. Place a generous tablespoon of almond paste in the middle of a square, lightly flatten, and spread the paste with your fingertips, leaving a ½-inch border of pastry. Place 2 tablespoons of the peach mixture on top of the almond paste.

5. Using a pastry brush, coat the edges of the pastry with some of the egg wash. Fold the pastry into a triangle. Using a fork, crimp the edges securely together to seal. Repeat the entire process with the remaining pastry squares and the second sheet of pastry (you will have 8 filled turnovers). Reserve the remaining egg wash.
6. Place 4 turnovers on each prepared baking sheet. Before baking, refrigerate the baking sheets with turnovers to chill uncovered for 30 minutes, or up to 2 hours.
7. Adjust two oven racks to the upper and middle positions. Preheat oven to 400°F.
8. Remove the turnovers from the refrigerator, brush the tops with the reserved egg wash, and sprinkle a few sliced almonds on top.
9. Bake the turnovers for 20 to 25 minutes, or until they are golden brown, rotating and switching the baking sheets halfway through baking. Allow to cool for 10 minutes, then sprinkle with the confectioners' sugar.

Note: Pure almond paste is sold in 8-ounce cans or tubes and can be found in the baking aisle of the grocery store. Leftover almond paste can be stored in the refrigerator in a plastic bag for use at a later time.

Peach Turnovers

There is nothing like fresh, juicy ripe peaches, though in a pinch, sliced frozen peaches are handy for a quick smoothie or for these tasty peach turnovers. This recipe is quick and easy! Use two prepared puff pastry sheets, sugar, cinnamon, and allspice, and finish with a sprinkle of turbinado sugar.

1 pound (4 to 5) fresh ripe peaches, or one 16-ounce bag sliced frozen peaches, thawed
¼ cup granulated sugar
⅛ teaspoon salt
¼ teaspoon ground cinnamon
⅛ teaspoon ground allspice

One 17.3-ounce package of 2 (9 x 9 x ½-inch) prepared puff pastry sheets, thawed according to package directions
1 large egg, lightly beaten with 1 teaspoon water
¼ cup turbinado sugar

1. To peel the fresh peaches, drop them whole into a pot of boiling water; boil for 2 to 3 minutes. Using a slotted spoon, remove the peaches, and when cool enough to handle, peel off the skin. (If using frozen sliced peaches, thaw according to package directions.) Divide the peaches in half. Chop half of the peaches into ½-inch cubes, and finely chop the remaining half.
2. In a large skillet, place the chopped peaches, the granulated sugar, salt, cinnamon, and allspice, and stir to combine. Cook the mixture over medium heat for about 2 to 3 minutes, until the sugar melts and the peaches give up their juices. Lower heat and cook for 3 to 4 more minutes (or longer if peaches are juicy), stirring often, until the mixture thickens. Pour the mixture in a bowl, cover, and refrigerate for 15 minutes.
3. Place parchment paper on two large baking sheets and set aside. To assemble the turnovers, unfold one sheet of the puff pastry onto a lightly floured counter, and using a rolling pin, gently roll the pastry into a 10-inch square. Using a pizza cutter or knife, cut the pastry into four 5-inch squares.
4. Place 2 tablespoons of the peach mixture in the center of a pastry square. Using a pastry brush, coat the edges of the pastry with some of the egg wash. Fold the pastry into a triangle. Using a fork, crimp the edges together securely to seal. Repeat the entire process with the remaining squares and the second sheet of pastry (you will have 8 filled turnovers). Reserve the remaining egg wash.

5. Place 4 turnovers on each prepared baking sheet. Before baking, refrigerate the baking sheets with the turnovers uncovered for 30 minutes, or up to 2 hours.

6. Adjust two oven racks to the upper and middle positions. Preheat oven to 400°F.

7. Remove the turnovers from the refrigerator, brush the tops with the reserved egg wash, and sprinkle with turbinado sugar.

8. Bake the turnovers for 20 to 25 minutes, or until they are golden brown, rotating and switching the baking sheets halfway through baking. Allow to cool for 10 minutes before serving. Peach Turnovers are best served the day they are made.

Banana Cream Pie

Banana cream pie is a dessert that screams comfort food to me! For added decadence, dark rum makes a tasty alternative to the vanilla extract. Use a prebaked pastry shell, or my favorite for this pie, a graham cracker crust.

1 cup sugar

½ cup all-purpose flour

¼ teaspoon salt

3 cups half-and-half or whole milk

3 egg yolks

2 tablespoons unsalted butter

2 teaspoons pure vanilla extract or dark
rum

4 large bananas, thinly sliced

1 prebaked 9-inch pie crust (½ recipe
Double Pie Crust, see recipe on
page 282), or 1 Graham Cracker Pie
Crust (see recipe on page 273)

1 cup heavy cream

2 tablespoons confectioners' sugar

1. To make the filling, in a large saucepan, whisk together the sugar, flour, and salt. Whisk in the half-and-half or milk, and place the saucepan over medium heat. Heat the mixture, whisking constantly, until it is steaming and slightly thickened. Remove pan from heat.
2. In a small bowl, lightly beat the egg yolks. Slowly whisk about 1 cup of the hot mixture into the egg yolks. Place the saucepan with the remaining hot mixture back on the stove. Over medium heat, while whisking constantly, slowly pour the egg yolk mixture into the hot mixture in the saucepan.
3. Using a heatproof spatula or flat-edged spoon, stir the mixture constantly until it has thickened and comes to a low boil. You will notice large bubbles starting to break the surface of the filling. Let the mixture boil for about 1 minute, stirring constantly. Remove pan from heat and allow the filling to cool slightly. Stir in the butter and vanilla extract or rum.
4. Arrange half the banana slices in a single layer on the bottom of the pie crust. Pour in half of the filling. Arrange the remaining banana slices on the surface of the filling. Pour in the remaining filling. Cover the pie with plastic wrap pressed onto the surface. Refrigerate to cool completely.
5. Just before serving, in a large bowl, whip the heavy cream until soft peaks form. Add the confectioners' sugar and whip again to incorporate the sugar. Spread the whipped cream evenly over the top of the pie. Keep chilled until serving, or serve immediately.

Bananas Foster Sundaes

This world-famous dessert recipe was created in 1951 in the city of New Orleans at Brennan's restaurant by Chef Paul Blangé for one of their loyal patrons and dear friends, Richard Foster. A tribute to friendships, this timeless dessert highlights the use of bananas, butter, brown sugar, and rum. Add a scoop of vanilla ice cream and serve in individual stemmed dessert glasses. A dollop of whipped cream with a sprinkle of nuts could take it over the top!

½ cup (1 stick) butter
¼ cup dark brown sugar
½ teaspoon ground cinnamon
¼ teaspoon ground nutmeg
½ cup dark rum, preferably high-quality
   100% Jamaican rum

4 medium firm, ripe bananas, peeled and
   sliced into ½-inch diagonal slices
1 pint vanilla ice cream
½ cup chopped toasted pecans or walnuts,
   optional for garnish

1. In a large nonstick skillet, place the butter, brown sugar, cinnamon, nutmeg, and rum, and stir to combine. Heat the mixture over medium-high heat, stirring constantly with a wooden spoon, about 2 to 3 minutes, until the sugar dissolves and the mixture is thick.
2. Reduce heat to medium and add the bananas to the skillet, gently spooning sauce over each piece. Cook for 3 minutes, or until the bananas are glossy and coated with the sauce.
3. Place ½ cup of ice cream into each of 4 stemmed dessert glasses. Place equal amounts of bananas and sauce over the ice cream. Garnish with chopped nuts, if desired, and serve immediately.

Freezing Bananas

You can freeze bananas in their skins until ready to use. Remove them from the freezer and run a little water over the peel to remove any frost. Peel them using a paring knife, and slice according to recipe directions.

Bananas Foster Sundaes Lite

Today, New Orleans is still a major port of entry for bananas shipped from Central and South America. Those of us living in the twenty-first century are very fortunate that we can pair our bananas with fat-free and sugar-free products while we indulge in this famous international dessert! This recipe will soon become one of your family's favorite "healthy lifestyle" desserts!

4 tablespoons (½ stick) margarine
2 tablespoons Splenda Brown Sugar Blend
½ teaspoon ground cinnamon
¼ teaspoon ground nutmeg
½ cup dark rum, preferably high-quality
    100% Jamaican rum

4 medium firm, ripe bananas, peeled and
    sliced into ½-inch diagonal slices
1 pint fat-free, sugar-free vanilla ice cream
    or fat-free, sugar-free vanilla frozen
    yogurt
½ cup chopped toasted pecans or walnuts,
    optional for garnish

1. In a large nonstick skillet, place the margarine, Splenda Brown Sugar Blend, cinnamon, nutmeg, and rum, and stir to combine. Heat the mixture over medium-high heat, stirring constantly with a wire whisk, for about 2 to 3 minutes, until the Brown Sugar Blend dissolves and the mixture is smooth and thick.
2. Reduce heat to medium and add the bananas, gently spooning sauce over each piece. Cook for 2 minutes, or until the bananas are glossy and coated with sauce.
3. Scoop ½ cup of the ice cream or frozen yogurt into each of 4 stemmed dessert glasses. Place equal amounts of bananas and sauce over the ice cream. Garnish with chopped nuts, if desired, and serve immediately.

Blackberry-Cardamom Cobbler with Crème Fraîche

Blackberries are such a classy fruit, elevating this basic cobbler to an upscale dessert! A tiny amount of cardamom, with its warm, sweet, ginger-like flavor, is an exciting replacement for cinnamon or allspice. The homemade crème fraîche should be made at least two days in advance, or up to a week before serving. Homemade is best, but store-bought crème fraîche will save time. Or you can serve the cobbler with a great vanilla ice cream for a heavenly touch.

Nonstick baking spray

¾ cup plus 2 teaspoons sugar, divided

1 tablespoon cornstarch (if using frozen blackberries, increase cornstarch to 2 tablespoons)

Zest of 1 lemon

6 cups fresh blackberries, washed and well drained, or frozen blackberries, thawed according to package directions

1½ teaspoons vanilla, divided

1 cup all-purpose flour

2 teaspoons baking powder

¼ teaspoon baking soda

¼ teaspoon salt

⅓ cup buttermilk

4 tablespoons (½ stick) unsalted butter, melted and cooled

⅛ teaspoon ground cardamom or ground cinnamon

Crème Fraîche (recipe follows), sour cream, or vanilla ice cream, for garnish

1. Preheat oven to 400°F. Prepare a 9-inch deep-dish pie plate or pan by spraying with nonstick baking spray, and set aside.
2. Place ½ cup of the sugar, the cornstarch, and lemon zest in a large bowl, and stir to combine. Add the blackberries and vanilla, and using a large spoon, gently toss the ingredients together until the sugar mixture is combined and the blackberries are coated. Pour the berry mixture into the prepared pie plate, evenly distributing the berries. Bake for 20 to 30 minutes, or just until the blackberries begin to release their juices. Remove the pie plate from the oven and leave the oven on.
3. While the blackberry mixture is baking, in a medium bowl, whisk together the flour, ¼ cup of the sugar, the baking powder, baking soda, and salt. In a separate bowl, combine the buttermilk, melted butter, and vanilla, stirring well to combine. Using a spatula, gently stir the buttermilk mixture into the flour mixture until just combined (the mixture will look like biscuit dough). Set aside until blackberry mixture is removed from the oven.

4. Pinch the dough into about 8 equal pieces and carefully place them on top of the hot blackberries, spacing about ½ inch apart. Combine the remaining 2 teaspoons sugar with the cardamom in a small bowl, stir to combine, and sprinkle over the dough.
5. Return the cobbler to the oven and bake for about 15 to 20 minutes, until the filling is bubbling and the biscuit tops are lightly browned and cooked through. Remove the cobbler from the oven and cool on a wire rack for 15 minutes before serving.
6. Serve the cobbler warm, garnished with a dollop of crème fraîche, sour cream, or vanilla ice cream.

Homemade Crème Fraîche

YIELDS I CUP

I rarely have the time to make crème fraîche, but I knew I had to include a recipe for it in this book. Homemade Crème Fraîche should be made at least two days ahead, or up to a week before serving, as the process takes anywhere from 24 to 36 hours, so I appreciate a container of store-bought crème fraîche as well as homemade. Serve it with a homemade dessert straight from the oven—and don't worry, we can keep a secret if you decide to purchase it at the store!

1 cup pasteurized heavy whipping cream (see Note)   *1 tablespoon buttermilk*

1. In a medium saucepan, warm the cream over low heat until it reaches 105°F on an instant-read thermometer.
2. Remove pan from heat and stir in the buttermilk. Place the mixture in a medium bowl and cover with plastic wrap. Allow the mixture to stand in a very warm location (for example, on top of the stove or near the oven, a heating vent, or a warming oven) until the mixture thickens to the consistency of sour cream. This process takes anywhere from 24 to 36 hours, depending on the temperature of your kitchen, or less time on a hot summer day.
3. When thickened, refrigerate the Homemade Crème Fraîche to chill before using. It can also be whipped, if desired. It will keep in a covered bowl or tightly sealed container in the refrigerator up to 1 week.

Note: Pasteurized heavy cream thickens more quickly than ultra-pasteurized heavy cream. Check the label carefully when purchasing. If only ultra-pasteurized heavy cream is available, allow extra time for the crème fraîche to thicken.

Bourbon Street Bread Pudding with Sweet Bourbon Sauce

YIELDS 10 TO 12 SERVINGS

Bourbon Street Bread Pudding is a huge hit in our restaurants! This recipe will easily become one of your family's favorite desserts. When you remove this warm and luscious pudding from the oven, serve it with a scoop of vanilla ice cream and a drizzle of easy-to-make, two-ingredient Bourbon Sauce. It can be baked in a large pan, or for a more elegant presentation, in individual ramekins (see Note); it's best served warm.

Nonstick baking spray

3 large eggs

1¾ cups sugar

1 teaspoon ground cinnamon, plus more
    for optional garnish

⅛ teaspoon salt

2 tablespoons pure vanilla extract

2 cups heavy cream

½ cup seedless golden raisins, or more
    to taste

1 pound good-quality egg bread, such as
    challah or brioche, or any dense
    bread, crust removed, cut into 1-inch
    cubes

3 tablespoons cold unsalted butter,
    cut into bits

Sweet Bourbon Sauce (recipe follows)

Confectioners' sugar, optional for garnish

Whipped cream, optional for garnish

1. Preheat oven to 350°F. Prepare a 13 x 9 x 2-inch baking dish by coating with nonstick baking spray. (To make individual bread puddings, see Note).

2. In the bowl of an electric stand mixer, or in a large bowl if using an electric hand mixer, place the eggs, sugar, cinnamon, salt, and vanilla. Beat the egg mixture on medium speed for about 5 minutes, until it is slightly thickened and forms a ribbon-like consistency. Add the heavy cream and mix on low speed until well combined.

3. Gently fold the raisins and bread cubes into the egg mixture until just combined, and allow to stand for 30 minutes. Gently toss the pudding mixture once or twice during the 30-minute standing time so the bread absorbs the moisture from the egg mixture, tossing carefully without breaking the bread pieces.

4. Pour the pudding mixture into the prepared baking dish. Dot the top surface with the butter. Bake the pudding for 60 minutes, or until the surface is golden brown and a knife inserted in the center of the pudding comes out clean. If the surface browns too quickly, loosely cover the pan with alu-

minum foil. When cooked, remove the pudding from the oven and allow to cool for 5 minutes.

5. Serve the pudding warm with Bourbon Sauce, and a dusting of cinnamon and confectioners' sugar or a dollop of whipped cream if desired. Cover leftover pudding with plastic wrap, refrigerate, and heat in a microwave before serving, or freeze leftovers by wrapping well in freezer paper; when ready to serve, defrost in the refrigerator, and proceed by heating in the microwave.

Note: If using individual ramekins, prepare as above, and reduce baking time to 30 to 35 minutes.

Sweet Bourbon Sauce

YIELDS 1½ CUPS

One 14-ounce can sweetened condensed milk

3 to 4 tablespoons bourbon, or to taste

1. Pour the sweetened condensed milk into a 2-cup microwavable measuring pitcher with a pouring spout. Microwave on high power in 30-second increments until warm.
2. Add the bourbon to the warmed milk, and stir well to combine. Serve warm over Bourbon Street Bread Pudding.

Candy Apple Grits Crème Brûlée

YIELDS 4 SERVINGS

I have always loved the aroma and found bright red candy apples very appealing. It takes you body and soul back to your childhood. I always keep grits in the house, and thought, "Why not try a dessert?" This dessert evokes images of the State Fair, or just a mild fall day—garnish with a small sprinkle of pistachio nuts in the center and you have a perfect dessert!

2 cups heavy cream
5 large egg yolks
³/₄ cups sugar, divided
3 tablespoons grits
1¹/₂ teaspoons pure vanilla extract

2¹/₂ tablespoons water
2 tablespoons light corn syrup
5 drops red food coloring
Chopped pistachio nuts, for garnish

1. Heat the heavy cream in a medium saucepan over medium heat until hot but not boiling.
2. Place the egg yolks in a medium bowl, and slowly pour in ¹/₄ cup of the hot cream, whisking constantly. Set aside.
3. Add ¹/₄ cup of sugar, the grits, and vanilla to the saucepan with the remaining hot cream. Whisk to blend well. Cook, keeping it at just a simmer over low heat, whisking occasionally, for 30 minutes, until nicely thickened.
4. Slowly pour the egg mixture into the saucepan, whisking quickly to blend well. Cook, keeping it at just a simmer over low heat, whisking constantly, for another 6 minutes. Remove pan from heat, and allow to cool in the saucepan for about 5 to 10 minutes.
5. Whisk the cooled mixture to incorporate any separation that occurred. Pour the custard into four 4 to 5-ounce round ramekins or custard cups, smoothing the tops with the back of a spoon. You can proceed with the recipe as follows, or allow the custard to cool completely, cover, and refrigerate up to 2 days before proceeding.
6. Make the candy crust by mixing ¹/₂ cup sugar with the water and corn syrup in a small saucepan; stir well to blend. Over medium heat, using a candy thermometer, bring the mixture to 250°F to 275°F, then remove the pan from the heat. Stir in the food coloring.
7. Working quickly, pour a thin layer of the candy crust over the tops of the custard, swirling the ramekins to cover the entire surface. Place the ramekins in the refrigerator for about 1¹/₂ hours to allow the crust to harden. Serve garnished with chopped pistachio nuts.

Chocolate Pecan Pie with Sweet Bourbon Whipped Cream

YIELDS 8 SERVINGS

You will love the combination of chocolate, pecans, and bourbon. This rich dessert is a welcome addition to dinner anytime of the year! Serve this decadent pie warm, with the Sweet Bourbon Whipped Cream or your favorite vanilla ice cream.

Pie Crust

1¼ cups all-purpose flour

2 teaspoons sugar

½ teaspoon salt

½ cup (1 stick) cold unsalted butter, cut into pieces

2 to 3 tablespoons ice water

Filling

2 cups (7 ounces) pecans

3 large eggs

¾ cup dark brown sugar

⅔ cup light corn syrup

1 teaspoon pure vanilla extract

2 tablespoons unsalted butter, melted

3 tablespoons bourbon

¼ teaspoon salt

¾ cup semisweet or bittersweet chocolate chips

Sweet Bourbon Whipped Cream (recipe follows), for garnish

1. To make the pie-crust dough, in a food processor fitted with the metal blade, pulse the flour with the sugar and salt. Add the cold butter and pulse until the mixture resembles coarse meal. Add the ice water, pulsing just until the dough begins to clump. Using your fingers, press the dough into a disk. Wrap in plastic and refrigerate for at least 30 minutes.
2. On a lightly floured surface, using a rolling pin, roll out the dough to a 12-inch round. Fit the dough into a 9-inch glass pie plate. Trim the overhang to ½ inch, fold the edge under itself, and crimp decoratively. Refrigerate for about 30 minutes, until firm.

3. Preheat oven to 375°F. To make the filling, on a rimmed baking sheet, toast the pecans for about 8 minutes, or until fragrant; cool slightly, coarsely chop, and set aside.

4. In a large bowl, whisk the eggs with the brown sugar, corn syrup, vanilla, melted butter, bourbon, and salt until blended. Stir in the pecans and chocolate chips until evenly distributed. Pour the filling into the pie shell.

5. Bake the pie on the bottom shelf of the oven for about 45 minutes, or until the center of the pie is set. Tent the crust with foil halfway through the baking time if the edges are browning too quickly. Transfer the pie to a rack and allow to cool, and serve warm, garnished with Sweet Bourbon Whipped Cream. The pie can be stored at room temperature for up to 1 day, and rewarmed at 325°F for 15 minutes.

Sweet Bourbon Whipped Cream

YIELDS ABOUT 2⅓ CUPS

1 cup heavy cream, chilled
3 tablespoons confectioners' sugar

3 tablespoons bourbon
¾ teaspoon pure vanilla extract

In the bowl of an electric mixer, pour the heavy cream and beat at medium speed until it becomes thick and frothy. Add the sugar and beat until stiff peaks form. Briefly beat in the bourbon and vanilla. Serve immediately.

Dan's Chocolate Chip Cookies

YIELDS 1½ DOZEN COOKIES

My husband, Dan, loves cookies, and I wanted to create a great-tasting cookie that the entire family could enjoy, so I used a few health-conscious substitutions: Spectrum-brand spread instead of butter; Splenda products instead of white and brown sugar; and an egg substitute instead of eggs. With semi-sweet chocolate chunks or chocolate chips, this cookie will definitely become a family favorite.

½ cup Spectrum Naturals Spread

½ cup Splenda Brown Sugar Blend, firmly packed

⅓ cup Splenda Granulated No Calorie Sweetener

½ teaspoon vanilla extract

¼ cup egg substitute, such as Egg Beaters

1¼ cups all-purpose flour

½ teaspoon baking soda

½ teaspoon salt

1 cup semisweet chocolate chunks or chocolate chips

1. Preheat oven to 350°F. Prepare two large baking sheets by lining with parchment paper or nonstick Silpat liners.
2. In a medium bowl, place the Spectrum spread, Splenda Brown Sugar Blend, Splenda Sweetener, vanilla, and egg substitute. Using a spatula, stir to combine the ingredients until the mixture is well blended and smooth. Add the flour, baking soda, and salt to the mixture; stir well to combine. Stir in the chocolate chunks.
3. Drop the cookie dough by rounded tablespoons onto the prepared baking sheets, spaced about 2 inches apart. Gently flatten the dough with the palm of your hand to about ½-inch thickness, or until each cookie is about 2½ inches round in diameter.
4. Bake for 12 to 15 minutes, or until golden brown. Remove pans from oven and let the cookies cool on the baking sheets for 5 minutes before transferring to wire racks. Cool cookies completely before storing in an airtight container.

Chocolate Chip Dessert Sliders

YIELDS 6 SERVINGS (3 SLIDERS PER SERVING)

1 recipe (1½ dozen) Dan's Chocolate Chip
    Cookies (see recipe on page 260)
Sugar-free coffee, vanilla, and chocolate
    ice cream or frozen yogurt
Raspberry sorbet

Chopped nuts such as pistachios
    or peanuts, or your favorite nuts,
    optional
Sugar-free shredded coconut, optional
Sugar-free cookie crumbs, optional

1. To assemble the Dessert Sliders, allow the ice cream, frozen yogurt, and/or sorbet to soften, then place a small scoop of desired flavor on the bottom (flat side) of one cookie. Make a sandwich by topping with a second cookie, flat side down.
2. Place the nuts, coconut, and cookie crumbs in separate shallow dishes if using. Roll the exposed ice cream along the edges of the slider in the nuts, coconut, or cookie crumbs, if desired. Serve immediately or freeze until serving.

Coconut-Pecan Cake

YIELDS 12 SERVINGS

My Coconut-Pecan Cake has been so popular with my family and friends that I had to include it again. It was the inspiration for my Coconut-Pecan Cupcakes (see recipe on page 264). With a snowy coating of shredded coconut, it looks perfect at the holidays, and I love the melt-in-your-mouth decadence of the coconut filling coupled with the light, airy texture of the cake. It's hard to wait until December for this cake!

Cake

Nonstick baking spray

3 cups cake flour, plus more for dusting
    pans

1 tablespoon baking powder

¼ teaspoon salt

1 cup (2 sticks) butter, softened

2 cups sugar

4 large eggs, at room temperature

2 large egg yolks

2 teaspoons pure vanilla extract

1¼ cups unsweetened coconut milk

Filling

1 large egg

⅓ cup granulated sugar

⅓ cup brown sugar

⅔ cup evaporated milk

6 tablespoons butter

¼ cup coconut-flavored rum

1 cup sweetened shredded coconut

1½ cups chopped toasted pecans

Frosting

1¼ cups light corn syrup
2 large egg whites
¼ teaspoon coconut extract

2 cups sweetened shredded coconut,
divided

1. Preheat oven to 350°F. To make the cake, coat three 9-inch round cake pans with nonstick baking spray, line the bottoms with waxed paper, and spray the paper. Dust the pans with flour, tapping out the excess. In a medium bowl, sift the flour, baking powder, and salt.
2. In a large bowl, using an electric mixer on medium speed, beat the butter until creamy. Gradually beat in the sugar. Beat for 2 minutes, until light and fluffy. Beat in the whole eggs, one at a time, until well blended. Beat in the yolks and vanilla.
3. With the mixer on low speed, alternately beat in the flour mixture and coconut milk, beginning and ending with the flour mixture, mixing until blended.
4. Divide the batter among the prepared pans, spreading evenly. Bake for 25 to 30 minutes, until a toothpick inserted in the center of the cakes comes out clean. Let the cakes cool in the pans for 10 minutes, then run a knife around the edges and turn the cakes out onto wire racks to cool completely.
5. To make the filling, in a medium saucepan, beat the egg with a fork. Add the granulated and brown sugar, evaporated milk, and butter, and stir well to combine. Cook over medium heat, stirring constantly, until the filling boils. Remove pan from heat and stir in the rum, coconut, and pecans. Transfer to a small bowl and let filling cool.
6. To make the frosting, in a small saucepan, bring the corn syrup to a boil.
7. In a large bowl, with the electric mixer on medium speed, beat the egg whites for about 4 to 5 minutes, until soft peaks form. With the mixer on high speed, gradually drizzle the hot corn syrup into the egg whites in a thin, steady stream. Beat for about 2 minutes, until stiff peaks form. Beat in the coconut extract. Gently fold in 1 cup of the coconut.
8. To assemble the cake, place one cake layer on a serving plate. Spread with half of the filling. Top with another cake layer and spread with the remaining filling. Top with the remaining cake layer. Spread the frosting completely over the sides and top of the cake. Sprinkle the entire surface with the remaining 1 cup of coconut, pressing gently so it sticks to the frosting.

Coconut-Pecan Cupcakes

I am always looking to come up with a twist on an old-fashioned favorite recipe, which inspired me to turn my moist, delicious Coconut-Pecan Cake (see recipe on page 262) into cupcakes with a surprise coconut-pecan filling that is sure to delight. Topped with a snowy frosting and more coconut, this dessert will make any celebration oh so much more special.

Cupcakes

3 cups cake flour
1 tablespoon baking powder
¼ teaspoon salt
¾ cup (1½ sticks) butter, softened

1½ cups sugar
3 large eggs, at room temperature
2 teaspoons pure vanilla extract
1¼ cups unsweetened coconut milk

Filling

1 large egg
⅓ cup sugar
⅔ cup evaporated milk

6 tablespoons butter, cut into pieces
1½ cups shredded coconut
1½ cups chopped toasted pecans

Frosting

1½ cups sugar
¼ teaspoon cream of tartar
½ cup water

2 cups sweetened, shredded coconut, divided
3 large egg whites, at room temperature
1 teaspoon pure vanilla extract

1. Preheat oven to 350°F. To make the cupcakes, line two 12-cup cupcake pans with paper cupcake liners. Take out the ingredients and bring to room temperature.
2. In a medium bowl, sift the cake flour, then whisk in the baking powder and salt.
3. In a large bowl, using an electric mixer on medium speed, beat the butter until creamy. Gradually beat in the sugar for 2 minutes, until the mixture is light and fluffy. Beat in the eggs, one at a time, until well blended. Beat in the vanilla.
4. With the mixer on low speed, alternately beat in the flour mixture and the coconut milk, beginning and ending with the flour mixture, mixing until blended.
5. To make the filling, in a medium saucepan, beat the egg with a fork. Add the sugar, evaporated milk, and butter. Cook over medium heat, stirring constantly, until the filling boils. Remove pan from the heat and stir in the coconut and pecans. Transfer the filling to a small bowl and let cool.
6. Fill each cupcake ¾ full with batter. Add 1 teaspoon of filling to each, then cover the filling with batter. Bake for 18 to 22 minutes, until a toothpick inserted in the center of the cakes comes out clean. Let the cupcakes cool for 10 minutes in the pan, then place onto wire racks to cool completely.
7. To make the frosting, in a small saucepan, whisk together the sugar, cream of tartar, and water until combined. Turn heat on high and allow the sugar to dissolve completely, stirring once as the mixture bubbles. Bring the mixture to a rolling boil, then remove from heat and set aside. Fold in 1 cup of the shredded coconut.
8. In a large bowl, with the electric mixer on medium speed, beat the egg whites and vanilla for about 5 to 6 minutes, until soft peaks form. (To check, stop the mixer and lift the beaters: the tips of the peaks should droop, but the peaks should be sturdy.) With the mixer on high speed, gradually drizzle the hot sugar mixture into the egg whites in a thin, steady stream. Beat for about 3 to 5 minutes, until stiff peaks form. (To check, stop the mixer and lift the beaters: the tips of the peaks should be stiff.)
9. Frost the cupcakes, and sprinkle the tops with the remaining 1 cup of shredded coconut.

Deep-Dish Apple Pie

Deep-Dish Apple Pie reminds me of my childhood. When I was young, these pies seemed huge, and the slices were so different from those of regular pies. Back then I loved warm apple pie with vanilla ice cream. This Deep-Dish Apple Pie is probably my new favorite. When I do indulge, I love the idea of the sugar glaze on the apple pie crust; I don't even need the ice cream!

2½ cups all-purpose flour

1 cup (2 sticks) cold butter, cut into large
    chunks

2 large egg yolks, plus enough ice water
    to make ½ cup of liquid

3 pounds (about 8 large) McIntosh or
    Jonathan apples, at room temperature

¾ cup granulated sugar

1 teaspoon cinnamon

Pinch of salt

1¼ cups crushed vanilla wafer cookies
    or graham cracker crumbs

1 cup confectioners' sugar

¼ cup whole milk

¼ teaspoon pure vanilla extract

1. To make the pie crust, in the bowl of a food processor fitted with the metal blade, pour the flour and add the butter. Pulse the mixture just until it resembles coarse crumbs. Add the egg yolk mixture and pulse just until the dough gathers into a ball. Remove the dough from the bowl and divide in half. (If making dough by hand, use a pastry blender or two knives to cut the butter into the flour until the butter is the size of small peas. Gradually drizzle in the egg yolk mixture, stirring with a fork, until the dough starts to come together into a ball.) Wrap each dough half in plastic wrap and refrigerate until well chilled, at least one hour or overnight. (Dough can be frozen until later use.)

2. Preheat oven to 375°F. Place a 9 x 13 x 2-inch ceramic or metal baking pan in the refrigerator to chill.

3. Meanwhile, to make the filling, peel, core, and thinly slice the apples into a large bowl. Add the sugar, cinnamon, and salt, and toss gently to combine.

4. On a lightly floured surface, using a rolling pin, roll out half of the dough into an 11 x 15-inch rectangle. Place the rolled dough into the prepared baking dish. Lightly ease the dough into the corners, and allow excess dough to hang over the edge. Sprinkle the bottom of the dough evenly with the crushed cookies or graham cracker crumbs. Add the apples.

5. Roll out the remaining piece of dough into an 11 x 15-inch rectangle. Cover the apples with the dough. Trim, crimp, and seal the edges of the top crust and bottom crust together.

6. Using a sharp knife, make three slits on top of the dough surface to allow steam to escape. Bake for 45 to 55 minutes, or until the crust is golden. Remove from oven and cool on a wire rack.

7. To make the glaze, in a small bowl, whisk the confectioners' sugar with the milk and vanilla until smooth and of drizzling consistency. Drizzle the icing over the surface of the pie. Use a pastry brush to spread the glaze to coat the entire top surface of the pie. Allow to stand for about 10 minutes, until icing forms. Serve warm or at room temperature.

Key Lime Crème Brûlée

The addition of Key lime juice from the tiny limes grown in the Florida Keys gives this crème brûlée a Southern flair. The bottled juice can be found year round at specialty markets and grocery stores. Always an impressive dessert, this custard topped with turbinado sugar (see Box) that's caramelized under a broiler or with a cooking torch aims to please!

2 large eggs
3 large egg yolks
½ cup granulated sugar
2 cups half-and-half

3 tablespoons bottled Key lime juice
1 tablespoon grated lime zest
⅓ cup turbinado sugar or brown sugar

1. Adjust two oven racks to accommodate two 13 x 9 x 2-inch baking pans. Preheat oven to 350°F. Place six ½-cup ramekins in each pan.
2. In a medium bowl, whisk the eggs and egg yolks together to combine. Add the granulated sugar and stir until the sugar is dissolved Add the half-and-half and Key lime juice and mix well to combine. Using a fine-mesh sieve, strain the mixture into a 4-cup measuring bowl. Stir in the lime zest. Pour the mixture into the ramekins. Pour hot water into each pan to reach about halfway up the sides of the ramekins.
3. Carefully place the pans in the oven and bake for 25 to 30 minutes, or until the mixture is set. Using a flat spatula to slide under each ramekin for control, carefully remove the ramekins from the water. Let cool on a wire rack for about 30 minutes.
4. Cover the ramekins by tenting with plastic wrap, making sure the plastic does not touch the surface of the crème brûlée, and refrigerate for at least 2 hours or overnight.
5. Just before serving, remove the number of ramekins you wish to serve from refrigerator. (Refrigerate the rest for use within 2 days.) Discard the plastic wrap, and sprinkle the top surface of each crème brûlée evenly with a generous teaspoon of the sugar. Use a cooking torch, following the manufacturer's instructions, until the sugar begins to brown and form a caramelized crust. Serve immediately, or if making in advance, refrigerate until ready to serve.

Turbinado Sugar

Turbinado sugar, also known as turbinated sugar, is a type of sugarcane extract. It is made by steaming, then crystallizing, unrefined raw sugar. Turbinado is similar in appearance to brown sugar, but is paler in color and has larger crystals. Generally, the two can be exchanged in recipes. A popular brand name is Sugar in the Raw, which is widely available in grocery stores.

Fat-Free Mango Ice Cream with Mango Sauce

YIELDS 12 SERVINGS

Here is a healthy homemade dessert using fat-free evaporated milk and yogurt as well as a sugar substitute. I've paired it with an easy-to-make Mango Sauce that can also be served with fish and poultry.

One 12-ounce can fat-free evaporated milk
⅔ cup Splenda Granulated No Calorie
    Sweetener
2 large egg yolks

One 16-ounce package frozen mango
3 cups cold fat-free plain yogurt
Mango Sauce (recipe follows), optional
    for serving

1. To make the custard, in a small saucepan, whisk together the evaporated milk, Splenda, and egg yolks. Heat over medium-low heat, stirring constantly, until the Splenda dissolves and the mixture thickens slightly. Do not allow to boil. Transfer the mixture to a large bowl, cover the surface of the custard with plastic wrap, and refrigerate until very cold.
2. In a food processor fitted with the metal blade, process the mango and yogurt until smooth. Pour the mixture into the cold custard and mix well to combine.
3. Freeze the mixture in an ice-cream maker according to the manufacturer's instructions. Store in the freezer. Let sit at room temperature for 10 minutes before scooping; serve with Mango Sauce if desired.

Low-Fat Mango Ice Cream

For a low-fat alternative to Fat-Free Mango Ice Cream, replace the ⅔ cup no calorie sweetener with ⅓ cup Splenda Sugar Blend (half Splenda, half sugar), and use low-fat vanilla yogurt instead of fat-free plain yogurt.

Mango Sauce

2 ripe mangos, peeled and diced
3 tablespoons Splenda Brown Sugar Blend
    or agave nectar, or to taste (see Note)

1 teaspoon vanilla or rum extract
1 teaspoon orange juice

1. In a blender, place the diced mango and cover tightly. Blend on high until smooth.
2. In a small microwavable bowl, stir together the Splenda Brown Sugar Blend, vanilla or rum extract, and orange juice. Microwave on medium for 25 to 30 seconds, then allow the mixture to come to room temperature before stirring into the mango purée. Place the Mango Sauce in a tightly covered container and refrigerate until serving.

Note: Depending on the ripeness or sweetness of the mango, you may want to add more or less Splenda or agave nectar to sweeten to taste. Agave nectar is a natural liquid sweetener made from the extract of the wild agave plant; it is similar to honey but low in glucose.

Orange Meringue Pie

1 teaspoon butter
2 tablespoons Cointreau or Triple Sec
2 tablespoons orange zest
2 tablespoons lemon juice
1¼ cups sugar, divided
¼ cup cornstarch
¼ teaspoon salt
¾ cup cold whole milk

¾ cup evaporated milk, at room temperature
4 eggs, separated
1 Graham Cracker Pie Crust (recipe follows)
¼ teaspoon cream of tartar
½ teaspoon vanilla extract, optional

1. Preheat oven to 350°F. In a small bowl, combine the butter, Cointreau or Triple Sec, orange zest, and lemon juice. Set aside.
2. To make the filling, in a medium saucepan, whisk 1 cup of the sugar with the cornstarch and salt. Add the whole milk and evaporated milk, whisking well to incorporate. Whisk in the egg yolks. Cook, stirring constantly, over medium heat for 5 minutes, or until the mixture thickens and begins to boil. Boil for 1 minute. Remove pan from heat and pour the hot mixture into the bowl with the butter-Cointreau mixture. Stir to combine. Pour the filling directly into the Graham Cracker Pie Crust and set aside.
3. To make the meringue, in a large bowl, use an electric mixer to beat the egg whites until foamy. Add the cream of tartar and continue to beat for about 4 to 5 minutes, until stiff peaks form. Gradually add the remaining ¼ cup sugar and continue beating until glossy and stiff. Add the vanilla extract, if desired.
4. Spoon the meringue onto the top of the pie. Using a spatula, spread the meringue to the crust edge to seal in the filling. Create decorative swirls on top of the meringue with the spatula.
5. Bake the pie for 15 minutes, or until the meringue is a delicate brown. Let cool to room temperature before serving.

Graham Cracker Pie Crust

YIELDS ONE 9-INCH PIE CRUST

This is a quick and easy pie crust. It was created for the Orange Meringue Pie (recipe above), though this recipe is a good basic graham cracker pie crust for many pies. If you like ice cream pies, fill this pie crust with Fat-Free Mango Ice Cream (see recipe on page 270) and serve with or without a drizzle of the Mango Sauce.

14 graham crackers
½ cup almond flour
2 tablespoons sugar

½ teaspoon nutmeg
4 tablespoons (½ stick) unsalted butter, melted

1. Preheat oven to 350°F. Place the graham crackers in a plastic resealable bag and tightly seal. Using a rolling pin, crush the crackers into fine crumbs.
2. In a medium bowl, pour the crumbs and add the almond flour, sugar, and nutmeg. Mix together with a fork. Stir in the melted butter and mix until incorporated.
3. Using the back of a spoon, press the mixture evenly into an ungreased 9 x 1½-inch pie pan. Bake for 5 minutes and let cool to room temperature before filling.

Pumpkin-Pecan Cake with Caramel–Cream Cheese Frosting

YIELDS 12 SERVINGS

This is a wonderful autumnal cake for Thanksgiving, or any special occasion! This multilevel pumpkin torte is full of spices, and the Caramel–Cream Cheese Frosting complements the pecans. The secret to successfully creating this four-layer cake is baking the layers in individual baking pans.

Nonstick baking spray
2 cups sugar
¾ cup canola oil
4 large eggs
One 15-ounce can pumpkin
2 cups all-purpose flour
2 teaspoons baking soda
2 teaspoons baking powder
½ teaspoon salt
2 teaspoons ground cinnamon

1 teaspoon ground allspice
1 teaspoon ground ginger
1 teaspoon ground mace
½ teaspoon ground cloves
½ cup baking raisins (see Note), optional
1 cup coarsely chopped pecans
Caramel–Cream Cheese Frosting (recipe
  follows)
¼ cup caramel sauce
1 cup finely chopped pecans, for garnish

1. If your oven is not large enough to fit four pans on one rack, adjust the two racks to the center of the oven. Preheat oven to 350°F.
2. Prepare four 8- or 9-inch metal cake pans, or four 8½-inch disposable aluminum cake pans, by spraying with nonstick baking spray.
3. In a large bowl, place the sugar, canola oil, and eggs, and beat with an electric mixer on medium speed for 10 minutes. Add the pumpkin and beat for 1 more minute, or until the mixture is combined.
4. In a large bowl, sift the flour, baking soda, baking powder, salt, cinnamon, allspice, ginger, mace, and cloves together. Gradually add the flour mixture to the pumpkin mixture, stirring together on low speed to combine. Beat the batter on high speed for 1 minute.
5. Using a spatula, fold in the raisins, if desired, and the pecans. Evenly divide and spread the batter into the four prepared baking pans.
6. Place the cakes in the oven and bake about 20 to 25 minutes, until the cakes spring back when lightly pressed with your finger or a toothpick comes out clean. Let the cakes cool on wire racks

for 20 minutes, then remove the cakes from the pans. (The cakes can be baked a day in advance. Wrap cakes in plastic wrap and refrigerate overnight before frosting.)

7. To assemble the cake, if necessary, cut the tops of the cake layers carefully with a serrated knife to even the surfaces. Place one layer of cake on a serving plate.

8. Spread a layer of Caramel–Cream Cheese Frosting on top of the first layer of cake, drizzle a tablespoon of the caramel sauce on top of the frosting, place another cake layer on top, and repeat the process for layers two and three.

9. Add the fourth layer to the top of the cake (do not frost), and immediately place the cake in the refrigerator for 30 minutes to help stabilize the layers for final frosting.

10. Remove the cake from the refrigerator, and frost the top and sides with the remaining frosting. Gently press the finely chopped pecans into the sides of the cake. Using a fork or a squeeze bottle, garnish the top surface of the cake by decoratively drizzling the remaining caramel sauce across the top. Store the cake in the refrigerator until serving.

Note: Specialty baking raisins are moister than regular raisins, so they remain soft and tender after baking. They can be found in the baking aisle of the grocery store.

Caramel–Cream Cheese Frosting

YIELDS ENOUGH TO FROST ONE 4-LAYER CAKE

Two 8-ounce packages cream cheese, at
   room temperature
1 cup (2 sticks) unsalted butter, at room
   temperature

¼ cup caramel sauce
4 cups confectioners' sugar, sifted

1. In a large bowl, place the cream cheese and butter. Using an electric mixer on medium speed, mix until combined. Scrape down the bowl. Add the caramel sauce and mix on low speed until combined.

2. Add the confectioners' sugar 1 cup at a time, mixing on low speed until each cup is combined. Scrape down the bowl and beat the mixture on medium speed for 5 minutes, or until creamy. Use immediately to frost Pumpkin-Pecan Cake.

Pumpkin Spice Mousse

YIELDS 6 SERVINGS

This is an easy dessert that can be prepared in advance. Spoon or pipe mousse into champagne flutes, goblets, mini-pumpkins, or chocolate cups that can be assembled in advance. Be creative: garnish with whipped cream, crumbled cookies, shaved chocolate, or candies.

1 teaspoon unflavored gelatin
1 tablespoon cold water
3 large egg yolks
1 cup sugar
1 cup canned pumpkin
1 teaspoon ground cinnamon
¾ teaspoon ground ginger
¼ teaspoon ground cloves
1½ cups heavy cream

1 teaspoon pure vanilla extract
⅓ cup finely chopped crystallized ginger, optional for garnish
Pumpkin pie spice, optional for garnish
Sweetened whipped cream, optional for garnish
Crumbled ginger cookies, optional for garnish

1. In a 2-quart glass bowl, sprinkle the gelatin over the cold water to soften. Whisk in the egg yolks and sugar, and set the bowl over a heavy 4-quart saucepan filled halfway with simmering water.
2. Cook the mixture, whisking constantly, until an instant-read thermometer inserted 2 inches into the mixture registers 160°F.
3. Carefully remove the hot bowl from the pan and beat the egg mixture for about 5 minutes, until it cools slightly. Beat in the pumpkin, cinnamon, ginger, and cloves.
4. Cover the pumpkin mixture with plastic wrap and refrigerate for about 45 minutes, until thickened and cooled.
5. In a medium bowl, using an electric mixer at medium speed, beat the heavy cream with the vanilla for about 4 to 5 minutes, until it just holds stiff peaks. Gently fold the whipped cream into the pumpkin mixture.
6. Spoon or pipe the mousse into ½-cup serving dishes, such as champagne flutes, martini glasses, jelly jars, pedestal goblets, or even fresh mini-pumpkins when in season. Cover tightly with plastic wrap and refrigerate for at least 3 hours, or overnight. (The dishes can be prepared a day ahead and refrigerated up to 2 days before serving.) Serve garnished if desired with the crystallized ginger, a sprinkle of pumpkin pie spice, a dollop of whipped cream, or crumbled ginger cookies.

Red Velvet Cake

Red Velvet Cake is such a Southern classic, I had to include it! The sign of a true red velvet cake is the deep red color that gives the cake its name. In original red velvet cakes, the reaction of the cocoa powder to the acids in buttermilk and vinegar created the red-brown hue. Today, to achieve the stunning deep red color, food coloring is used, which offset by the rich white frosting makes a gorgeous holiday or picnic centerpiece!

Vegetable oil or nonstick baking spray
2 cups cake flour, plus more for coating
    pans
3 tablespoons unsweetened cocoa powder
2 teaspoons baking powder
1 teaspoon salt
¾ cup (1½ sticks) butter, softened

1¾ cups sugar
4 large eggs
1 cup whole milk
3 teaspoons red food coloring
1 teaspoon vanilla extract
Buttercream Frosting (recipe follows)

1. Preheat oven to 350°F. Using vegetable oil or nonstick baking spray, coat two 9-inch cake pans. Dust each pan lightly with flour and shake out excess.
2. In a large bowl, mix together the flour, cocoa, baking powder, and salt.
3. In another large bowl, cream together the butter and sugar until light and fluffy. Beat in the eggs one at a time.
4. In a small bowl, combine the milk, food coloring, and vanilla.
5. Using a spatula, alternate folding the flour mixture and the milk mixture into the butter mixture, ending with the dry ingredients. Pour the batter into the prepared pans and bake for 30 to 35 minutes, or until a toothpick comes out clean. Let the cakes cool in the pans for 5 minutes before turning out onto wire racks to cool completely.
6. When the cakes are completely cool, place one layer on a serving plate. Frost the top of the layer with Buttercream Frosting. Place the remaining cake layer on top and frost the sides and top of the cake.

Buttercream Frosting

6 cups confectioners' sugar
1 cup (2 sticks) butter, softened

4 to 6 tablespoons heavy cream
2 teaspoons pure vanilla extract

In a large bowl, mix all the ingredients until light and fluffy. Use immediately to frost the Red Velvet Cake.

Red Velvet Cake Roll with Peanut Butter Frosting

YIELDS 10 SERVINGS

Here is a fun Southern twist on the traditional red velvet cake that children and grownups will both enjoy. The good news, no butter is needed in this cake roll recipe. It's all about the Peanut Butter Frosting and a garnish of chopped peanuts with a drizzle of melted chocolate.

Nonstick baking spray
¾ cup all-purpose flour
1 teaspoon baking powder
2 tablespoons unsweetened cocoa powder
¼ teaspoon salt
5 large eggs, at room temperature
¾ cup sugar

½ teaspoon pure vanilla extract
2 teaspoons red food coloring
Peanut Butter Frosting (recipe follows)
½ cup chopped peanuts, for garnish
½ cup (2 ounces) dark chocolate, melted,
　　for garnish

1. Preheat oven to 350°F. Prepare an 18 x 13 x 1-inch rimmed baking sheet by spraying with nonstick baking spray. Line the pan with a sheet of parchment paper.
2. In a medium bowl, sift the flour, baking powder, cocoa powder, and salt, and set aside.
3. In a large bowl, beat the eggs with an electric mixer on low speed for about 1 to 3 minutes, until bubbles form around the edge and the mixture becomes foamy. Increase the speed to medium and slowly add the sugar in a steady stream. Increase the speed to high and continue to beat for about 5 to 10 minutes, until the eggs are very thick and pale yellow. Using a rubber spatula, scrape down the sides of the bowl. Reduce the speed to low, add the vanilla and red food coloring, and mix until combined.
4. Gently fold the flour mixture into the egg mixture with the rubber spatula until all of the flour is thoroughly combined. Pour the batter into the prepared cake pan. Spread the batter to the edges of the pan in an even thickness.
5. Bake the cake for 10 to 15 minutes, or until it feels firm and springs back when touched with your fingertip.
6. Remove the cake from oven and run a knife around the edges to loosen, then carefully invert the cake onto a large sheet of parchment paper (cut slightly larger than the size of the baking pan). The bottom of the cake should now be right-side-up. Slowly peel off the parchment paper that is

attached to the cake. Starting at a short end, gently roll the cake and the large parchment sheet up together into a tight log. Let the cake cool seam-side-down for 15 minutes.

7. Carefully unroll the cooled cake. Spread about 1½ cups of Peanut Butter Frosting over the surface of the cake, leaving about a 1-inch border at the edges. Reroll the cake carefully but tightly around the frosting, leaving the parchment paper behind. Using a serrated knife, carefully trim about 1 inch from both ends of the cake, and frost or pipe the entire cake roll with the remaining frosting. Garnish the ends of the roll with chopped peanuts, and sprinkle a few on the top. Drizzle the melted chocolate over the roll.

Peanut Butter Frosting

YIELDS ENOUGH TO FROST 1 CAKE ROLL

½ cup (1 stick) unsalted butter, at room temperature
1¾ cups smooth or chunky peanut butter

3 cups confectioners' sugar, sifted
½ cup heavy cream
1 teaspoon pure vanilla extract

1. In a large bowl, beat the butter and peanut butter with an electric mixer on medium-high speed until blended.
2. Alternately add confectioners' sugar and heavy cream to the butter mixture and beat on medium-high speed until the mixture is smooth, or to spreading consistency. Add the vanilla, mix to combine, and use to frost the Red Velvet Cake Roll.

Strawberry Rhubarb Pie

I grew up with my mom picking and cooking fresh rhubarb. She made rhubarb apple sauce and rhubarb pies, and I think she would be very happy with my Strawberry Rhubarb Pie! I like to serve this classic combination with a scoop of vanilla ice cream or fat-free vanilla frozen yogurt.

1 cup plus 2 teaspoons sugar
⅓ cup flour
¼ teaspoon salt
½ teaspoon ground cinnamon
3 cups sliced rhubarb
2 cups hulled strawberries, halved and
    quartered if large

2 teaspoons freshly squeezed lemon juice
1 teaspoon pure vanilla extract
1 Double Pie Crust (recipe follows)
2 tablespoons unsalted butter, cut into bits
1 tablespoon milk

1. Preheat oven to 425°F. Position an oven rack in the lower third of the oven.
2. In a small bowl, mix together 1 cup of the sugar, the flour, salt, and cinnamon.
3. In a large bowl, mix the sliced rhubarb and strawberries, and sprinkle with the lemon juice and vanilla. Add the sugar mixture to the fruit and toss gently until the fruit is well coated with the sugar. Set aside for about 10 minutes, until the fruit softens slightly.
4. Place one pie crust into the bottom of a 9-inch pie dish. Spoon the rhubarb mixture into the pie crust and distribute the butter over the fruit. Cover with the top crust and trim the overhanging dough to ¾ inch all the way around. Turn the edges under so they're flush with the rim of the pie dish, and crimp or flute to seal. Use a sharp knife to cut several steam vents into the top crust. (Alternatively, cut the top crust into 1-inch strips and weave a lattice crust, crimping the edges to the bottom crust.) Brush the top crust with the milk and sprinkle with the remaining 2 teaspoons of sugar.
5. Bake the pie for 30 minutes. Reduce oven temperature to 350°F and bake for 25 to 30 minutes, until the crust is a rich golden brown, the fruit is tender, and juices bubble through the vents. Let cool on a wire rack for at least 1 hour before serving.

Double Pie Crust

YIELDS I DOUBLE CRUST FOR ONE 9-INCH PIE

2¼ cups pastry flour
¼ teaspoon salt
¼ teaspoon baking powder

14 tablespoons (1¾ sticks) cold butter,
    cut into pieces and refrigerated
    for 30 minutes
5 to 7 tablespoons ice water
1 tablespoon cider vinegar

1. In a food processor fitted with the metal blade, place the flour, salt, and baking powder. Pulse to combine. Add the butter little by little, pulsing until the mixture resembles coarse meal.

2. Add 5 tablespoons water and the vinegar to the processor and pulse just until the dough comes together and rolls up off the sides of the food processor. (If the dough is not coming together, add 1 to 2 more tablespoons water, one at a time, just until dough combines.) Do not overmix, or the crust will be tough.

3. Divide the dough into 2 equal parts, forming each into a flattened disk. Wrap tightly in plastic wrap and refrigerate for at least 45 minutes, or preferably overnight.

4. Roll out the dough into two 9-inch rounds. Place one round into a pie pan, and reserve the other for the top of the pie once filled.

Sweet Potato Pie with Brown Sugar Pecan Topping

YIELDS 8 SERVINGS

This pie has a spicy vanilla flavor and is made with a butter pie crust that requires a 9-inch deep pie pan. The combination of the butter crust, sweet potato filling, and brown sugar pecan topping is a winner. Due to the deep-dish nature, I prefer to allow the pie to cool before serving.

6 medium (about 3 pounds) sweet
    potatoes
Nonstick cooking spray
1 Butter Pie Dough crust (recipe follows)
¾ cup heavy cream
2 large eggs
½ cup light brown sugar, packed
¼ cup granulated sugar

1 tablespoon pure vanilla extract
1 teaspoon ground cinnamon
½ teaspoon allspice
6 tablespoons butter, melted
¾ cup brown sugar
½ cup all-purpose flour
1 cup chopped pecans
½ teaspoon salt

1. Preheat oven to 350°F. Position a rack in the lower third of the oven.
2. Wash and dry the sweet potatoes. Spray a baking sheet with nonstick cooking spray. Place the sweet potatoes on the baking sheet and bake for 1½ hours, or until soft when pierced with a fork and some juices are starting to run. Remove the sweet potatoes from the oven and allow to cool. (Turn off the oven if you are letting the potatoes cool completely before proceeding.)
3. Meanwhile, roll the Butter Pie Dough into a 12-inch circle and place in a glass pie plate. Trim excess dough, leaving 1 inch overhanging the edge of the pie plate. Fold the dough under to form a high rim. Flute the edges as desired. Refrigerate the crust while the filling is prepared.
4. Preheat oven to 375°F. Using a pot holder if necessary to hold the potatoes, cut an opening in the top of each potato and squeeze the potato pulp into a food processor fitted with the metal blade. Process to mash the potatoes until they are smooth and cooled, scraping down the sides of the bowl at least once.
5. Add the heavy cream and process again until well blended. Add the eggs, light brown sugar, granulated sugar, vanilla, cinnamon, and allspice. Process the filling until well blended and smooth.
6. Pour the filling into the refrigerated pie shell and bake for 30 minutes.
7. Meanwhile, make the topping. In a small bowl, mix together the melted butter, ¾ cup brown sugar, flour, chopped pecans, and salt. Set aside.

8. After the pie has baked for 30 minutes, quickly remove it from the oven and close the oven door. Sprinkle the topping evenly over the surface of the pie. Return the pie to the oven and bake for 20 more minutes.

9. Reduce heat to 350°F and bake the pie for about 10 to 15 minutes more, or until the topping is bubbly and the crust is golden brown. Serve warm if desired, but the deep slices cut better if allowed to cool before serving.

Butter Pie Dough

YIELDS TWO 9-INCH PIE CRUSTS

This pastry recipe can easily be halved for one pie crust. And I always think it's a good idea to prepare the dough at least two days in advance. One more thing checked off the to-do list!

2½ cups all-purpose flour
1 teaspoon salt

1 cup (2 sticks) cold unsalted butter, thinly sliced
½ cup ice water

1. In a large bowl, whisk together the flour and salt. Add the butter slices and toss with the flour to separate the slices.

2. Using a pastry blender or two knives, cut the butter into the flour until the butter is the size of small peas.

3. Gradually drizzle in the ice water, stirring with a fork, until the dough starts to come together into a ball. Divide the dough in half and wrap each half in plastic wrap. Refrigerate for at least 30 minutes before rolling on a lightly floured countertop.

Walnut Molasses Tart

YIELDS 8 SERVINGS

This is a rich, sweet tart full of walnuts and molasses. It's what I call a real special-occasion dessert, with its rich crust and filling. A thin slice goes a long way! I must admit this tart was a crowd pleaser—a bit decadent, but definitely a new classic.

Crust

⅓ cup ground walnuts
1¼ cups cake flour
¼ cup sugar
½ teaspoon nutmeg
Pinch of salt

6 tablespoons butter, chilled and cut into pieces
1 tablespoon ice water
½ teaspoon vanilla
Nonstick cooking spray

Filling

4½ tablespoons molasses
3½ tablespoons light corn syrup
¾ cup light brown sugar, packed
½ teaspoon salt
¼ cup butter

2 egg yolks
1 teaspoon vanilla
1½ cups chopped walnuts
1½ cups walnut halves

1. Preheat oven to 350°F. To make the crust, in the bowl of a food processor fitted with the metal blade, place the walnuts, flour, sugar, nutmeg, and salt, and briefly pulse to mix them together. Add the butter, ice water, and vanilla, and pulse just until a ball of dough forms.
2. Spray a 10-inch removable-bottom fluted tart pan with nonstick cooking spray. Spread the dough evenly along the bottom and up the sides of the pan. Cover and refrigerate the crust for about 1 hour, until firm (or freeze crust briefly).

3. Bake the crust for 15 minutes, or until very lightly browned and just set. Remove the crust from the oven and let cool for about 5 minutes. Keep oven on.
4. To make the filling, in a small saucepan, combine the molasses, corn syrup, sugar, salt, and butter. Cook over medium heat, stirring often, until the butter is melted and the mixture begins to simmer. Remove pan from heat and allow the filling to cool briefly. Quickly whisk in the egg yolks and vanilla. Stir in the chopped walnuts.
5. Pour the filling into the prepared cooled crust. Arrange the walnut halves on top of the filling.
6. Bake the tart on a sheet of aluminum foil for about 25 minutes, until the crust is nicely browned. Remove from oven and allow to cool on a wire rack before serving.

Chapter 12

Beverages

As an owner of restaurants and one who's had a glass of wine or two and enjoys cocktails, no way could my cookbook not include recipes for beverages, both alcoholic and non-alcoholic.

My parents weren't drinkers. My father was diabetic, and my mother preferred candy to cocktails. We didn't keep a bar in our home, but my Uncle Jessie had one at his house. He made it by converting an old television cabinet into a bar. When he opened the doors, the bar would light up. My Uncle Jessie was as cool and sophisticated as his bar.

The only thing that came close to alcohol in our home was the wine made from our grape arbors. We had green and purple grapes, and my parents called the wine the purple grapes yielded "grape wine." This was shared with family and friends when they came to visit or for special occasions.

Even when I started traveling with the Ebony Fashion Fair, I wasn't interested in cocktails. That took a while. Food was my passion. It was when I discovered brunch in New York that I started to have "something" with my meal, and it was always a Mimosa.

When my modeling career took off, invitations for parties flooded in no matter where I was—Paris, Milan, or Vienna. It was so exciting! Champagne and cocktails were the preferred beverages at these gatherings, and I enjoyed them. I learned that while drinks are an important factor at a party, it's not a party without food. And since food was an important part of my life, I started dreaming about owning my own restaurant where I could bring food, drink, and great music together, ensuring a good time for all.

The restaurant business has been a big part of my life. I learned the ropes in a huge downtown restaurant where I worked evenings and weekends for a year and a half. I worked the front of the house, the back, and even the coat check. By the end of my training, I had a clear idea of the kind of restaurant I wanted to have. I'd envisioned the look and the feel of the restaurant and kept notes and pictures in a folder—my folder of dreams. I knew I wanted to create an exciting bar that would be a part of the restaurant but have its own distinct space, with its own compatible atmosphere with the main dining room. I designed a polished aluminum bar that could be seen gleaming from large picture windows. The bar's terrazzo floor sparkled like a jewel when light hit it at various times of the day.

I didn't just open my first restaurant on Forty-seventh Street and Eighth Avenue in Manhattan's theater district; I produced it, directed it, and paid special attention to casting it. I looked for beauty, brains, and personality—a must in the business. One of my best friends, Steve Bagby, was a Ford model. In between assignments, he sharpened his bartending skills. I talked him into becoming my head bartender and promised that he'd be able to continue his modeling career. Steve was a hit; he was warm, friendly, and terribly handsome. We became family and we still are to this day, even though he lives in California. Steve and I never run out of fond memories when we see each other once or twice a year.

A few years after my first restaurant opened, I started dating Dan, and one of our first trips together was to New Orleans. After a night out on the town, the Funky Butt being the last stop, naturally the next morning we headed to Café Du Monde. We needed a hit of their wonderful chicory coffee. Chicory, the root of the endive plant, was used by the French as an addition to coffee that was scarce during their own civil war. It gave coffee an added rich flavor and full body, and at Café Du Monde it pairs well with their famous beignets. Food with the right beverage is a great way to start the day.

No matter how plain or fancy a meal, beverages, alcoholic or non-alcoholic, are a must. In my last book, *Rituals & Celebrations*, I featured a "Bid Whist Card Party for Eight." The theme was based around a basic brown bar with beautiful decanters full of bourbon, brandy, cognac, rum, and Scotch whiskey, and of course, non-alcoholic mixers, fruit garnishes, and plenty of ice.

One of my favorite movies is *Cat on a Hot Tin Roof*. I was too young to understand all of the nuances when I saw it for the first time, but I didn't care. Elizabeth Taylor was so glamorous and beautiful, and no one was more handsome than Paul Newman. When an all–African American cast of *Cat on a Hot Tin Roof* opened on Broadway in 2008, I was ecstatic. B. Smith's is now located on Forty-sixth Street's Restaurant Row, and my staff has been showing off their creativity ever since we moved there. They're always coming up with drinks based on currently playing shows. When *Cat* opened, they had a ball. They created The Big Daddy cocktail, Big Mama's Mango Mojito, the Maggie the Cat Martini, The Dixie Star, and The No-Necked Monster, a non-alcoholic drink for kids who came to the restaurant.

One night some of the cast members were in the restaurant, and I sat there and watched everyone having a good time. A movie from long ago had turned into something close and special to me.

In this chapter, I've included sweet and savory cocktails as well as punches. There's nothing like good party punches, such as Mango Pear Tea Punch or Wild Sweet Orange Tea Punch. There's always a place for good iced tea. I've included a recipe for Georgia Peach Iced Tea; it's a really refreshing thirst quencher. And who says sangria always has to be red? White Sangria holds its own with rich, fruity flavor, as does fresh Strawberry Sangria with Rose Geranium. Try the refreshing Cucumber and Green Tea Martini with fresh ginger. In our garden on Long Island, we grow cucumbers and mint. There is nothing I love more than the taste and scent of fresh mint. Wait, that's not true . . . there's nothing I love more than fresh mint in a nice, tall Mint Julep.

Cheers, everyone!

Hot Tin Roof Cocktails

Cat on a Hot Tin Roof is one of those classic Southern plays by Tennessee Williams, and when it came back to Broadway in 2008 with an all–African American production directed by Debbie Allen, my restaurant couldn't wait to get creative and put together drink specials and menu features. Film star Terrence Howard made his Broadway debut as Brick, alongside stage veterans James Earl Jones (Big Daddy), Phylicia Rashad (Big Mama), Anika Noni Rose (Maggie), and Lisa Arrindell Anderson (Mae), who was my first assistant at B. Smith's restaurant—I know how to hire talent! They all truly made this a spectacular production of such a classic. These cocktails were inspired by their amazing performances.

Maggie the Cat Martini

YIELDS 1 SERVING

This orange and ginger martini is almost as feisty as Maggie herself.

2 ounces vodka

1½ ounces Triple Sec

2 ounces orange ginger mix (see Note)

1 maraschino cherry, for garnish

1. Fill a martini glass with ice and water, and let stand for about a minute to chill the glass.
2. Fill a cocktail shaker to about one-third with ice, pour in the vodka, Triple Sec, and orange ginger mix, and cover and shake vigorously.
3. Pour the ice and water out of the martini glass. Using a cocktail strainer, pour the liquid into the chilled glass. Garnish with a maraschino cherry.

   Note: To make the orange ginger mix, use 2 parts orange juice to 1 part sour mix, and add Monin ginger syrup to taste.

The Big Daddy

YIELDS 1 SERVING

Inspired by my beloved husband, Dan Gasby, the patriarch of B. Smith's restaurants, this drink features vodka, Cruzan coconut rum, and cranberry juice in a "big boy" glass. This is a BIG DRINK, so be ready!

1½ ounces vodka
1½ ounces Cruzan Coconut Rum

Cranberry juice

Fill a 12-ounce soda glass with ice. Add the vodka and the coconut rum. Fill to the top with cranberry juice.

Big Mama's Mango Mojito

YIELDS 1 SERVING

Big Mama always stood by her man. We hope that you'll love this drink as much as she did him.

4 mint leaves, plus 1 sprig for garnish
1 teaspoon sugar
2 lime wedges
2 ounces Cruzan Mango Rum

Splash of orange juice
Soda water
Sprite

1. In a mixing glass, muddle (lightly crush and stir) the mint, sugar, and 1 lime wedge. Add the rum and orange juice, and top off with equal amounts of soda water and Sprite.
2. Fill a rocks glass with ice and strain the liquid over the ice. Garnish with the remaining lime wedge and mint sprig.

The Dixie Star

YIELDS I SERVING

This drink's name is a tribute to Brick and Skipper's team. The Dixie Star features Absolut Raspberri, Raspberry Pucker, peach nectar, and a kick of Sprite.

1 ounce Absolut Raspberri Vodka
½ ounce Raspberry Pucker
½ ounce Triple Sec

Peach nectar
Splash of Sprite
1 lemon wedge, for garnish

1. Fill a 12-ounce glass with ice and add the vodka, Raspberry Pucker, and Triple Sec.
2. Fill the glass almost to the top with peach nectar, and top with the Sprite. Garnish with the lemon.

The No-Necked Monster

YIELDS I SERVING

Maggie may not have been fond of Mae and Gooper's children, but lots of folks are fond of this non-alcoholic cherry lemonade!

1 ounce fresh lemon juice
½ ounce grenadine

Soda water
Maraschino cherries, for garnish

1. Fill a 12-ounce glass with ice and add the lemon juice and grenadine.
2. Add soda water to fill, stir, and garnish with maraschino cherries.

Cajun Mary

This is one of my favorite savory spiced mixed drinks. The Old Bay Seasoning on the lip of the glass gives it a nice, spicy kick, while the blue cheese–stuffed olives add a nice twang. Alternatively, try garnishing it with cherry tomatoes or with Spicy Baby Okra and Olives. I must say, they are pretty tasty with the Cajun Mary. Tennessee Williams would surely approve!

Old Bay Seasoning
1 lime wedge
2½ ounces Absolut Mango or Peppar
    Vodka
Bloody Mary mix (homemade or store-
    bought)

3 blue cheese–stuffed olives, Spicy Baby
    Okra and Olives (see recipe on page
    38), or cherry tomatoes,
    for garnish

1. Sprinkle the Old Bay Seasoning onto a small saucer. Wet the lip of a 12-ounce glass with the lime wedge, and dip the wet rim into the Old Bay.
2. Fill a separate 12-ounce glass with ice and pour in the Absolut Mango or Peppar Vodka. Fill the glass with Bloody Mary mix and stir thoroughly. Carefully pour the entire drink into the rimmed glass, leaving the Old Bay intact.
3. For a garnish, thread a toothpick or skewer with the stuffed olives, Spicy Baby Okra and Olives, or cherry tomatoes.

Sweet Libations

Southerners have a sweet spot for cool, refreshing cocktails, and this group of drinks aims to please. Whether they're smooth and fruity or have a candy-flavored kick, these delicious libations will give anyone with a sweet tooth cause to swoon.

Orange Cherry Drop

This drink is as refreshing as its name! Triple Sec is an orange-flavored liqueur; paired with vodka and sweet cherries, it reminds me of an adult Shirley Temple.

2½ ounces vodka
1 ounce Triple Sec
Simple syrup, to taste (see Box)

2 or 3 maraschino cherries, plus 1 cherry
for garnish
Splash of soda water

1. Fill a martini glass with ice and water and let stand for about 1 minute.
2. Fill a cocktail shaker to about one-third of the way with ice. Pour in the vodka, Triple Sec, and simple syrup. Add 2 or 3 cherries, squeezing them to release some of their juice; cover the shaker and shake vigorously.
3. Pour the ice water out of the martini glass. Using a cocktail strainer, pour the cocktail into the chilled glass. Garnish with a cherry.

Making Simple Syrup

Simple syrup is a mixture of sugar and water that's heated so the sugar crystals dissolve. To make simple syrup, in a small saucepan, combine 2 parts sugar to 1 part water. Bring to a boil, stirring often, until sugar is dissolved. Remove the pan from heat, and allow the syrup to cool completely before using. Store in a bottle in the refrigerator for up to 2 weeks.

Lime Rickey

If you love the taste of lime, this is a quick and easy drink. This recipe is prepared with vodka, though you could also use gin or tequila.

1 lime, divided
1½ ounces vodka

½ ounce simple syrup
Soda water

1. Cut the lime in half, reserve half and cut the other into wedges.
2. Fill a 12-ounce glass with ice and pour in the vodka and simple syrup. Add the juice of the reserved ½ lime, fill with soda water, and garnish with a lime wedge (save the remaining lime wedges for another use).

Almond Joy

Amaretto is an almond-flavored liqueur; here it is mixed with white crème de cacao, which is vanilla bean based, and dark crème de cacao, which adds a chocolate flavor. Shake it up with half-and-half and you truly have what I call an Almond Joy!

1 ounce amaretto
½ ounce white crème de cacao
½ ounce dark crème de cacao

5 ounces cold half-and-half
Shaved chocolate, for garnish

1. Fill a cocktail shaker to about one-third of the way with ice. Pour in the amaretto, white crème de cacao, dark crème de cacao, and half-and-half. Cover and shake well.
2. Pour into an 8-ounce glass, and garnish with shaved chocolate.

Peppermint Pattie

YIELDS I SERVING

This is a liquid version of that peppermint-pattie candy that we all grew up with. It's full of flavor, with vanilla vodka, dark crème de cacao, a splash of Bailey's Irish Cream, and peppermint schnapps. If you can find fresh chocolate mint leaves, they add a pleasant surprise.

2 ounces Stolichnaya Vanilla Vodka
1½ ounces dark crème de cacao
1 ounce peppermint schnapps

Splash of Bailey's Irish Cream
5 ounces half-and-half
Fresh mint sprig, for garnish

1. Fill a martini glass with ice and water and let stand for about 1 minute.
2. In a martini shaker filled one-third of the way with ice, pour in the vanilla vodka, dark crème de cacao, peppermint schnapps, Bailey's Irish Cream, and half-and-half. Cover and shake well.
3. Pour the water and ice from the martini glass and using a cocktail strainer, pour the liquid into the chilled glass. Garnish with the sprig of fresh mint.

Mint Julep

YIELDS I SERVING

On long, hot summer days at the beach in Sag Harbor, I serve icy-cold mint juleps. Originated in the South, this Kentucky Derby classic is all about the bourbon and fresh mint. It's traditionally served in a silver julep cup.

12 leaves fresh mint
2 ounces simple syrup
Crushed ice

2 ounces Kentucky bourbon whiskey
Fresh mint sprig, for garnish

1. In a silver julep cup or a highball glass, combine the mint leaves and simple syrup. Muddle (lightly crush and stir) the leaves and syrup, then fill the glass with crushed ice.
2. Add the bourbon and stir the drink until the outside of the glass becomes frosted. Garnish with the sprig of fresh mint.

Lemon Meringue Pie

YIELDS 1 SERVING

This drink is the liquid version of lemon meringue pie, light and refreshing. If you love the pie, you'll find this elegant drink equally soul satisfying.

1½ ounces citrus vodka
½ ounce limoncello
½ ounce Triple Sec
½ ounce simple syrup, or more to taste

Splash of half-and-half
Lemon twist, for garnish (see Note for
 alternative garnish)

1. Fill a martini glass with ice and water and let stand for about 1 minute.
2. In a martini shaker filled one-third of the way with ice, pour in the citrus vodka, limoncello, Triple sec, simple syrup, and half-and-half. Cover and shake well.
3. Pour out the ice and water from the glass and using a cocktail strainer, pour the liquid into the chilled glass. Garnish with the lemon twist.

Note: If you are missing the taste of pie crust, eliminate the lemon twist garnish. Before preparing the cocktail, wet the rim of the martini glass with simple syrup, then dip the rim into a saucer filled with ground graham cracker crumbs. Strain the cocktail into the prepared glass.

Make Mine a Martini

Martinis are a personal taste, and come in all types of personalities. They can be shaken—James Bond style—or stirred, made with gin or vodka, and flavored with any number of liqueurs or garnishes. Here are some truly creative takes on the original.

Tapioca Martini

YIELDS 1 SERVING

Tapioca brings back a lot of childhood memories, but this is definitely a cocktail for adults only.

2½ ounces Stolichnaya Vanilla Vodka, chilled
1 ounce Chambord
2 ounces tapioca pudding, at room temperature

Generous splash of Godiva white chocolate liqueur
1 maraschino cherry, for garnish

1. Fill a martini glass with ice and water and let stand for about 1 minute.
2. In a martini shaker filled one-third of the way with ice, pour in the vanilla vodka and Chambord. Cover and shake well.
3. Strain the vodka mixture into a clean cocktail shaker; add the tapioca pudding and Godiva liqueur, and shake well.
4. Pour out the ice and water from the glass, then pour the liquid into the chilled glass. Garnish with the cherry.

Pistachio Margarita-tini

YIELDS 1 SERVING

If you love pistachios and creative cocktails, this Pistachio Margarita-tini will really impress your guests!

1 lime, divided
1 tablespoon shelled pistachio nuts
¼ teaspoon coarse salt, or more to taste
3 ounces Patron Silver Tequila

1¼ ounces Dumante Verdenoce Pistachio
  Liqueur
Splash of orange juice

1. Fill a martini glass with ice and water and let stand for about 1 minute.
2. Cut 1 small wedge and 1 wheel from the lime, then squeeze the juice from the rest of the lime to measure ¾ ounce; set aside.
3. In a food processor, combine the shelled pistachios and coarse salt and grind until pistachios are broken down to a coarse powder. Place the ground pistachios on a saucer.
4. Pour out the ice and water from the martini glass. Use the lime wedge to wet the rim of the chilled glass, then dip the rim of the glass into the ground pistachios.
5. Pour the tequila, pistachio liqueur, lime juice, and a splash of orange juice into a cocktail shaker filled with ice. Shake well. Strain into the prepared martini glass. Garnish the rim of the glass with the lime wheel.

Watermelon Martini

YIELDS 1 SERVING

Martinis are very popular in our restaurants. This watermelon martini is refreshing and beautifully presented with a cool wedge of fresh watermelon. Another round for the table, please!

1½ ounces vodka
½ ounce Midori
1½ ounces fresh watermelon juice

Splash of grenadine
Watermelon wedge, for garnish

1. Fill a martini glass with ice and water and let stand for about 1 minute.
2. Fill a cocktail shaker to about one-third of the way with ice, then pour in the vodka, Midori, watermelon juice, and grenadine. Cover and shake well.
3. Pour out the ice and water from the glass. Using a cocktail strainer, pour the liquid into the chilled glass. Garnish with the watermelon wedge.

Cucumber and Green Tea Martini

YIELDS 1 SERVING

My friends at Moët Hennessy are always coming up with interesting new cocktails. Their mixologist was kind enough to share this recipe. You will love the combination of fresh garden flavors paired with green tea and Cytrus Vodka. When using fresh ginger, start with a small amount and add more to taste.

One 2-inch slice cucumber, plus a thin
  slice for garnish
Fresh ginger, peeled and diced, to taste
Pinch of salt
Splash of simple syrup

1½ ounces Belvedere Cytrus Vodka
Splash of lemon juice
¾ ounce green tea
2 basil leaves

1. Fill a martini glass with ice and water and let stand for about 1 minute.
2. In a cocktail shaker, place the cucumber and ginger with the salt and simple syrup and muddle (lightly crush and stir). Add ice to fill about one-third of the way, then add the vodka, lemon juice, green tea, and basil leaves. Cover and shake vigorously.
3. Pour the ice and water from the glass. Using a cocktail strainer, pour the liquid into the chilled glass. Garnish with a thin slice of cucumber.

Crème Brûlée Martini

Here is a wonderful, sweet end to a meal. This liquid dessert makes it difficult to stop at just one.

Caramel sauce

2 ounces Stolichnaya Vanilla Vodka

1 ounce Bailey's Irish Cream

1 ounce Monin caramel syrup

1. Line a martini glass with the caramel sauce of your choosing.
2. Fill a cocktail shaker about one-third of the way with ice, and add the vodka, Bailey's Irish Cream, and caramel syrup. Cover and shake well.
3. Using a cocktail strainer, pour the liquid into the martini glass.

Fresh and Fruity Coolers

It's a Southern tradition to sit on the porch and cool off with a cold beverage on a languid afternoon. Here is a collection of refreshing iced teas, punches, and sangrias that make the most of seasonal fruit. They're perfect for sipping on a hot day, or serving up at backyard gatherings.

Wild Sweet Orange Tea Punch

YIELDS 8 SERVINGS

This non-alcoholic drink blends tropical and exotic flavors to create a refreshing summer treat. With lemongrass, blackberry leaves, rose hips, spearmint, orange peel, safflower, hibiscus flowers, rose petals, ginger, and licorice root, it makes you feel like you've escaped to the markets of Marrakesh or to the streets of Sumatra for this fantastic tea.

8 Wild Sweet Orange Tazo tea bags, or
    your favorite orange tea bags
4 cups boiling water

Simple syrup, agave nectar to taste,
    or your favorite sugar substitute
    (see Box)
4 cups chilled mandarin orange seltzer
Orange slices, for garnish

1. Place the tea bags in a large heatproof pitcher or container. Add the boiling water and let steep for 10 minutes. Remove the tea bags and add the sweetener while the tea is hot, stirring well to dissolve. Cover and refrigerate until ready to use.
2. Just before serving, add the orange seltzer to the tea. Serve in tall glasses over ice, garnished with orange slices.

Diabetes-Friendly Punch

For a diabetes-friendly version of the Wild Sweet Orange Tea Punch, there are many sugar substitutes; my new favorite is agave nectar, which is made from the juice of the salmiana variety of agave. It has a mild flavor, a long shelf life, and a low glycemic index that is beneficial to many. It is easy to pour, and dissolves quickly in drinks. It's widely available at Trader Joe's and other natural food stores, though if you can't find it you can alternatively sweeten the punch with Splenda Brown Sugar Blend or your favorite sugar substitute.

Mango Pear Tea Punch

YIELDS 8 SERVINGS

This exotic tea is flavored with rose hips, hibiscus flowers, orange peel, roasted chicory, licorice root, and natural mango. Sweeten the punch with sugar or your favorite sugar substitute. It looks beautiful served with the fruit floating in a large pitcher.

8 mango-flavored herbal tea bags
4 cups boiling water
1 cup sugar or your favorite sugar
    substitute
One (750 ml) bottle chilled sparkling pear
    cider
1 cup fresh diced mango
1 cup fresh diced pear
Orange slices, for garnish

1. Place the tea bags in a large heatproof pitcher or container. Add the boiling water and let steep for 10 minutes. Remove the tea bags and add the sugar or sugar substitute while the tea is hot, stirring well to dissolve. Refrigerate until ready to serve.
2. Just before serving, add the sparkling pear cider and the diced mango and pears. Serve over ice in tall glasses garnished with orange slices.

Georgia Peach Iced Tea

YIELDS 1 SERVING

This drink should be prepared with strong iced tea. It can be sweetened with simple syrup or agave nectar, which pours and dissolves quickly, and has a low glycemic index that's beneficial to many. It tastes great and enhances the flavor of this adult iced tea! For a non-alcoholic version, fresh peach purée can be substituted for the peach schnapps.

2½ ounces peach schnapps
½ ounce simple syrup or agave nectar
Strong fresh-brewed iced tea

Lemon wedge and fresh mint sprig,
  for garnish

1. Fill a 12-ounce glass with ice, then pour in the peach schnapps and the simple syrup.
2. Fill the glass with iced tea, stir thoroughly, and garnish with the lemon and fresh mint.

Chamomile Cooler

YIELDS 1 SERVING

Here is another recipe from my friends at Moët Hennessy that gives soothing chamomile tea a kick of citrus vodka.

2 ounces Belvedere Cytrus Vodka
½ ounce honey water (½ honey plus ½ hot
  water)
¾ ounce lemon juice

Splash of simple syrup
2 ounces strong fresh-brewed chamomile
  tea
1 lemon wedge, for garnish

1. Place the vodka, honey water, lemon juice, simple syrup, and tea in a cocktail shaker. Cover and shake well.
2. Pour the cocktail into a rocks glass and garnish with the lemon wedge.

Strawberry Sangria with Rose Geranium

YIELDS 8 SERVINGS

This refreshing summer cooler contains no alcohol, yet the wild-berry tea and puréed strawberries give it that great sangria color. For guests who prefer their beverages with a bit of a kick, add a little white muscat or light rum to taste. Unless you already grow them, you'll most likely have to visit a nursery to find rose geraniums. They make great potted plants and of course smell wonderful, too. The aromatic, rose-scented leaves are often used to infuse their flavor in sorbets, ices, and beverages. If you can't find rose geranium, it can be substituted with fresh mint, basil, lemon balm, or lemon verbena.

4 cups water
4 wild-berry tea bags
1 cup sugar or your favorite sugar
substitute
Two 1-pint baskets strawberries, hulled

One (750 ml) bottle chilled sparkling apple cider
8 fresh rose geranium leaves, or ¾ teaspoon rose water (see Note)

1. In large saucepan, bring 2 cups of the water to a boil. Add the wild-berry tea bags; cover and let steep for 10 minutes. Discard the tea bags.
2. Add the sugar to the hot tea and stir until dissolved. Stir in remaining 2 cups of water, and pour into a large pitcher or container. Cover and refrigerate the tea until cold, about 3 hours or up to 1 day.
3. In a food processor, purée 1 pint of the strawberries. Slice the remaining strawberries. Place the puréed and sliced berries into a large pitcher (or divide between 2 pitchers). Add the chilled tea to the pitcher.
4. Lightly crush the rose geranium leaves to release their aromatic oil. Add them to the sangria, and serve over ice in tall glasses.

Note: Rose water is available at Middle Eastern markets and specialty food stores.

White Sangria

I love sangria year round. It's the perfect drink for a crowd. There are no hard rules for making it, so just be creative. White and red sangria are both crowd pleasers. Serve it in a large clear glass pitcher, and be sure to put some fresh fruit in each serving.

1 bottle dry white wine
¾ cup Cointreau or Triple Sec
¾ cup brandy
Juice from 2 lemons
Simple syrup or agave nectar to taste

1 bottle sparkling apple-pear cider, chilled
1 cup seedless white grapes
1 cup peeled and diced pears or white peaches

1. In a large pitcher or container, combine the white wine, Cointreau or Triple Sec, brandy, lemon juice, and simple syrup or agave nectar. Cover and refrigerate until ready to serve.
2. Just before serving, add the sparkling cider, ice cubes, grapes, and peaches to the sangria. Serve in wine goblets or tall glasses, adding some fruit to each serving.

Acknowledgments

Writing a cookbook is like that old proverb "It Takes a Village"—of talented people to be sure! My husband Dan Gasby is at the top of the list and is truly the wind beneath my wings! Dan wears many hats and was my literary agent for this project. Just one of the many reasons I said, "Thank you, Dan," at the end of our television show.

Many thanks to Beth Wareham, Vice President and Director of Lifestyle Publishing at Scribner. She believed in the project and was a guiding force through thick and thin!

And I couldn't have gotten the book to my publisher without my Executive Assistant, Michele Peppers, who was also my diligent Project Manager, as well as my candid photographer!

My friend television producer Adrienne Hammel has worked on my TV shows and on my last book, so I was delighted she had time to do some research for me on this book. It is wonderful to have talented friends that you enjoy working with; writers Yvonne Durant and Diana Murphy both jumped right on board!

Daniel Green has been invaluable as a trusted friend, confidant, and second set of eyes. During the past decade and a half he has been my makeup artist and photographer extraordinaire (he shot the cover for this book!). But most of all Daniel has been a trusted friend for many years, and a member of the B. Smith family!

I met photographer Colin Cooke while working on another project and had seen some of his beautiful photographs, and when it was time to shoot the food for this book, he was the first person I called. As you can see in the book, he did a fabulous job with his retoucher Mike Marquand and prop assistant Don Purple.

When you own restaurants and write cookbooks you really understand the importance of chefs, recipe developers, and recipe testers as well as food stylists! In alphabetical order:

Kersti Bowser, Jeannie Chen, Abby Dodge, Karen Ferries, Maggie Green, Paul Lowe (food and prop stylist), Executive Chef John Poon, Stephanie Rose, Whitney Stewart, Rhonda Stieglitz, Nancy Vaziri, Jeannie Voltz, and Patty White.

I had lots of help with the beverage chapter from our creative restaurant bar staff! Just like restaurant chefs, good bar staff members continuously create new and exciting drink recipes. A big thanks to Lonnie Barnett, John Laubenthal, Emily Petrain, Dartel McRae, Chris Van Hoy, and Sonja Williams at B. Smith's Restaurant in New York City! Also, thanks to Robin Piro of B. Smith's Sag Harbor. Cheers to Tom Townsend and of course Mike Wyche, Bar Manager and creative drink genius at B. Smith's Restaurant, Union Station in Washington, D.C. Also, a special thank-you to Noel Hankin, the Senior Vice President of Multicultural Relations at Moët Hennessy USA and their talented mixologists for sharing their recipes for the Chamomile Cooler and Green Tea Martini.

And I couldn't forget the rest of my Executive Team: Regina Briganti, Russell Brown, Adam Caswell, and Greg Wyman!

Index